PSYCHOANALYTIC CASE STUDIES

PSYCHOANALYTIC CASE STUDIES

G. PIROOZ SHOLEVAR, M.D.
EDITOR

JULES GLENN, M.D.
ASSISTANT EDITOR

LEO RANGELL, M.D.
Introduction & Overview

INTERNATIONAL UNIVERSITIES PRESS, INC.
MADISON CONNECTICUT

Library of Congress Cataloging in Publication Data

Psychoanalytic case studies / Jules Glenn, G. Pirooz Sholevar.
editors.
p. cm.
Includes bibliographical references and indexes.
ISBN 0-8236-4405-7
1. Psychoanalysis—Case studies. I. Glenn, Jules. II. Sholevar,
G. Pirooz.
RC504.P758 1991 90-36401
616.89'17—dc20 CIP

Manufactured in the United States of America

To the memory of Victor Calef, M.D.

Whose enthusiastic dedication to Psychoanalysis inspired many younger colleagues.

CONTENTS

ACKNOWLEDGMENTS

I wish to thank Jacob A. Arlow, M.D. for his valuable guidance and encouragement, and Albert J. Solnit, M.D. and John Gado, M.D. for their assistance and encouragement with this book.

GPS

CONTRIBUTORS

SAMUEL ABRAMS, M.D.

Dr. Abrams is Clinical Professor of Psychiatry and Training and Supervising Analyst in Psychoanalytic Institute, New York University Medical Center. He is the past-Director of Psychoanalytic Institute of New York (1981–1984); Editor, *Psychoanalytic Study of the Child;* Associate Editor of *Psychoanalytic Quarterly;* and on the Editorial Board of *International Journal of Psycho-Analysis.*

ISIDOR BERNSTEIN, M.D.

Dr. Bernstein is Clinical Associate Professor of Psychiatry and Training and Supervising Analyst with Psychoanalytic Institute, New York University Medical Center. He is the past-President of Long Island Psychoanalytic Society (1965–1966; 1976–1977).

CALVIN A. COLARUSSO, M.D.

Dr. Colarusso is Clinical Professor and Director of Child Psychiatric Training, University of California in San Diego, La Jolla, California. He is Training and Supervising Analyst in Adult and Child Analysis in San Diego Psychoanalytic Institute in La Jolla, California. He is the author of the *The Race Against Time* and co-author of *Adult Development: New Dimension in Psychodynamic Theory.*

ALAN J. EISNITZ, M.D.

Dr. Eisnitz is Clinical Professor of Psychiatry and Training and Supervising Analyst in Psychoanalytic Institute, New York University Medical Center. He is past-Director of Psychoanalytic Institute of Downtown Medical Center (1972–1975).

JULES GLENN, M.D.

Dr. Glenn is Clinical Professor of Psychiatry and Training and Supervising Analyst, The Psychoanalytic Institute, New York University Medical Center. He is the past-President of Association for Child Analysis (1984–1986) and the Psychoanalytic Association of New York (1987–1989). He is the editor of *Child Analysis and Therapy*, and co-editor, *Freud and His Self-Analysis* and *Freud and His Patients.*

EDWARD D. JOSEPH, M.D.

Dr. Joseph is Professor of Psychiatry at Mount Sinai School of Medicine in New York and Training and Supervising Analyst in New York Psychoanalytic Institute. He is the past-President of American Psychoanalytic Association (1973–1974; 1984–1986) and International Psychoanalytic Association (1977–1981).

RUDOLPH M. LOEWENSTEIN, M.D.

The late Dr. Loewenstein was a Training and Supervising Psychoanalyst at the New York Psychoanalytic Institute. He had served as the President of American Psychoanalytic Association (1957–1958) and Vice President of International Psychoanalytic Association. His extensive publications include the book of *Practice and Percept in Psychoanalytic Technique.*

LEO RANGELL, M.D.

Dr. Rangell is Clinical Professor of Psychiatry at UCLA School of Medicine in Los Angeles, California and Clinical Professor of Psychiatry and Psychoanalysis, University of California in San Francisco. He is Training and Supervising Analyst in Los Angeles Psychoanalytic Institute. He is the past-President of American Psychoanalytic Association (1961–1962; 1966–1967) and International Psychoanalytic Association (1969–1973). He has been on the Editorial Board, *Journal of American Psychoanalytic Association* (1956–1984).

IRWIN C. ROSEN, Ph.D.

Dr. Rosen is Clinical Professor, Department of Psychiatry, University of Kansas Medical Center, and Training and Supervising Psychoanalyst, Topeka Psychoanalytic Institute, Topeka, Kansas.

G. PIROOZ SHOLEVAR, M.D.

Dr. Sholevar is Professor and Director, Division of Child, Adolescent and Family Psychiatry at Jefferson Medical College, Thomas Jefferson University, Philadelphia, Pennsylvania. He is the President-Elect of Society of Professors of Child and Adolescent Psychiatry and councilor of the American Academy of Child and Adolescent Psychiatry, past-President of Council of Child and Adolescent Psychiatry for Pennsylvania, Delaware and Southern New Jersey and The Council for Advancement of Psychoanalytic Education (CAPE). He is a graduate of the Institute of Philadelphia Association for Psychoanalysis in Child and Adolescent Psychoanalysis as well as Psychoanalysis of Adults. His eight published books includes a major text on emotional disorders in children and adolescents.

AUSTIN SILBER, M.D.

Dr. Silber is Clinical Professor of Psychiatry and Training and Supervising Analyst in Psychoanalytic Institute, New York University Medical Center. He is a past-Director of Psychoanalytic Institute of New York University and past-Secretary, American Psychoanalytic Association (1985–1987).

VANN SPRUIELL, M.D.

Dr. Spruiell is Clinical Associate Professor, Tulane University Medical School and Clinical Associate Professor in Louisiana State University Medical School, New Orleans, Louisiana. He is Training and Supervising Analyst in Louisiana Psychoanalytic Institute. He is the past-Secretary, Board on Professional Standards, American Psychoanalytic Association (1979–1981) and past-President, New Orleans Psychoanalytic Association (1983–1985).

EDWARD M. WEINSHEL, M.D.

Dr. Weinshel is Clinical Professor of Psychiatry, University of California in San Francisco, School of Medicine. He is Training and Supervising Analyst in San Francisco Psychoanalytic Institute. He is the past-Chairman, Board of Professional Standards, American Psychoanalytic Association (1972–1975); past-Vice President, International Psychoanalytic Association (1975–1981); and past-Secretary, International Psychoanalytic Association (1985–1987).

PREFACE

This book was planned to satisfy the crying need for clinical data detailing the course of analysis from beginning to end. Only with such data can the serious scholar or the careful clinician get an accurate sense of what comprises an analysis. The data will enable the reader to evaluate the intermeshing work of patient and analyst and the mode of therapeutic action of a successful psychoanalysis. Such data will illustrate the psychoanalytic process as the sequence of steps which proceed within the analytic situation and "in the mind of the patient as the treatment moves forward" (Abrams, 1988).

Case reports are an excellent vehicle for reviewing the broad sweep of analysis. They illustrate the process of analysis, the defenses employed, and the gradual uncovering of the hierarchy of the patient's important fantasies; the resistances to those phenomena; the flow of the treatment process with periodic advancements, heightened defensiveness, and regressive shifts; the vicissitudes of the transference; and the effect of the analyst's interventions upon the analytic process. During the course of treatment, the patient's diagnosis can be confirmed or modified, his motivations for treatment evaluated, and responsiveness to the analytic process in order to promote change can be determined (Eisnitz, chapter 3, discussion).

We were guided in our attempts by the high standards of analytic reports established by Freud's writings on the analysis of Little Hans, Dora, the Rat Man, and the Wolf Man. Freud's literary genius, which allowed him to capture the essence of the analytic events, including the human qualities of the protagonists and their exquisite interaction, his eschewal of jargon in his expositions, and focus on clarity to explain the complex tales of inner turmoil and environmental conflict and compliance, also served as a guide. His clarity has allowed modern analysts to review his cases in the light of current understanding and to reassess the development of his patients' neuroses and Freud's therapeutic procedures.

Following Freud there have been many attempts at presenting analytic case reports to illustrate the psychoanalytic process. There is, for example, Dewald's book, *The Psychoanalytic Process* (1972), describing an entire analysis, with verbatim statements, which shows how one analyst conceives of analysis. Dewald's book permits critique and discussion of the therapeutic process but it is the rare reader who would not be overwhelmed by the inevitable repetitions—the patient's production and the analyst's comments are fully recorded.

The present volume is different from the limited number of previous reports of psychoanalytic treatment because it allows the examination by the treating analyst and two discussants of each selected clinical summary of the therapeutic process. The criteria for the selection of the case reports included selection of case summaries which read clearly so that the analytic process can be perceived and understood. The reader had to be able to distinguish between what the patients said and felt and what the analyst said and did. If possible, the reader had to feel in harmony with the analyst as he empathized with and understood his patients. Theory was not to be excluded, but it is clearly differentiated from the here and now of the analysis itself.

Describing psychoanalysis is a difficult and demanding task. The free associations of the patient on the couch during a lengthy treatment course with frequent sessions make for somewhat meandering and disjointed data. The analyst as a *participant* observer must seek the silver thread that runs through the varied descriptions of immediate external events, recollections of past occurrences, and recitations of fantasies, including those of the analyst himself. The impediments to the successful description of the analytic report include the presentation of too much detail that overwhelms the reader and makes him unable to follow the lines of thought and the feelings of analysand and analyst. This deprives the reader of an overview of the patient's struggle with painful interactions and memories and the analyst's attempts to put himself in the patient's place to understand those struggles. Too much detail may lead the reader down the many blind alleys that patients enter without clear understanding of the resistances that may temporarily obfuscate the analytic journey.

The decision for discussion of each case report by two experienced analysts was made in order to allow complementary views on the clinical phenomena and psychoanalytic process as well as inclusion of appropriate theoretical formulations. It was intended that the discussants' examination of the details of the analysis should place the treatment in a perspective beyond that of the treating analyst. Their discussions were intended to call attention to the new thoughts the cases would force upon the reader, current theory, technical engagements, and even errors and how they had affected the treatments. The discussions were to be freewheeling and unrestricted.

A number of case reports were examined by three analysts but quite a few did not meet the above criteria. The cases chosen were two classics, by Rudolph Loewenstein (the analysis of a patient treated in the 1930s but published in 1956) and Leo Rangell (published in 1952). These cases were supplemented by two more recent analyses: that of a patient with personality disorder treated by Irwin Rosen and a child analytic case by Calvin Colarusso.

Considering the significance of the termination phase, we made sure that this stage of treatment has been described in at least some of our cases. During the termination period the insights and therapeutic effects stabilize themselves. Even when they weaken with the threat of losing a formidable person—the analyst—the analysis of the significance of that loss prepares the way for postanalytic consolidation. In addition, although no analysis is fully complete, many loose ends are clarified during the final period. The patient, realizing he will be on his own, is often motivated to analyze previously neglected areas. Ideally he also masters the art of self-analysis which he can later invoke when faced with difficulties or the frightening traumatic events that life can mete out.

The book is intended for a wide range of readers interested in psychoanalysis. The reader may be a student of psychoanalysis trying to learn and master the fundamentals of psychoanalytic technique as it is actually practiced, or an experienced analyst expanding his vistas. The book is intended to supply basic and palpable information and the subtle evaluation of the analytic process sought by the reader. We also hope it conveys to the reader the excitement of participating in a highly dynamic and intricate process undertaken by two people, the analysand and the analyst, who are attempting to unearth the living past as it affects the patient's present-day character and behavior. On this journey, the traumatic events are uprooted from the past and freshly integrated in a more mature psychic organization.

Jules Glenn, M.D.
G. Pirooz Sholevar, M.D.

REFERENCES

Abrams, S. (1988), The psychoanalytic process in adults and children. *The Psychoanalytic Study of the Child,* 43:245–261. New Haven, CT: Yale University Press.

Dewald, P. A. (1972), *The Psychoanalytic Process: A Case Illustration.* New York: Basic Books.

INTRODUCTION AND OVERVIEW

Leo Rangell, M.D.

A volume of clinical case reports is always welcome on the psychoanalytic scene. Theory stems from clinical practice but theories can acquire a life of their own over long periods of time. Although psychoanalytic theory is said to rest upon a clinical base, the description of the original material from which theories stem, in relation to the intricacies and specificities claimed, remains in a secondary position. Theories are described, even spun out to elaborate degrees without the corresponding clinical material upon which they are based. Supporting clinical data, when forthcoming, is presented as brief excerpts or incomplete summaries. Fuller clinical reports, centered upon descriptions in depth of patients in treatment, are infrequent.

It would be refreshing to have more clinical reports in the psychoanalytic literature. Whatever theoretical considerations stem from them would then be secondary to the data rather than the reverse. Validation and conviction would be more solid. There would be many examples of a single theoretical point instead of an elaborate theoretical construction from a meager point of origin. A pyramid would be built with its base on the bottom rather than, as happens with elaborately spun-out theories, a pyramid standing on its point.

This book is a compilation of clinical cases, a selected record of patients in treatment. It represents an aggregate of the clinical experiences of the analysts who treated the patients, coupled with the clinical–theoretical opinions of eight discussants, two for each case. Such a collection of clinical cases and their discussions is of particular benefit in the current theoretical climate. This is an era dominated by theoretical systems, highly developed and much debated, with strong affective and often divisive polarization. Thus, calling attention to the bedrock experiences of a group of patients in psychoanalytic treatment can add basic observations to be appreciated and utilized. Past as well as current theorizing can be monitored, measured, and checked against data accumulated daily and reported here by psychoanalytic clinicians.

When I was a psychoanalytic candidate in the 1940s, a book by Helene Deutsch, written in 1932, was particularly useful in demonstrating the observational clinical material from which the author's theoretical knowledge up to that time had derived. Psychoanalytic education, both of the individual candidate and the field in general, proceeding in logical, intellectual sequence, has always been based initially on observational data, normal and abnormal. In a manner parallel to Freud's own development, psychoanalytic education stands first upon Freud's great case histories (1905, 1909a, 1911, 1918) and his *The Interpretation of Dreams* (1900). Our continuing theoretical development needs such a periodic refueling. While clinical excerpts are not uncommon and in fact appear in many papers, full case histories are much more rare, and it is hoped that this collection will fill an existing gap.

The cases selected are both special ones, compelling in their contents, and typical, run-of-the-mill clinical experiences. They are florid and dramatic, and also ordinary and low key. They are vividly presented, readable, and hold the attention of those whose interests center on psychoanalytic understanding. The cases are of a widely mixed variety from many points of view. They provide a wide range of psychopathology, from obsessions through phobia and character disorders, to a latency child with a variety of phobic, obsessive, and aggressive symptoms. An empirical fact from which an added bonus can be expected to accrue is that the patients, who span forty years, did not follow theoretical trends or vary with them; they spoke their troubles directly and uncoached to the attending psychoanalysts. It may be seen and examined, however, how the analysts differ in each decade. It would also be of interest to know how the analysts themselves would see their performances and orientations then as compared to now.

Besides the span of the ages of the patients and different historical periods of psychoanalytic thinking, the analysts themselves were in different phases of their analytic careers. The respective analysts, at the times of the treatments, ranged from candidates to young analysts to those at the peak of their professional careers. The types of discussants are also varied.

Dr. Loewenstein's patient was treated in the 1930s when Dr. Loewenstein was a young man, but it was reported in 1956. My own case of the doll phobia was treated when I was a candidate; the paper was my graduation thesis in 1950. The religious adult patient treated by Dr. Rosen, and the latency child treated by Dr. Colarusso, bring us by increments to modern and current issues.

By serendipity, the reader will benefit from a historical review as well. The styles of the times and of the analysts, and of the nature and types of clinical presentations, are visible here. In the case of the fulminating obsessional patient, a previous iatrogenic input is analyzed and dissolved. In the case of the doll phobia, the psychopathology as fixed in the symptom and manifested in the underlying character structure was filtered through a net of theoretical understanding and traced developmentally to its etiologic origins. The intervening processes between origins and current manifestations were exposed, interpreted, and set into place in relation to each other. The central goal and interest in the mixed character neurosis of the religious counselor is the detailed ramifications of the psychoanalytic process as revealed in the transference and reconstructed into the past. In the case of the latency child, the psychoanalytic interchange between patient and analyst is similarly attended to, with typical hours described to present a continuity of treatment. In addition, the special problems and techniques of child analysis are demonstrated, including the issue of the analyst's working relationship to the parents of the patient.

By today's standards Dr. Loewenstein's patient was without question a borderline case or worse, yet was analyzed in a standard manner, an empirical observation worth noting in terms of current views. This patient was reminiscent in many ways of Freud's Rat Man (1909b) or Wolf Man (1918). Some clinical flashes at times remind us of other earlier cases, Dora (1905), Anna O. (Breuer and Freud, 1893–1895), or Little Hans (1909a). It is worth noting that errors committed in previous analytic treatments were not necessarily due to countertransference mistakes but iatrogenic inputs from other factors.

The patient had undergone three previous analyses, all ending in traumatic experiences. One analyst broke the patient's confidentiality to her husband, the second abruptly dismissed the patient when the latter expressed suicidal thoughts. The third analyst, Dr. Z., gave unanalytic suggestions which amounted to advising the patient to falsify data and experiences to herself. In relation to these, and to inappropriate fee arrangements, Loewenstein speaks of intellectual integrity, a subject I came to from a theoretical standpoint many years later (Rangell, 1974). There are good contrasts and combinations demonstrated in this case report of past, present, and transference data.

In the doll phobia patient, the unconscious intrapsychic process is traced, of drives being tested by the ego, the experience of anxiety, and then, through a series of unconscious intrapsychic steps, the processes identified which caused symptom formation and character pathology. The therapeutic process is in the reverse direction. To use a phrase in current consciousness from a recent film, the direction is "Back to the Future." I used in this case the metaphor of a wheel, with the symptom at the hub, etiologic spokes in a radial direction, and concentric interconnecting links. The therapeutic and diagnostic paths are to and fro, up and down, back and forth. As Dr. Abrams pointed out in his discussion of this paper, "Outwards and inwards, past and future . . . taking apart and putting together . . . all of this happens in a good analysis" (pp. 120–121).

The cases give evidence of their historical times and are surrounded phenomenologically and therapeutically by their sociocultural envelopes. Of the case reports presented, Dr. Rosen's rigid, religious, obsessional patient is perhaps the most illustrative of an average, modern adult analysis. The analysis is low key, less dramatic than some of the others, but persistent, reliable, and effective, a combination of the cognitive with the fully and properly affective. There is an automatic and natural blend between transference and reconstruction, past and present. The patient reveals hysterical and phobic features, with phallic and oedipal etiologic inputs along with and added to oral, anal, and narcissistic ones. Both transference and extra-transference material are in evidence and utilized, all helped by a series of copious and strategic dreams and their associations. While Dr. Eisnitz, in his discussion, points to the difficulty in summarizing and convincingly presenting the course of an analytic case, Rosen appears to have done just that.

Dr. Colarusso's latency child, treated from ages nine to twelve, suffered from phobias, temper tantrums, and nightmares, with fears of rattlesnakes, conflicts over masturbation, and accompanying fantasies. The case is preceded by a thorough, conventional diagnostic workup, indicating the issues to be faced in deciding upon child analysis (perhaps the thoroughness of the preliminary steps reflects a teaching institution). There were four interviews with the parents, followed by two diagnostic and evaluative interviews with the boy, psychological testing, and a summary conference with the parents. The parents are bright, concerned, from intact families themselves, and particularly willing and cooperative. The course of the analysis was followed and reported by thoroughly detailed process notes, with the presentation of almost verbatim accounts of selected serial analytic hours. Oedipal themes are stressed, with castrative wishes, anxieties, and derivatives in the transference and within the patient's family constellation. There are regular and active parental conferences. The analysis was a moving and effective one, with not only symptoms removed, but with a growth process and developmental progression resumed. In the last hour, the analyst noticed how tall the boy had become.

The full and at times dramatic case is subjected to careful, thoughtful, and even sparkling discussions. The discussants are seasoned analysts working from the vantage point of distant observers, immersed in the daily experiences of the detailed analytic work. Their commentaries are frank and helpful, and continue the analytic process of thought, in each instance advancing the level and scope of understanding.

The fear of rattlesnakes revealed in the initial evaluation, which had been absent from the analytic course, entered analysis in the second year, and the patient's associations revealed his connection with his fear of losing his penis in retaliation for his interest in women and his mother. This was followed by further revelation of the patient's masturbation fantasies and the details of his oedipal development with clear interest in his mother and the wish to have his father out of the way.

The termination process has been well described by Colarusso. The wish for termination was initiated by Jim after resolution of his symptoms, concomitant with Colarusso's further analytic work on Jim's castration anxiety and construction of his oedipal feelings. The positive feelings toward the analyst and the father became more readily apparent at this time. The process and date for termination were mutually established by the patient and analyst and a range of feelings and issues was expressed and worked through during this period.

Discussing the compelling case described by Dr. Loewenstein, Dr. Silber finds that it reads "like a turn of the century melodrama . . . [and is] vaguely old fashioned." Examining the problems of reanalysis, Silber carefully dissects the intricacies of transference and countertransference issues, and differentiates transference problems from the many other iatrogenic inputs intruded into this case by the three faulty analysts who had previously treated the patient. Silber points to Loewenstein's correct analytic attitude in resolving the unanalyzed transferences and other residual conflicts of the previous analyses, along with the newly evolving transference neurosis of his present analysis. Interpretations both inside and outside of transference proved clinically useful. Silber notes the importance Loewenstein attributed to understanding the structure of Mme. N.'s symptom. Going further than Loewenstein, Silbert observes the uncovering of childhood conflicts which had taken place.

Discussing the same case, Dr. Weinshel notes the qualities of Victorian drama throughout this clinical experience, the lies, deception, deceit, betrayal, tyranny, infidelity, incest, and how these were handled and analyzed in the phase of treatment conducted by Dr. Loewenstein. Following a useful review of Loewenstein's contributions and evolution as an analyst, Weinshel sets out not to be a supervisor, but an explorer, to note especially what changes in theory and technique have taken place in the intervening years. His observations are grouped into seven categories: the nosological, oedipal, and preoedipal developmental goals of analysis; resistances; the psychoanalytic process; transference; and superego conflicts. Weinshel points also to the frequency of problems of morality, integrity, and responsibility in analysis, and that betrayals in this case by the previous analysts should not be confused with countertransference. Recent emphases on the latter "or its cousin, empathic failure, has in some quarters become so extreme that at times it would appear that the patient and his problems are considered to be a superfluous complication" (p. 73).

Dr. Spruiell, in his discussion of the paper on doll phobia, places at the hub of the wheel "a small number of important unconscious fantasies." He also notes the presence of overt and covert perverse symptomatology, simultaneously with the psychoneurotic organization. More specifically, Spruiell points to the link between the phobic object and the fetish. Stating that "it is characteristic of our present time that there is insufficient interest in the analysis of symptoms," Spruiell emphasizes the central position and approach taken in this paper. He also notes how this case presages future writings of mine on intrapsychic conflicts, and on outcomes resulting from superego conflicts.

Dr. Abrams, in his discussion of the same paper, adds a good and interesting description of the psychoanalytic process as a side contribution, and integrates this case into it clearly and helpfully. His linear description of the psychoanalytic process, in which four stages are described, is not an alternative but complementary to my circular model of neurosogenesis and of the treatment process. I incidentally wrote on the total psychoanalytic process in a paper (Rangell, 1968). Coincidentally, in relation to Abrams's including a phase of "postanalytic consolidation" in the psychoanalytic process, I myself, in a paper (Rangell, 1966), also described a postanalytic phase following termination.

Discussing the more typical current type of psychoanalysis reported by Dr. Irwin Rosen, Dr. Alan Eisnitz comments first on the value of such posttreatment reviews of psychoanalytic cases for teaching purposes. He compares the broad sweep of this case, coupled with the detailed, day-by-day reporting, with attendance at a clinical–pathological conference or grand rounds. I would add the interesting value of this method for research, understanding, and theory building as well.

While tracing the deepening of the unconscious themes in the analytic progression, with cogent comments on many significant dreams, Eisnitz points out and discusses the atypical and challenging features in this case, the patient's prior intellectual knowledge of psychoanalysis, his professional religious involvement, and the issue of the analyst having outside information. The patient's prior knowledge was effectively connected with affects and the transference neurosis. An observation of Eisnitz's I find worth emphasizing is that today's intellectualization may provide a firm foundation for effective insight later. Outside information here could be brought within the analysis, particularly with regard to significant and meaningful contradictions. There is a particularly good and informative discussion of the different role of religion in psychoanalytic thinking today, with various possible outcomes following the removal of the defensive use of religious beliefs and attitudes. In this case, the analyst was able to show the relation between the transference and the patient's religious devotion. Subtle observations are made on the analysis of the transference, extratransference material, the developmental history, regressions, and oedipal and preoedipal elements. Areas less analyzed in this case report, according to Eisnitz, are sexuality and the nature of the postanalytic religious residuals.

Dr. Edward Joseph, discussing the same presentation, starts out by observing that after the analysis the patient's colleagues were just beginning "to like the guy." Joseph points out the complicated, slow, cumulative, multilayered development of insight and the difficult vicissitudes of arriving at these. The patient and analyst have common goals but different expectations. Joseph emphasizes the analyst's work on the resistances, his avoidance of defensive intellectual traps, and how transference led to the genetic origins in producing this successful outcome. He stresses the role of unconscious fantasies, and their successive developmental levels of formation, in arriving at explanatory interpretations and insights.

Discussing the one child case included in this volume, that of Dr. Colarusso, Dr. Jules Glenn observes that the clinical presentation illustrates well the psychoanalytic process, with the systematic and alternating analysis of defenses and drives. The understanding of the transference opened the process to the full range of communications, including a natural bridge to play, story-telling, and drawing, along with speech, dreams, and free associations. The patient's capacity for insight was not due to his brightness but resulted from tactful interpretations given with the necessary empathy. The issue of giving gifts to the child patient was discussed, the dangers inherent in this or in other forms of excessive encouragement, as well as the way in which the analyst felt it useful and necessary to help the working alliance. A similar alliance was formed with the parents, while always maintaining the patient's confidentiality. The patient's need to cheat in play, in the transference, and in his extra-analytic family life was analyzed in terms of his pathological conflicts. Glenn discusses the positive relationships of the analyst to the parents, and the constructive use to which this was put in the analysis. Resistances were exposed and worked through up to and including the resistance to continuing treatment, until the end.

Dr. Isidor Bernstein, reviewing the same case presentation, expresses his feeling of an intimate participation in a dynamic ongoing process. Bernstein selects three specific issues for discussion and comment, indications and contraindications for child analysis, interpretations and reconstructions in child analysis, and, as with Dr. Glenn, the role of the parents in the ongoing process. Disagreeing with Colarusso on some fine points, Bernstein pointed out that the child was not suffering and that play is not the equivalent of free associations. The analyst's analytic attitude succeeded in bringing about basic trust. While a psychoanalytic process was clearly engaged with, an ongoing transference analysis, drives and defenses, sexual and aggressive, continued actively toward the parents, unlike with adult analysis. Bernstein felt that very little reconstruction was in evidence regarding certain data, such as details of the obviously important anal phase, other preoedipal forerunners to the oedipal conflicts, and reactions to the births of the patient's two younger siblings.

Each discussant adds a significant dimension and elaboration to the cases presented, to aspects of the psychoanalytic method, whether of understanding or technique. Some discussants, such as Eisnitz, Glenn, and Abrams, discuss the psychoanalytic process in a global and continuous way, while others, such as Weinshel or Bernstein, select more specific and circumscribed topics which the material brings out. Taken together these give a multisided view of the analytic process as it carries out the psychoanalytic goals by the psychoanalytic method.

Since one of the four clinical cases presented is my own, I must resist the temptation to address the two discussants of that paper as one typically responds to the official discussants after presenting a paper. Since I am also, however, the only author of the original papers here to comment on my own case, I will not lean over to ignore the discussants, I will instead limit myself to reflect, as might be the case with the authors of the other selected papers, upon what would remain the same today, and what changes might have occurred in the handling of my own or other cases in the decades since.

A number of interesting thoughts occur to me which I believe might add a perspective in considering these cases. One is that I still feel satisfied, even good about my own clinical experience which is presented here. I do not feel I would necessarily do better today. I confess to what might be an awkward feeling of satisfaction in spite of the case having an obviously antiquated quality. The description appears, and is, dated; cases are not "described" that way any longer.

Major theoretical observations or questions press themselves upon me. Formative analytic attitudes and stances which were set down back then for the most part have survived the test of time. The main thrust of the analytic work was toward what the patient suffered from, and the dynamic substructure uncovered as causing it. By this I mean not only the symptoms but the character, which includes what was originally ego syntonic but which became dystonic as a result of the analytic unfolding. The case report, even as I look back at it four decades later, seems to reveal that emphasis. The patient did not enter treatment suffering from a transference neurosis; this came later during the treatment to a greater or lesser degree. And the transference neurosis never did recapitulate the original neurosis in its entirety, with all its ramifications.

There is a profound point about technique and the practical and theoretical aspects of therapy intrinsic to this observation. The analysis was not basically an interactional experience but a reconstructive process. This is a definitive statement on a much debated issue today. There was incidentally no later recurrence on that account, from any insufficient attention to the here and now. Dr. Abrams correctly notes the relative paucity in this paper of a report on process compared to attention to products and procedures. This might be somewhat related to the style and content of "then" compared to now, what was presented and how it was presented being characteristic of that time. Not that process was less important in the 1940s and 1950s, but it was regarded as the means to the end rather than the end in itself. Of more interest was the meaning, the reconstruction, and the outcome of the patient's condition and characterological makeup. The psychodynamics of the case was a more common concept then than it is today. However, I did, relevant to these questions, write specifically in a paper years later on "The Psychoanalytic Process" (Rangell, 1968), as well as specific papers on technique, such as what transpires "From Insight to Change" (Rangell, 1981).

I would make some further observations about then and now stemming from these cases. Certain empirical data are to be noted which may cast light on future issues and debates. Preoedipal determinants are prominent in these early cases alongside of and in reciprocal relationships with oedipal–phallic etiologic factors. Dr. Spruiell points out correctly that my case of the doll phobia—this certainly applies as well to Dr. Loewenstein's case, and probably to most others of the past treated by psychoanalysis—would by today's standards be considered narcissistic and "very disturbed," thereby eligible for various parameters of technique. Also to be noted is that castration anxiety was indistinguishable from fragmentation anxiety, so commonly described in recent years, and was in fact the form through which total body fragmentation would result. This did not eliminate its phallic roots.

These data and their meanings coming from patients were the same then as now. The metaphor of the wheel I introduced and first used in my case to explain clinical data has served me in good stead for decades of later writings. In terms, however, of what I would see differently today, my concept of the wheel has evolved in that I have come to see differently what is at the hub. In the case reported it was the presenting symptom, actually the phobic object, which started me on the path to this overriding concept. This was seen to be similar to the onion peel metaphor utilized earlier by Breuer and Freud (1893–1895).

In later years the metaphor remained and continued to be useful, but underwent a metamorphosis as to its composition. The specific symptom which was at first at the hub of the therapeutic quest and direction gave way at one point in my conceptualization to the infantile neurosis. This was still a symptom but now the original and universal one, developmentally en route to all the others. Dr. Spruiell interestingly suggests that nodal unconscious fantasies might exist at the hub of the wheel. Since these are antecedent even to symptom formation, such a suggestion has logical merit. But by now, over the years, I have gradually conceived as the source even of unconscious fantasies what I have called in a series of later papers "the unconscious intrapsychic process" (Rangell, 1963a,b, 1969). This starts and continues the dynamic movement toward symptom formation, and is the path traveled in the reverse direction in the therapeutic analytic process. This dynamic center developed further into the concept of "the human core" (Rangell, 1967).

I agree with Dr. Spruiell's observation that perversion is always reciprocally present with the phobia (Rangell, 1975). This is where my conviction of the simultaneous and reciprocal presence in common of neurosis and perversion was born. Perverse impulses or actions, overt or latent, can exist in partial and shallow to complex and highly organized forms in both neurosis and psychosis, as they do universally in normal sexual foreplay. Preoedipal and oedipal, oral and anal components, existed intermingled with oedipal determinants in this case forty years ago, and in all of the clinical cases reported in this volume from then until the present. This empirical fact might be compared with the separate entity of narcissistic personality on today's psychoanalytic scene, and the explanations proffered about a damaged self based on the commonly adduced etiologic focus of the unempathic mother. The spectrum of patients whose analyses are described here may also be compared with the two analyses of Mr. Z. (Kohut, 1979), found necessary as a prelude and technical model of self psychology in the early 1970s. By serendipity, one of the offending analysts in Loewenstein's case was called by him Dr. Z., over fifty years ago! In this case, Loewenstein undid the errors of the previous analyst not by another analysis under a new theory but by correcting the errors in another standard analysis.

Every analyzed patient we treat or study makes us listen differently to all others. Just as each of us learns from our own past cases, we can also derive experience and insight from one another's cases, analyzed and reported in depth. We also extrapolate from clinical insights to the widest social and cultural phenomena. I learned from this patient with a phobia for dolls the unconscious meaning of high heels in female dress and in the fantasies and sexual activities of males and females. From another patient I derived an understanding of the multilayered meanings and emotional valences of fingernails in feminine attire. This I learned from a patient who called himself a "trans-cosmetologist," a variant of transvestitism. He would make up girls and then himself as a prelude to his sexual foreplay and seductions. An extension of my education into the meanings of this part of female anatomy, and the repressed determinants behind the widespread interest in what has by now become a specialty within the wider cosmetic industry, came from an eventual understanding of another patient and why his divorcing wife opened a nails care boutique, which went on to become very successful.

As one of the discussants, Dr. Bernstein, put it, immersion in these cases is like participating in a dynamic, ongoing psychoanalytic treatment. Readers have an opportunity to sit in on and participate in these varied ongoing analyses, both to vicariously supervise and be supervised as they read and think along. From this overall view, historically, temporally, diagnostically, and of a variety of individual analytic styles, the reader has an opportunity to synthesize as well as differentiate for himself, and to attempt to answer problems which have been under current debate in recent decades. How has knowledge of transference and countertransference advanced? A lesson separate from but contiguous to countertransference is that of iatrogenic inputs. To me a most important question is what light do these cases shed on the crucial question of the qualitative and quantitative relationships between transference and reconstruction. Is the present analytic experience decisive in and of itself and/or as a replica of the reconstructed past? How does the "new" current experience influence the old previous ones?

Many of these questions will not be answered by the clinical experiences reported. These cases for the most part did not lead to new interactional methods, or to reductionism to one aspect of the past, but can be said rather to represent the development of the mainstream itself. But the reader might well be stimulated to examine more closely his own amassed clinical material, past, present, and ongoing into the future. This overall look can be compared to the theoretical yield from the progression of recent alternative theories and methods, with their differences in understanding and derivative treatments. How have the contents of psychodynamic psychopathology, and the methods of understanding and treating them, changed, if at all? Has the psychoanalytic method changed from reconstructive to interactional, from transference as a reflection of unconscious conflicts of the past to a new corrective reparative experience in the present? What endures about psychoanalysis from this overall view of clinical material as given here over five decades? Has increased complexity of theory advanced or complicated "progress"?

This volume will not necessarily provide the answers, but can well serve to start the reader looking to his own experience for directions and convictions. Reading this material is not only engaging but in my opinion can be an instruction exercise for any practicing psychoanalyst, as well as to the gamut of therapists and other mental health professionals to whom psychoanalytic theory and principles serve as a model. The journey undertaken cannot help but be a fascinating and, I trust, useful one. It can also add to the enjoyment of practicing analysis and therapy.

REFERENCES

Breuer, J., & Freud, S. (1893–1895), Studies on Hysteria. *Standard Edition,* 2. London: Hogarth Press, 1955.
Deutsch, H. (1932), *Psycho-Analysis of the Neuroses,* ed. E. Jones. London: Hogarth Press and The Institute of Psycho-Analysis.
Freud, S. (1900), The Interpretation of Dreams. *Standard Edition,* 4 & 5. London: Hogarth Press, 1953.
——— (1905), Fragment of an analysis of a case of hysteria. *Standard Edition,* 7:3–124. London: Hogarth Press, 1953.
——— (1909a), Analysis of a phobia in a five-year-old boy. *Standard Edition,* 10:3–152. London: Hogarth Press, 1955.
——— (1909b), Notes upon a case of obsessional neurosis. *Standard Edition,* 10:153–265. London: Hogarth Press, 1955.
——— (1911), Psychoanalytic notes on an autobiographical account of a case of paranoia (dementia paranoides). *Standard Edition,* 12:3–84. London: Hogarth Press, 1955.
——— (1918), From the history of an infantile neurosis. *Standard Edition,* 17:3–124. London: Hogarth Press, 1955.
Kohut, H. (1979), The two analyses of Mr. Z. *Internat. J. Psycho-Anal.,* 60:3–27.
Rangell, L. (1963a), The scope of intrapsychic conflict—Microscopic and macroscopic considerations. *The Psychoanalytic Study of the Child,* 18:75–102. New York: International Universities Press.
——— (1963b), Structural problems in intrapsychic conflict. *The Psychoanalytic Study of the Child,* 18:103–138. New York: International Universities Press.
——— (1966), An overview of the ending of an analysis. In: *Psychoanalysis in the Americas,* ed. R. Litman. New York: International Universities Press.
——— (1967), Psychoanalysis, affects, and the "Human Core"—On the relationship of psychoanalysis to the behavioral sciences. *Psychoanal. Quart.,* 36:172–202.
——— (1968), The psychoanalytic process. *Internat. J. Psycho-Anal.,* 49:19–26.
——— (1969), The intrapsychic process and its analysis—A recent line of thought and its current implications. *Internat. J. Psycho-Anal.,* 50:65–77.
——— (1974), A psychoanalytic perspective leading currently to the syndrome of the compromise of integrity. *Internat. J. Psycho-Anal.,* 55:3–12.

——— (1975), Psychoanalysis and the process of change. An essay on the past, present and future. *Internat. J. Psycho-Anal.*, 56:87–98.
——— (1981), From insight to change. *J. Amer. Psychoanal. Assn.*, 29:119–141.

1. THE ANALYSIS OF AN OBSESSIONAL NEUROSIS

Introduction

Dr. Loewenstein's analysis of Mme. N., a woman with severe obsessional neurosis, took place in the early 1930s. Mme. N. had three previous unsuccessful therapeutic encounters with three different therapists. The analysis with Dr. Z., which lasted for eleven years, was particularly significant in shaping the course and symptomatology of Mme. N.'s neurosis. Dr. Loewenstein reversed the deteriorating course of the analysis by addressing the unrecognized and complicated transference reaction of the patient, and her extensive resistances, which effectively incorporated the methods of psychoanalytic inquiry into the structure of her neurosis, using it as a potent resistance to the unfolding of the psychoanalytic process.

The failure of Dr. Z. to recognize Mme. N.'s transference neurosis resulted in significant omissions as well as faulty interventions in the analytic situation. Dr. Loewenstein recognized and interpreted the impact of Dr. Z.'s inappropriate and nonanalytic interventions with Mme. N. at the height of the transference neurosis. These interventions had undermined the therapeutic relationship and brought about a regression in the patient from a hysterical neurosis to an obsessional neurosis with florid symptomatology. The maintenance of analytic neutrality and adherence to a proper analytic stance helped Dr. Loewenstein to forge a productive course of analysis. He was assisted in the achievement of his goal by focusing on Mme. N.'s ego reactions to interventions in order to judge the effectiveness of interpretations. Dr. Loewenstein also respected Mme. N.'s individual uniqueness which served as the broader context for her psychopathology and psychoanalytic treatment.

Dr. Silber's discussion underlines Dr. Loewenstein's neutrality, the proper analytic posture, and focus on the patient's unanalyzed transference neurosis toward Dr. Z. In addition, Dr. Silber examines Mme. N.'s transference reaction toward Loewenstein. He describes in detail the countertransference phenomenon in both analyses and the differential ways it was handled by the two analysts. Dr. Silber examines the nature of the therapeutic change without the discovery of infantile neurosis and its resolution, a necessary phenomenon described by Freud. A possible mechanism proposed is the analysis of here and now in transference (see Gill [1979] in Silber's discussion) and the interpretation of the patient's hostility toward her mother outside of transference. The central issue of Mme. N.'s homosexual feelings toward her mother, sister, young maids, and daughter, and in transference toward her previous analyst, Dr. Z., was not addressed in analysis. Dr. Silber proposes that Dr. Z.'s forbidding attitude toward sexual activities in real life had intensified Mme. N.'s homosexual fantasies toward her female analyst which remained unconscious and brought about further regression toward an obsessional neurosis. Dr. Silber also discusses the technical alteration by Dr. Loewenstein to accommodate the severity of Mme. N.'s neurosis.

Dr. Weinshel underlines Dr. Loewenstein's success in addressing the broad range of events in the life of the patient—infantile, intermediate, and present. Dr. Loewenstein's recognition and emphasis on resistance, autonomous ego functions, and enhancing the tolerance of the ego to the patient's unconscious drives is apparent. Dr. Weinshel emphasizes the prominence of betrayal in Mme. N.'s history and the impact of Dr. Loewenstein's meeting with the patient's husband which placed Mme. N. in a childlike position. In spite of Dr. Z.'s inexcusable contamination of the analytic situation, Mme. N. appears to have had the characteristic of inviting betrayal by others which had been part of her personality structure and neurosis.

Dr. Weinshel discusses the gradual shift in emphasis in many areas in psychoanalysis since Freud's original constructions. He comments on several areas. In the area of diagnosis, there is less emphasis on the symptoms and more on the patient's character structure, ego strength, and the developmental level of her conflicts. There is more emphasis on the relationship between the oedipal and preoedipal pathology, the phobic and obsessional neuroses representing the different phases of the same process, and the role of aggression in both neurotic phases and the patient's intra- and extra-analytic life.

The goal of analysis includes the discovery and reconstruction of the patient's character development and its role in the overall psychic structure by connecting the patient's external and internal worlds and its place in the tripartite psychic apparatus. Helping the patient gain insight into her resistances has become more significant than merely uncovering the content of repressed conflicts. There is more focus on countertransference issues which played a significant role in shaping the interventions of Drs. Z., X., and Y. and may have influenced Dr. Loewenstein's technique in the application of the rule of abstinence.

THE OLD WOMAN'S TOUCH: REFLECTIONS ON THE TREATMENT OF A CASE OF OBSESSIONAL NEUROSIS

Rudolph M. Loewenstein, M.D.

Over twenty-five years ago an analyst living abroad asked me if I would take care of one of her patients during the latter's visit to her sister in Paris.

Some time later the patient in question came to see me. She was a married woman of about thirty, with symptoms of a serious obsessive–compulsive neurosis. She had such a dread of having perhaps "touched the old woman" that she could not get along without seeing her analyst every day. She would not let me question her in any detail on the history of her life and illness because she said it upset her too much and made her anxiety unbearable. Knowing that my role during the few weeks

From *Revue Française de Psychanalyse* (Freud Centenary Issue), 22/3 (July-September 1956):384–404. "Réflexions sur le traitement d'un cas de névrose copulsionnelle." Reprinted by permission of R. Loewenstein Estate. English translation by Vera Dammann, 1958.

I would be seeing her should be that of a temporary crutch, and that the responsibility for her treatment was in the hands of her regular analyst, I decided to accept the passive role the patient imposed on me, and to observe and help her as much as I could.

The patient began each session by relating a dream of the preceding night and followed it up with "associations." Mainly through these "associations" I discovered that she had been in treatment for a considerable number of years without much result. But I will give the biographical data further on in my description of the case, since it was only later that I learned many more details about her history.

Some months after the patient had returned to her country I received another letter from her analyst, this time asking me if I would be willing to take over her patient, who was showing no improvement at all. I wrote for details of the case and in reply received a letter from the analyst in which she enumerated a number of the patient's "complexes." It was a fairly comprehensive list containing, among others, the unconscious neeed for punishment—then a comparative newcomer in the categories of pathogenic factors described in the psychoanalytic literature of the period. The reason I am stressing this letter is because it made rather an unfavorable impression on me at the time, but it was not until much later that I realized why: the list of "complexes" she had sent me could have applied equally well to a large number of patients and did not read like the description of a particular case. There was nothing in the letter that referred to the specific problems of this patient and made her recognizable as an individual or distinguished her from the general group of people suffering from the same "complexes." I had a premonition that this lack of attention to the personal peculiarities of the patient might be partly responsible for the lack of success in the treatment. However, I was cautious about passing judgment in view of the seriousness of the patient's symptoms which had persisted for many years: continuous and excessive anxiety; an extreme degree of *folie du doute;* endless compulsive ablutions; total absorption in her "touchings" and her treatment to the exclusion of all other activities. Therefore, when her husband came to see me, I offered to analyze his wife for a period of six to eight months and then tell him whether I felt myself capable of continuing with any chance of success. It is hardly necessary to mention that all the medical examinations the patient had undergone, both in her own country and in France, had failed to discover any somatic disorder. However, I did keep in mind the possibility that she might be suffering either from one of those neuroses which are inaccessible to psychoanalysis or from a latent psychosis in the guise of obsessional neurosis; hence my reservations in making a prognosis. Such possibilities had to be contemplated in the presence of symptoms which had been growing steadily worse over the years. Fortunately, my fears were to prove unfounded.

I have already mentioned the patient's fears and her obsessive dread of having "touched the old woman." I also mentioned her ablutions, or to use her own expression, "washings." It became clear to me later that the fears were not lest she had touched some real old woman, but lest she had touched someone or something that might have been in contact with an old servant, a maid she had had six years previously. It made no difference whether the object in question was a man or a young woman or a table, or whether the person or object was quite close to her or several yards away. What mattered was that she had the idea, the obsession, that she might somehow have been in contact with this person or thing that had been touched by the "old woman," the maid in question. To avoid being "contaminated" by such "touches," she isolated herself from all sorts of objects—including the psychoanalytic couch by spreading out innumerable pieces of tissue paper. Every morning, following an established ritual, she scrubbed herself for hours with soap and water. And if during these "washings" she had the obsessive thought that she might somehow have touched "the old woman," she was compelled to start all over again. The result was that she walked around with her red, chapped hands held away from her body, avoiding contact with any of the furniture, in a state of continual panic anxiety. One of her constant preoccupations was the problem of getting herself new clothes. Although she had a great many dresses hanging in her closets, each one carefully separated from the others by layers of tissue paper, she was unable to touch them because they had been contaminated by "the old woman's touch." She was continually faced therefore with the terrifying task of buying a new dress. Curiously enough, but typical of the ambivalence in this type of obsessional patient, side by side with this exaggerated cleanliness in her clothes and her person, she only washed her hair once or twice a year, and wore the same underwear for several months without a change. "It is clean," she used to say, "because I wash myself so often." Her life was completely taken up with her neurosis; she had no time for recreation, rest, or occupation.

II

At about this time I learned a few details about the patient's history, and although the complete story only came out during the course of her treatment, I propose for the sake of clarity to give a consecutive summary here, and will come back to certain facts in more detail later.

Mme. N. was the second youngest of four children. There was a considerable gap in age between the older brother and sister and herself, and she had always been closest to the younger sister, with whom she was now living in Paris. She herself had been her father's favorite and used to protect her younger sister from his injustices. The two sisters had remained extremely close. The parents had been a united couple; they had managed to impose their way of life on their children, although not their small-town bourgeois opinions. Later, after the patient's marriage, the father's authoritarian attitude was greatly modified as the result of financial reverses, a fact which was to have considerable influence on the patient's neurosis.

The first signs of neurosis appeared when the patient was sixteen.[1] She was studying the piano and planning to make a

[1]There was no way of ascertaining the existence of a childhood neurosis and the patient never mentioned recollection of neurotic symptoms in childhood.

career in music. Her father objected violently to her plans; "he was not going to allow a daughter of his to become an artist; she must marry and have children." The patient did not relinquish her plans, but from that time on she had "concentration difficulties" and this effectively prevented her from doing as good work on the piano as before. She was treated by a well-known psychotherapist and her condition improved. Some years later her parents decided to marry her to a young man they had selected, the son of family friends. He was an amiable, pleasant young man, but the patient neither respected nor admired him. She rebelled and refused to consider the marriage. She left with her sister to spend a weekend in the mountains and there had an affair with a young man she had never met before and never met again. When she returned home, tearful and conscience-stricken, she told her mother all about the episode as proof that she could not possibly marry the young man her parents had picked out for her. Her father remained adamant and threatened to make her knuckle under. She gave in.

During the honeymoon her neurosis erupted definitively in the form of continuous states of anxiety and depression. For two years she was under the care of Dr. X., who used a kind of "cathartic" technique. When there was still no improvement after two years of treatment, Dr. X. told her husband about his wife's premarital affair, which he considered responsible for her anxiety state. Fortunately, the patient had already related the whole episode to her husband a few weeks previously so that he did not show too much resentment. She then went into treatment with Dr. Y. The patient related—whether accurately or not I had no means of knowing—that after about two years of treatment, when she began to express suicidal thoughts, Dr. Y. abruptly broke off the analysis without giving her any other suggestions or advice. Her anxiety grew worse. She then went to Dr. Z., with whom she remained in analysis for eleven years prior to coming to me. During the first five years of treatment her life was a succession of anxiety crises, depressions, and phobias. Among other things, she was afraid to enter any street or public square if the name contained an allusion to rust or red. During the course of analysis it came out that this color was contained in the name of the boy she had the weekend affair with.

After five years her condition suddenly worsened and the neurosis took the acute form described earlier. Immediately preceding the aggravation of her symptoms some important life events had occurred. Her father, who had been having business difficulties, lost all his money with the result that the whole family was now in serious financial straits. Perhaps as a result of his financial misfortunes, Mme. N.'s father permitted her younger sister to marry the man she was in love with, an artist with neither money nor position. This had a profoundly disturbing effect on the patient. And while the financial situation of her own family was growing more and more critical, her husband inherited a fortune from his father. Thus the patient became the only member of her family in easy circumstances, a situation which she found very distressing. Her humiliation was complete when her father, whom she had always admired and feared, borrowed money from her husband and failed to pay it back. Mme. N.'s condition suddenly deteriorated. She had recently engaged a maid whom she hated and feared. She only kept her for four weeks but by the time she dismissed her the damage had been done, and she was already in the grip of the obsessional neurosis in which, as we have seen, this maid becomes the old woman who haunted her. Mme. N. could not bear to touch anything in the house—furniture, clothes, etc.—that this woman might have touched. Henceforward her clothes remained hanging in their closets. She could not even bear to sleep in the same bed as her husband unless she was separated from him by layers of tissue paper, so that intercourse between them occurred even less frequently than before. Her anxiety was intolerable, and in order to rid herself of any trace of contact with the old maidservant, she started the ritual of daily ablutions described earlier. In all fairness to Dr. Z. it should be stated that the latter tried several times to get her to go to another doctor but the patient refused. And Mr. N. told me later in confidence that, unknown to his wife, Dr. Z. had not charged any fees for the last six years.

III

As I mentioned in the beginning, the patient's behavior during her analytic sessions followed a fairly regular pattern. She avoided coming into contact with any furniture, covered the couch with pieces of tissue paper, stretched out on it, and then began by beseeching me tearfully to reassure her that she had not "touched the old woman." Then she would relate a dream and follow it with "associations." The "associations" were of a very special nature. They resembled fantasies based on symbolic interpretations of the dream, interspersed with wisps of memories from her life. It was obvious that she was continuing a routine pattern she had grown accustomed to with Dr. Z. At first I had no inkling of what this way of behaving represented. After a few weeks my interpretation of one of her dreams seemed indirectly to impress the patient; the next day she brought a new dream and associations which seemed to confirm my interpretation of the previous day exactly. I was very pleased about this. But when a few weeks later the same thing occurred again with the interpretation of another dream, my satisfaction became tinged with uncertainty. There was something strange about this: it was not usual to see one's interpretations so readily confirmed, without struggle or resistances on the part of the patient, and particularly such a seriously sick patient. When soon the same thing happened a third time I was sure I was on the wrong track. Subsequently these initial interpretations were shown to be more or less irrelevant. It then became clear to me that everything concerned with the treatment, the sessions themselves, her "associations," my interpretations, had been absorbed into her obsessional neurosis and had become part of a sort of magic ritual which, like her ablutions, she used to help ward off the "old woman's touch." The treatment had lost all character of psychoanalytic cure and had become an integral part of her neurosis.

The patient had a peculiar habit which gave me the first clue to the enigma. At the end of every session she would insist on my repeating my last interpretation several times, on the pretext either that she had not understood a word of it, or that she did not get the full meaning, or because she could not remember the exact phrasing. She claimed that she had to get my interpretation by heart so that she could remember and use it to help her cope with her doubts and fears until the next session. I then recalled how Freud had interpreted this type of obsessive symptom in his patient known as the "Rat Man." Freud explained that this type of obsessive doubt expresses an unconscious lack of confidence in the interlocutor—a sort of derisive doubt. Only much later did I realize that my patient's mockery and unconscious distrust were directed against her last analyst, Dr. Z., and that she had had good reason to question the latter's interpretations and to deride her counsels. When I suggested to her—with great circumspection in view of her extreme anxiety—the possibility that she had such feelings, she was seized with panic. I concluded that I had guessed right, but also that I would have to exercise extreme caution in probing further in that direction. I then chose another line of approach. I decided to use the "rule of abstinence" and in future not to repeat my interpretations so many times. At first I repeated them five times instead of six, then four times instead of five, and so on. It was hard for the patient to tolerate this frustration.

I shall not go into all the details of this analysis; but I should like to mention that this progressive breaking up of her ritual, through deprivation, brought some aggressive reactions closer to the surface. The first two valid and relevant interpretations of her obsessions had similar results. On her way to my office the patient had to pass the window of a pastry shop. She was often tempted to go in and buy some candy, both for herself and to take home to her mother, but she always resisted the impulse for fear of "touching the old woman." One day she plucked up sufficient courage to get as far as the door, but there she recoiled in horror; someone had passed near her, whether man or woman she did not know, but she was seized with a horrible dread that perhaps it was the "old woman." I told her quite simply that she did not really want to buy candy for her mother. She refused to believe this, but the interpretation bore fruit; the patient gradually became able to express hostile thoughts toward her family and her analysts. Another of Mme. N.'s obsessions, as we have mentioned, was to buy herself new dresses because she could never wear again any dress that she had once put in a closet, where it would hang along with all her other dresses of the past six years, separately wrapped in tissue paper. The purchasing of material for a new dress was preceded by weeks of preparation during the analytic sessions. She had to "associate" and obtain assurance through magic interpretations that she was justified in buying a new dress that would not be contaminated by contact with the old woman. After a few months of analysis she found the courage to buy some silk for a new dress. Just as she was passing the cashier's desk with her parcel under her arm, she was suddenly obsessed with the idea that the cashier had stretched out a long arm and touched the parcel. Once again she was seized with panic and resolved not to touch the silk for a long time. She added that on leaving the shop she found herself humming over and over the melody of a children's song. I insisted that she tell me the words. It was the nursery rhyme, "J'ai du bon tabac dans ma tabatière. . . . Tu n'en auras pas." (I have good tobacco in my pouch. . . . You shan't have any.) This, then, was the meaning of her symptom. She, the only wealthy member of her family, wants to buy a new dress; the old maidservant, her mother, her sister—all jealous, all poor—want to take it away from her. Overcome with guilt and anxiety she has to renounce the dress, just as she has to deprive herself of candy, because she ought, but does not want to share it with her mother and sister and feels too guilty to eat it alone. Once I had understood this, I could tell Mr. N. when he came to see me again that I would undertake to treat his wife.

Here I should like to leave the analysis for a moment in order to complete the account of the events which preceded the appearance of the obsessional neurosis in the middle of her treatment with Dr. Z. I was gradually able to reconstruct these during the three-and-a-half years that Mme. N. was in analysis with me. At the end of that period her analysis was, with my approval, interrupted for extremely important external reasons. However, there had already been very considerable improvement in her condition.

After the death of her father-in-law, when the question of dividing the inheritance came up, the mother-in-law came to live with them and the patient had to spend a great deal of time with the old lady. The patient disliked her intensely but had to appear outwardly civil and amiable. All this took place soon after her own family's financial ruin, and after her father had permitted her younger sister to marry the poor man she was in love with. Dr. Z., who had been kept informed of all matters pertaining to the inheritance, at this point suggested that the patient and her husband get the help of a lawyer. This they did, with the result that her husband's share of the inheritance was considerably increased.

Mme. N., who had never found sexual satisfaction in her marriage, was always tempted to take a lover, but fear of guilt feelings prevented her from succumbing to the temptation. She always felt that if she had a satisfactory love life she might perhaps be cured of all her ills. With the thought that she might one day have a lover, she surrounded herself with young, attractive, flirtatious maids. She would imagine their love affairs and think that they would not blame her if she had an extramarital love life of her own. The "old woman"—ugly, forbidding, straitlaced—was the first "old maid" she had ever hired. She wanted to dismiss her at once, but Dr. Z. advised her to keep her, we have seen with what result: a few weeks later Mme. N. was seized with such intolerable anxiety that she was unable to touch anything in the house and her husband finally had to dismiss the old maidservant. Thus the patient, while not actually disobeying Dr. Z., obtained her ends through her neurosis.

About that time Dr. Z. intervened in still another matter. My patient told me about it quite casually, without realizing its significance, when she was well on in her analysis. She had made the acquaintance of an attractive young man who courted her assiduously. She decided to go to a masked ball where she knew she would meet him, in the hope that a liaison would develop. Dr. Z. advised her to give up the idea. She went even further; when Mme. N. later reproached her and said she would never stop regretting having given him up, Dr. Z. suggested that she tell herself that she might have caught a venereal disease from him if she had become his mistress. Here then was the source of the patient's obsessive fear of being "contaminated by the old maid's touch." But in her obsession it was no longer a man who might contaminate her, but a woman—an old woman. The maid in fact was a substitute for her analyst: both had red hair and both were spinsters—"old maids." Now her horror of the "old woman's touch" and the latter's domination over her both become understandable as violent, affective conflicts with the analyst as object. All the patient's rage against her, all her distrust and unconscious derision had been displaced onto the old servant, seemingly sparing her analyst. I say seemingly because in actual fact the patient took her revenge by unconsciously making a mockery out of the treatment, and punished the analyst by burdening her with her pitiable and incurable presence.

IV

Before continuing discussion of the technical problems involved in Mme. N.'s case, I should like to say a few words about the structure of her neurosis. I shall not go into details about her childhood history, but concentrate rather on the relation between her neurosis and the events described above.

We have seen that during the first five years of analysis her anxiety hysteria centered around the conflict between her sexual desires on the one hand, and her obedience and attachment to her father on the other. Her symptoms represented guilt on account of her sexual escapade and a constant effort to avoid the temptation of being unfaithful to her husband and thus to her father. But with the episode of the old maid and the resulting symptoms, a very different picture emerges. True, the horror of red hair continues the old phobia, but it has now become displaced to the "old woman." The difference is striking: the fear refers no longer to contact with a man, but with a woman; and it is no longer a fear of sexual contact but of some horrible contamination or pollution. Moreover, the analysis revealed that during the period of the obsessional neurosis the "touches" invariably expressed two things: on the one hand a hostile contact, or assault, by the "old woman," and on the other it represented touching money. As we saw earlier, her obsessive fears represented the impossibility of deriving satisfaction from the money she had come to possess in spite of herself. During a considerable part of her analysis the material centered around the secondary gains from her neurosis, which consisted in depriving her mother and sister of reaping any benefit from her wealth. She often promised to give her sister discarded dresses or other possessions of hers; but the "old woman's touch" prevented her from making the gift. On such occasions her obsession took the following form: "If I give these dresses to my sister she will be contaminated by the 'old woman's touch'; she will become the 'old woman.' " This can be interpreted in the following way: "If I give her my dresses she will not only have a husband whom she loves but also beautiful clothes to please him; I would hate her so much that I would be afraid what she might do to me." She deprived her sister of looking attractive and pretty without being to blame: it was the fault of her neurosis which she could not help; moreover she also deprived herself and suffered terribly from anxiety. The incident of the candy is a good illustration of this mechanism. After her neurosis took the obsessive–compulsive form, she was no longer tempted to have a love affair. One might say that the old conflict centering around sexual temptation had regressed into a conflict centering around money, aggression, defilement, and guilt connected with a woman. This change clearly confirms the distinction Freud made between anxiety hysteria (phobia) and obsessional neurosis. Her former neurosis, a phobia, had been based predominantly on conflicts of the phallic stage, but it had regressed into a neurosis based on the anal–sadistic stage of libidinal development. One can also observe her regression from the oedipal to the preoedipal stage: from interest focused on the man in the phobic phase of the patient's neurosis to absorption in the woman in the obsessional phase. It is this latter element that contains the explanation of some otherwise puzzling aspects of her symptoms, namely that it could be either a man or a woman who reminded her of the "old woman" in her "touch" obsessions; sometimes even her husband. She would reveal this by telling me, "I loathe his physique." In her derogatory fantasies about her husband she saw him as the son of the "old woman"; hence she had to make a barrier between them, in bed, with layers of tissue paper.

The strength of her aggressive tendencies during the obsessional period can be gauged by her inability to tolerate the slightest aggressive impulse or hostile feeling in herself. At first my slightest hint that she might have such feelings stirred up intolerable anxiety and guilt which only gradually became bearable. As for the anal component in the structure of her neurosis, we have seen it at work in her ablutions and in her constant concern with pollution and contamination. We have seen how Dr. Z. precipitated this symptom by suggesting that the patient tell herself that genital contact might result in venereal disease. The intensity of ambivalence toward money is particularly striking in this case.

From her adolescence on, her father had opposed the idea of her marrying for love; she must have an arranged marriage with a man who was comfortably off. Through attachment to her father she submitted outwardly to his will. But in actual fact the neurosis which broke out during her honeymoon was a blow at her father and represented a sort of unconscious revenge, which she in turn paid for dearly in terms of anxiety and guilt. Later, after the loss of his fortune, this father for whom she had sacrificed her love life was to betray her by allowing her younger sister to marry the man she loved. Everything then conspired to depreciate love in favor of money: she had to go about in the company of her mother-in-law—another "old woman"—instead of a lover; her father borrowed money from her husband and did not pay it back. Dr. Z. added the finishing stroke by advising her to get a lawyer, who increased her husband's inheritance, while at the same time she advised her to reject a lover but to retain a disagreeable, ugly old maid in her service. As with her father, the patient outwardly submitted, and her revolt took the form of the obsessive–compulsive neurosis.

The question arises to what extent Dr. Z.'s suggestion that she imagine herself contaminated as a result of sexual intercourse is enough in itself to explain the patient's fear of "touches." We know of course that there are many cases with similar obsessive symptoms which cannot be traced back to a similar source. It is true also that fear of venereal disease is often a component in the pathogenesis of such cases, but not always; and it is often only a rationalization of other underlying anxieties. The fear of touching or being touched has extremely complex connotations. Generally speaking, contact with the hand can represent the whole gamut of human behavior extending from affection to aggression. It may mean proximity, tenderness, sexual contact, taking possession, etc. So, too, in Mme. N.'s case the obsession was overdetermined. In the incident of the cashier, the cashier's long arm and hand which seemed to reach out and touch the parcel signified a sort of *mainmise* or seizing of the silk, forbidding the patient to use it. The obsession in this instance implied that the "old woman" exercised her power over the patient unscrupulously and forbade her to be an attractive woman; and that she was jealous and wanted to steal her silk. On other occasions touching had the meaning of "touching money" with similar underlying affects: she had no right to have money or to benefit by it; the old woman wanted to touch her money and take it away from her. It is interesting that in Mme. N.'s case the sysmbolic meaning of the act of touching that is usually so important—masturbation—played only a secondary role. What was important was the fantasy of being at the mercy of a sexual gesture on the part of a hated and feared woman. The patient's unconscious thought on hearing Dr. Z.'s advice might be translated as follows: "You want me to give up my life as a woman, to lie to myself by imagining I might have been contaminated by the man I love; at the same time you want me to submit to a forbidding, ugly old maid like yourself; I can just as easily imagine that you are the one who has contaminated everything I possess, you 'old woman.' So you want me to imagine contaminations? All right I am going to imagine some. If this is the kind of help you give me to get well, just you wait and see the results."

While Dr. Z.'s advice may not have been sufficient in itself to determine the form of the patient's neurosis, it was certainly an important factor in bringing it about.

V

There were a few special features about Mme. N.'s treatment that have a bearing on some important problems of psychoanalytic technique.

Her pattern of behavior when she first came into treatment with me, that is, reporting a dream every day and following it up with associations that implicitly invited an interpretation of the dream, was clearly a continuation of a routine she had developed during her preceding treatments. We have seen how I was taken in at first by this insidious form of resistance. The interesting thing about her associations was that they more or less compelled interpretations in terms of childhood problems: attachment to her father; jealousy; sexual games with her sister; guilt feelings about masturbation. We have seen, too, how my interpretations of this material stimulated further dreams and associations which appeared to confirm them, but without producing the slightest effect on the patient nor any modification in her symptoms. She neither denied nor confirmed the validity of my interpretations. Her one invariable reaction was to ask me to repeat them several times at the end of the session. She seemed to have no resistance: she was always punctual and talked freely; her outward manner betrayed none of the well-known little signs of resistance. It was precisely this apparent absence of all resistance that led me to discover that her defenses were camouflaged in a much subtler way. I gradually realized that her associations tended to prompt me to the interpretations she wanted or expected from me. Furthermore, in this first period my interpretations were centered almost exclusively around the patient's distant past, as I suppose Dr. Z.'s had been. She contributed little and gave only the scantiest information on events in the present or recent past. At first I was never able to explain to my own satisfaction why a certain dream had occurred on a certain night, or what it was in the present that had evoked or reactivated a particular childhood memory. And we know that to get at the true meaning of a dream it is essential to know this. All this helped to convince me that Mme. N. was using the routine recital of her dreams as a resistance to the analysis. We have already seen how she had absorbed the analytic treatment into her obsessional rituals, so that it had become an integral part of a sort of transference neurosis. We also know that unconsciously she made a mockery out of her analysis, thereby unconsciously expressing her lack of confidence in her doctors and her treatment. She had had good reason not to have much confidence in them: Dr. X. had betrayed her confidence; Dr. Y. abruptly dismissed her when she started to talk about suicide; as for Dr. Z., the reasons for the patient's mistrust were more complex. Dr. Z. had certainly stepped out of her role of analyst in some of her recommendations. I do not know if she had given the patient advice on other occasions besides the three already mentioned, but in the three we know about, although not of equal importance, there was one element in common: in all three instances Dr. Z. had sided with money against sexuality. She was evidently not sufficiently aware of the meaning and impact this had for her patient, namely, that of definitely discouraging any aspirations toward a satisfactory love life and thereby reinforcing the regressive tendencies that were stimulated by outward events that occurred at that time. Dr. Z.'s recommendation to keep the old maid and to renounce the love affair certainly betray her own lack of confidence in the efficacy of analytic procedure, and there can be no doubt that this undermined the patient's own confidence in it. One of her recommendations had a quite special significance that is worth discussing in some detail: her advice to her patient to console herself for renouncing the lover by imagining she might have been contaminated by him. It is as if Dr. Z. told the patient to lie to herself. Now intellectual dishonesty in an analyst is a fault that inevitably does irreparable damage. The patient, of whom total frankness and sincerity are asked, will never be able to give them to an analyst who has given proof of lack of intellectual integrity himself.

Dr. Z. had also lent herself to another subtle deformation of the analytic technique, which the patient exploited every time that she wanted to buy a dress for example. For weeks beforehand Mme. N. asked her doctor for reassurance through analyzing her dreams that she would be able to make the contemplated purchase without danger of the "old woman's touch." As a matter of fact when she did finally decide to buy a dress the transaction was almost always interrupted by the "old woman's touch," which was a way of giving the lie to her analyst's assurances. Thus Dr. Z. had let herself be maneuvered into allowing the patient to use the analytic procedure as a sort of magic ritual to exorcize her obsessive fears. The patient faced me with the same problem. I told her frankly that I could give her no assurance that the sessions preceding the purchase of the dress would insure her against the "old woman's touch." I did however advise her to behave as much as possible as she would want to behave when she was cured; to judge for herself the risk of so doing, but not to be afraid to go counter to her apprehensions. This advise was based on Freud's recommendation in the analysis of phobic patients—to suggest to the patient, once the analysis is sufficiently advanced, to confront the object of the phobia little by little.

Mme. N. also tried to gain the complicity of her analyst in extracting secondary benefits from her neurosis. One day she asked me to write to her husband to ask him to send her extra money so that she could come to analysis in a taxi, and thus avoid the "old woman's touch." I refused categorically, telling her that coming in a taxi could have no influence whatsoever on the progress of her treatment. From that day forward her analysis made great progress. On another occasion she tested me out in a different way: she suddenly started to mention suicidal thoughts. Her intention of scaring me was quite transparent and there was obviously no real danger; so I assured her that I was not going to interrupt the treatment as Dr. Y. had done. Her suicidal thoughts disappeared immediately and never recurred.

I do not think I am mistaken in saying that one of the flaws in Dr. Z.'s method had been to concentrate her interest and effort exclusively on the analysis of the patient's childhood. That was why her interpretations of the dreams, and mine during the first months of treatment, were mainly centered on events or affects which had hardly any bearing on the patient's later life experiences. They might be said to hang in midair, unrelated to her present life. Dr. Z.'s habit, too, of analyzing the dreams for themselves and not her patient through the dreams had accentuated still further the divorce of the analysis from the patient's psychological reality. In fact Mme. N. reacted as if the interpretations did not concern her; in other words, she did not react to them at all. We have seen how my first interpretations, which suffered from the same defect, also failed to reach her. By this mechanism she was following a pattern of behavior adopted toward her father at the time of her marriage: outward compliance coupled with stubborn inner resistance. Her passivity toward interpretations continued for so long, albeit in a somewhat attenuated form, that I later took the step of requiring her to tell me whether she agreed or disagreed with them and why.

Because of her excessive concentration on the patient's childhood, Dr. Z. failed to give enough attention to analysis of the transference, as is clearly shown by the fact that she had never made the connection between the old maid and herself. When toward the end of the third year of analysis I finally confronted the patient with this connection, she was quite shocked at first, as if such an idea had never occurred to her. During her treatment with me she also had numerous ambivalent transference reactions toward me. I was fortunate enough, however, to be able to analyze them correctly before they could endanger the treatment. It was then quite a common fault among some analysts to concentrate, as Dr. Z. had done, exclusively on events in the patient's remote childhood. Generally this was due to a confusion between interest in scientific research and its application in the treatment of patients. Because a neurosis derives from early childhood conflicts it was thought that only these early conflicts were important in analyzing the patient's symptoms. Yet Freud had warned analysts long ago against just such a mistake. He had stressed the vital importance of the relation between the past and the present—the past being only important, in an analysis, insofar as it is carried into the present, and the present insofar as it reactivates the past. He also said that it is not enough to discover the source of the original conflicts, but it is also necessary to retrace all its subsequent vicissitudes in later life, in which the ego and the superego as well as the instinctual drives are involved. He used the following metaphor: when a building is damaged by a fire, it is not always at the seat of the fire that the worst damage is found; sometimes flames spreading from the first fire may start fires in other parts of the building that cause much more serious damage. There are times in therapy when it is more important to repair the damage from these later fires before turning our attention to the earlier damage.

In Mme. N.'s case the main conflicts were expressed in a compulsive–obsessive form which had developed while she was in analysis with Dr. Z. It was imperative to deal with these relatively recent conflicts first, and only through them could their origins in childhood be approached. It was not possible in the relatively short time at my disposal to elucidate this patient's early conflicts sufficiently, which accounts for the incomplete results of the analysis. We have seen that the only effective interpretations were those which included her ego reactions as well as her aggressive and libidinal drives. As a general rule interpretations are only effective when they are concrete and personal and apply specifically to the individual case.

Recently it has become more common to see patients with variations of Mme. N.'s type of resistance. I am referring to patients who use psychoanalytic jargon in their sessions, glibly making use of analytic terms that they have picked up in psychoanalytic books or that their analyst has rather rashly imparted to them. They unconsciously make use of these terms to disguise their real psychological experiences. Frequently it is not easy to overcome such paradoxical intellectualized resistances. It is of course essential in scientific work to describe problems of psychopathology in generalized terms and to use such concepts as, for instance, the Oedipus complex. But it is equally essential in the treatment of an individual patient to retranslate these concepts into concrete terms of the patient's personal life. Dr. Z.'s original letter to me showed that she had failed to make such a retranslation, and her analysis of Mme. N. suffered in consequence. Whenever a patient makes use of analytic terms as a means of resistance, the analyst should be particularly careful to express his patient's experiences in simple, nontechnical language, and the terms he uses should correspond exactly with the thoughts and affects of the patient. The following experience with Mme. N. is an illustration. On the way home from my office, during the third year of analysis, she sometimes took a taxi from the subway station to her sister's apartment. Sometimes when she got into the taxi she was seized with the horrible dread that she was "sitting on the old woman." She invariably associated these obsessions with a sexual game she used to indulge in with her sister, when they took turns sitting on each other's knees in the bathroom. She had often reported these memories before, but neither the obsession nor its accompanying anxiety had lessened. Moreover, she had always retained conscious memory of these games and felt neither guilt nor anxiety about them. Therefore these episodes as such were not sufficient to determine her obsession. They had to be considered screen memories. Gradually I elicited more details about the little incidents that preceded the occurrence of the obsession. It was generally either the sight of a beggar to whom she had just refused money, or an old news vendor watching her get into the taxi; other incidents were connected with having to control her resentment against her mother, who was also living in her sister's apartment. It then became possible to reconstruct the repressed thought behind the obsession. The repressed thought centered round the meaning of the colloquial expression, "*Je m'asseois dessus*" (literally, "I sit on them," an expression of contemptuous indifference that might perhaps be conveyed by, "I don't care two hoots about them"). Thus it meant that she was not going to feel sorry for the old beggar, nor for her impoverished mother nor for her sister, but was going to indulge in the extravagance of a taxi. But her hostile impulse aroused such guilt that she immediately punished herself in the place where she had sinned: she sat down on the old woman whose contact disgusted her so much. It was only from that point that the thread led back to the sexual games with her sister, which indirectly represented scarcely disguised fantasies of sexual contact between the father or mother and the child sitting on their lap. The latter fantasies had been completely repressed and the patient was filled with horror when they were mentioned in the analysis. They also led back to the old jealousy of her sister which had been repressed and overcompensated. Nevertheless it was only very gradually that I learned to translate accurately the thoughts underlying the obsession about "sitting on the old woman." One day she greeted my interpretation with the comment, "It's almost that, but not quite." And after I changed the wording slightly she blushed, burst out laughing, and said, "That's it exactly." The obsession disappeared for a few days. But we had to work these conflicts through again and again before the symptom disappeared for good.

Mme. N.'s treatment took place more than twenty-five years ago. One may speculate how the analysis would have developed had it taken place today. There has been such a great advance in psychoanalytic technique with the acquisition of a deeper and more refined insight into the psychology of the ego.[2] Nowadays, of course, I am much quicker to recognize resistance that uses the technique which Mme. N. managed to impose on me for several months. And while the technique that I later employed successfully in her case was along the lines of ego analysis, it seems certain to me now that had I then possessed a greater knowledge of ego psychology I would have avoided needless mistakes and loss of time. In particular one may ask whether, in the light of our present knowledge of the ego, it was necessary to apply the "rule of abstinence" in the way described. It is difficult to know for certain. But it seems to me probable that this rule should have been applied, but with more subtlety. Whenever a patient finds a way to act out his resistances within the analytic procedure itself by means of a transference neurosis, then almost inevitably the rule of abstinence has to be used. However, it is then necessary to give the patient plenty of time (as I in fact did in the case of Mme. N.) and to conduct the analysis *lege artis,* with a great deal of tact and respect for the patient, so as to make it possible for the patient's ego to learn to tolerate the warded off drives, and to transform acting out into insight.

I treated Mme. N. for three-and-a-half years, at the end of which she showed very considerable improvement. She was able to wash and dress in a normal manner. Her anxieties and obsessions occurred less and less frequently and were tolerable. At the end of this period she received letters from her husband announcing his intention of getting a divorce in order to marry his mistress. I encouraged her to return to her country, where she remained about eight months until the divorce proceedings

[2]These advances are in a very large measure due to the work of Anna Freud.

were finished. Mme. N. was mainly upset by the hostility of her daughter, who sided against her violently. During the whole period of the divorce proceedings Mme. N. had no psychiatric help, and when she returned to Paris her improvement appeared to be consolidated. It was not possible for me to take her back into analysis at that time; so I sent her to a colleague, under whose treatment she continued to improve. I saw her some time later when she had just spent some time with her daughter, with whom she was now on better terms. She was leading a normal, though lonely and not very happy, life, and was thinking of returning to her own country. Her fears had diminished to the point where they hardly hampered her at all. Then the war broke out and I lost touch with Mme. N.

BIBLIOGRAPHY

Fenichel, O. (1939), *Problems of Psychoanalytic Technique.* Albany, NY: Psychoanalytic Quarterly.

Freud, A. (1936), *The Ego and the Mechanisms of Defense.* New York: International Universities Press, 1946.

Freud, S. (1909a), Analysis of a phobia in a five-year-old boy. *Standard Edition,* 10:5–149. London: Hogarth Press, 1955.

——— (1909b), Notes upon a case of obsessional neurosis. *Standard Edition,* 10:155–318. London: Hogarth Press, 1955.

——— (1912), The dynamics of the transference. *Standard Edition,* 12:97–108. London: Hogarth Press, 1958.

——— (1913), The disposition to obsessional neurosis. *Standard Edition,* 12:311–326. London: Hogarth Press, 1958.

——— (1914), Remembering, repeating, and working through. *Standard Edition,* 12:145–156. London: Hogarth Press, 1958.

——— (1937), Analysis terminable and interminable. *Standard Edition,* 23:209–253. London: Hogarth Press, 1964.

Glover, E. (1953), *The Technique of Psycho-Analysis.* New York: International Universities Press.

Hartmann, H. (1951), Technical implications of ego psychology. *Psychoanal. Quart.,* 20:31–43.

Kris, E. (1951), Ego psychology and interpretation in psychoanalytic therapy. *Psychoanal. Quart.,* 10:15–30.

Loewenstein, R. M. (1951), The problem of interpretation. *Psychoanal. Quart.,* 20:1–12.

——— (1951), Ego development and psychoanalytic technique. *Amer. J. Psychiat.,* 107:617–622.

——— (1954), On defences, autonomous ego and psychoanalytic technique. *Internat. J. Psycho-Anal.,* 35:188–193.

Nacht, S. (1950), *De la Pratique à la Théorie Psychoanalytique*. Paris: P.U.F.
Reich, W. (1933), *Character Analysis*. New York: Farrar, Straus, & Young, 1949.

A DISCUSSION OF "THE OLD WOMAN'S TOUCH: REFLECTIONS ON THE TREATMENT OF A CASE OF OBSESSIONAL NEUROSIS" BY RUDOLPH M. LOEWENSTEIN

Austin Silber, M.D.

It is a pleasure to discuss this most interesting case study by Dr. Loewenstein. Published in 1956 it describes an analysis conducted for a period of three-and-a-half years in the early 1930s. It reads like a turn-of-the-century melodrama. The symptomatology is florid, dramatic, and vaguely old-fashioned.

The case report has its share of villains. High on the list are therapists X., Y., and Z. The patient, Mme. N., spent most of her adult life in therapy. After a brief, successful stint of psychotherapy at sixteen years of age, she underwent a two-year, unsuccessful "cathartic" type of treatment with Dr. X. This longer period of therapy was necessitated by the eruption of her neurosis which was characterized by continuous states of anxiety and depression. Her next two years were spent in analysis with Dr. Y. This analysis ended abruptly and traumatically for the patient. For the next eleven years of her life Mme. N. remained in analysis with Dr. Z. The last six years of her treatment with Dr. Z. involved the full-blown obsessional neurosis so graphically described by Dr. Loewenstein.

Mme. N.'s therapeutic encounters with Drs. X., Y., and Z. were most significant in shaping her experience prior to her analysis with Dr. Loewenstein. Dr. X. told her husband about a premarital affair which should have been kept confidential. Dr. Y. abandoned her after two years of analysis when she began to express suicidal thoughts. Her illness became more florid after five years of analysis with Dr. Z. Dr. Loewenstein felt he was confronted with a severe obsessional neurosis which had formed out of a preexisting anxiety hysteria. He emphasized that this alteration in her symptomatology was an indication of the regression which had ensued during the course of her analysis with Dr. Z. Both the libidinal regression from the phallic to the anal phase and the concomitant regression of ego functions were amply documented in the protocol.

What makes this obsessional neurosis unique is that its resolution does *not* require any understanding of its infantile sexual roots. (In a footnote Dr. Loewenstein states, "There was no way of ascertaining the existence of a childhood neurosis and the patient never mentioned recollections of neurotic symptoms in childhood" [p. 28].) This is in marked contrast to Freud's (1909) "Notes Upon a Case of Obsessional Neurosis" where he makes it clear that the factors that enter into the formation of an obsessional neurosis "are to be found in the patient's *infantile* sexual life and not in his present one" (p. 165). Freud also states that the understanding and study of the Rat Man's infantile neurosis can "alone enable us to obtain a grasp of the complicated organization of his subsequent illness" (p. 162).

We are thus confronted with the rather remarkable resolution of severe obsessive–compulsive symptoms brought about by an understanding of the meaning and structure of these symptoms as they affected the patient in the transference neurosis which evolved during her analysis with Dr. Loewenstein. Essential for this understanding was the patient's newly formed appreciation of the meaning of her relationship with her previous analysts, an ongoing analysis of her relationship with Dr. Loewenstein, as well as a different appreciation of her involvement with the other significant people in her life.

In this case report we can observe how an unanalyzed transference neurosis is instrumental in aggravating the severity and depth of a patient's illness. However, the analyst's recognition and interpretation of his patient's resistance, when combined with an equal appreciation of the newly evolving transference neurosis, can lead to the resolution of severe neurotic symptomatology.

Dr. Loewenstein's case report raises many interesting questions in regard to how analysts formulate their understanding of a patient's illness. The ways in which this understanding can then modify their technical handling of the resistances encountered during the analysis is depicted. The susceptibility of the analytic process to the analyst's personal prejudices, limitations, and deficiencies is unfortunately etched in the progressive worsening of Mme. N.'s neurosis under the ministrations of Drs. X., Y., and Z. This case report highlights the effect of certain therapeutic indiscretions: a betrayal of a confidence; an unanalytic approach to the expression of a wish in lieu of an effort to analyze it (the suicide threat); and, finally, the failure to recognize the transferential implications of the analyst's behavior within the analysis (Dr. Z.). These indiscretions all contribute to the patient's regressively deepening neurotic symptomatology. The potential dangers inherent in a poorly conducted analysis are graphically depicted. This all forms a fitting background to an appreciation of the tact and skill Dr. Loewenstein was able to use in a seriously compromised therapeutic situation.

It also makes clear why specific variations in technique were indicated in order to attempt to get this patient into a more usual analytic regimen. Thus, there was Mme. N.'s initial refusal to supply in any detail either the history of her life or her illness, coupled with her special treatment of the analytic couch (covering it with tissue paper). Then there were her demands for reassurance from the analyst that she had not "touched the old woman" at the beginning of her sessions. These problems placed upon the analytic situation limitations related to the compelling nature of the patient's severe symptomatology. Thus, the patient's illness, and the analyst's concern about its severity, modified the beginnings of the analysis. Unfortunately, we never do learn when the couch was no longer covered with tissues, but we must assume that at some later point in the treatment, Dr. Loewenstein's technique was modified. Certain other variations in technique that seem specifically related to the severity of the patient's symptomatology apparently necessitated Dr. Loewenstein's meetings with the patient's husband and learning from him, in confidence, the fact that Dr. Z. had not accepted payment for the last six years of her treatment with Mme. N. That money had special meaning to Dr. Z., and that this entered into some countertransference problems, may have been linked up with Mme. N.'s regression from the phallic to the anal phase. Dr. Loewenstein had commented that the patient's primary symptoms (concern with pollution, contamination, and resort to ablutions) had been precipitated by Dr. Z.'s suggestion "that the patient tell herself that genital contact might result in venereal disease" (p. 37).

Another variation in technique had to do with Mme. N.'s "passivity toward interpretations" (p. 42) which lasted so long that Dr. Loewenstein "took the step of requiring her to tell me whether she agreed or disagreed with them [interpretations] and why." These efforts on Dr. Loewenstein's part to help his patient overcome her passivity could have led to the patient feeling forced to comply with his verbal demands. This could have reinforced her retreat to the anal phase (which it apparently did not), it also could have been viewed as a command and led to a hypnotic compliance. In this instance the verbal forcing could be viewed as a variation of the "laying on of hands" in a hypnotic induction. Dr. Loewenstein's direct questions could have been viewed as a possible countertransference response to his patient's demand for verbal repetitions of reassurance. (In some ways he treats Mme. N. as an analyst might treat a child—note his contact with her husband.) It is easy to see that Mme. N.'s treatment made many demands on her analyst to broaden his concept of analytic neutrality as he more actively became involved in trying to help his patient shed her pathological symptomatology.

Dr. Loewenstein describes his gradual understanding of the meaning of his patient's behavior in her analysis.

> It then became clear to me that everything concerned with the treatment, the sessions themselves, her "associations," my inter-

> pretations, had been absorbed into her obsessional neurosis and had become part of a sort of magic ritual which, like her ablutions, she used to help ward off the "old woman's touch." The treatment had lost all character of psychoanalytic cure and had become an integral part of her neurosis [p. 31].

It is obvious that the recognition of this resistance had not been available to her previous analyst and had instead become incorporated in the continually evolving transference neurosis.

Dr. Loewenstein began to recognize the defensive meaning of Mme. N.'s insistence that he repeat his interpretations many times at the end of her sessions. This "derisive doubt," which also touched upon her unconscious hatred and distrust helped bring some of her angry reactions to the fore. He was able, after some months of analysis, to understand the *meaning* of her obsessional symptom. He reached this understanding by interpreting the hostility in her obsessional actions (hostility toward her mother and toward her family) and by insisting that Mme. N. not withold the content of a nursery song (thus, knowingly mobilizing the negative transference). Once Dr. Loewenstein had this understanding, he felt he could treat and cure Mme. N.'s obsessive–compulsive illness. The analyst's *conviction* that he can understand his patient's symptomatology and his confident reliance on his own analytic skills and understanding may be an important element amongst the many that lead to an analytic "cure."

That Dr. Loewenstein sensed this possibility is inherent in his statement that "Dr. Z.'s recommendation to keep the old maid and to renounce the love affair certainly betray her own lack of confidence in the efficacy of analytic procedure, and there can be no doubt that this undermined the patient's confidence in it" (p. 40). What makes this assumption noteworthy is the implication that the analyst's theoretical convictions can have a significant effect in influencing the outcome of an analysis. Suggestion and persuasion must be considered part of the analytic armamentarium in this special instance. At the same time, however, the analyst's technique needs also to nurture the patient's developing autonomy. The complex nature of this patient's analytic experience is easy to note but most difficult to fully understand. In this case report, the patient's primary obsessional symptom was resolved. However, Mme. N. was left in an unhappy state with her fears much reduced, thus she still was in need of further analysis.

Dr. Loewenstein had strong feelings about Dr. Z.'s advice to Mme. N. in regard to renouncing her lover "by imagining she might have been contaminated by him." He goes on to say: "It is as if Dr. Z. told the patient to lie to herself. Now, intellectual dishonesty is a fault that inevitably does irreparable damage. The patient, of whom total frankness and sincerity are asked, will never be able to give them to an analyst who has given proof of lack of intellectual integrity himself" (p. 40). What seems at least equally significant about Dr. Z.'s behavior, but which doesn't incur quite as much indignation on Dr. Loewenstein's part, is that Dr. Z. is indicating that sex in the real world with a lover is both dangerous and bad, thus, unconsciously, encouraging the patient's sexual involvement with her analyst in the ever-deepening, unanalyzed transference neurosis. Dr. Z. is urging her patient to give precedence to fantasy over reality—encouraging her patient to move away from involvement in her real life and instead to live in her neurosis with her analyst. The living out of her unconscious fantasies with her analyst, and these likely were masturbatory fantasies of a homosexual nature, were then woven into the analytic process in the obsessional manner Loewenstein had discerned.

The patient's illness, which regressed sharply into the fulminating obsessional neurosis from the milder anxiety hysteria, seemed induced by Dr. Z.'s incapacity to recognize and then analyze her transference relationship with Mme. N. Thus, an analyst's inability to recognize her own countertransference involvement with her patient directly contributes to her patient's estrangement from reality and her more serious immersion in neurotic illness. Dr. Loewenstein's "unfavorable impression" of Dr. Z., by virtue of her letter which stressed "complexes" rather than the "personal peculiarities" of her patient, seems to presage the countertransference difficulties that so dominated the treatment. The unconscious homosexual masturbatory fantasies the patient lived out in the treatment with Dr. Z. were likely displaced from her mother toward her sister who, at a critical period in the analysis with Dr. Z., and with the patient's father's sanction, married an artist. This left the patient, who in her youth was a frustrated artist, even more deeply bound to her old maid analyst. This sister also had been the patient's companion during her ill-fated weekend with the red-headed stranger, and perhaps this sister had been the real unconscious object of Mme. N.'s affection. The masturbatory fantasy aspect of Mme. N.'s relationship with her sister seems apparent in the sitting-on-knees games played in the bathroom, "which indirectly represented scarcely disguised fantasies of sexual contact between father and mother and the child sitting on their lap" (p. 44).

The masturbatory equivalents of her sexual fantasies were carried over in the analysis with Dr. Loewenstein in a more disguised verbal form by means of the insistently demanded repetitions, a specified number of times, at the end of the sessions. The gradual reduction of the repetitions of these remarks and the identification of this behavior as a resistance led to the gradual diminution of the gratification of (sexual) fantasies within the analysis and coincided with Dr. Loewenstein's instructions forcing his patient to face the external world to an increasingly significant degree. Thus, the analyst's grasp of a resistance occurring within the therapeutic situation and its technical handling which moves the patient away from the unanalyzed gratification of this fantasy in the transference, when coupled with the analysis of the transference as a resistance, furthers the development of the analytic process.

A central question in regard to the homosexual component in Mme. N.'s illness is never directly addressed in the paper, although it seems to have very marked significance. It is only when the young maids are supplanted by the old maid that the illness really flourishes. The patient's relationship with her mother (with whom she lived during her analysis) and her own daughter were hardly mentioned in the protocol. Our more recent knowledge of the significance of the adolescent phase of development, especially Blos's emphasis on the need to analyze the negative oedipal configuration in adolescence (Blos, 1979), seems very applicable to this young woman whose neurotic symptomatology became manifest at age sixteen.

The analyst's ability to cull out resistances that became part of the analytic process, and also to define unanalyzed transferences to the previous analyst, had the effect of undoing the primary neurotic symptomatology which seemed to have been derived from the treatment process itself. That this neurotic element seemed to be so readily separable from the infantile neurosis proper as Loewenstein understood it is very dramatic. Some analysts (Loewald, 1980, p. 245) feel that the infantile neurosis becomes technically revived at the time of the development of the transference neurosis. This raises questions about what was taking place in the analysis with Loewenstein that led to the resolution of the patient's obsessive–compulsive symptom. It is necessary to refer once again to Dr. Loewenstein's footnote, "There was no way of ascertaining the existence of a childhood neurosis and the patient never recollected neurotic symptoms in childhood" (p. 28). Are we seeing an example of what Gill (1979) calls the analysis of the here and now in the transference? Gill is concerned with how the patient experiences the actual situation with the analyst as a manifestation of the transference. If by actual situation is meant the actual situation with Mme. N.'s *previous* analyst rather than present analyst, that certainly seems to apply in this case study. At the same time, it was the interpretation of Mme. N.'s hostility toward her mother in the present ("I told her quite simply that she did not really want to buy candy for her mother" [p. 32]) that began to move the treatment along. So it was not the interpretation of the here and now in the transference but the clarification of the patient's attitude toward her mother (an interpretation outside of the transference), which made her aware of her unacknowledged hostility. It was making the patient conscious of an unacceptable wish that seemed to be so clinically useful.

It seems easier to analyze the missed transferences of a previous analyst than to be as discerning in identifying the transference reactions, especially the negative ones, that relate to the treating analyst.

Dr. Loewenstein correctly points out that "Dr. Z. failed to give enough attention to analysis of the transference, as is clearly shown by the fact that she had never made the connection between the old maid and herself" (p. 42). He then goes on to take note of important details about incidents that preceded the occurrence of the patient's obsession, "It was generally the sight of a beggar to whom she had refused money, or an old news vendor watching her get into a taxi . . ." (p. 44). These figures were connected with members of her family and then to figures and events in childhood. Dr. Loewenstein, however, does *not* connect these figures to himself in the transference. Even though he was likely to be the beggar whom his patient didn't pay and certainly was the old news vendor watching her get into the taxi, which, in the protocol, was clearly connected with her treatment. It would seem that the analyst's understanding of the meaning of a symptom, even without taking into account its transference implications, can be sufficient, at times, to cause the disappearance of an obsession. All this points to how difficult it is to clearly understand just which factors, or combination of factors, and in what setting and sequence, contribute to the curative effect of analysis. It also underlines why Freud never did write a general technique for psychoanalysis. Anna Freud (1977) takes note of "Freud's growing conviction that the psychoanalytic process is too complex, too different in each individual case, and too variable to be pressed into a definitive systematic presentation" (p. 257).

Anna Freud (1977) in commenting upon the recent significant changes in the handling of the transference itself notes:

> What in Freud's method appeared as an autonomous revival of the past and was the spontaneous production of the patient is today all too often a phenomenon which the analyst has foisted upon the patient from the very beginning, behind which the patient's other spontaneous contributions to the analysis, such as his free associations, his memories, disappear and remain excluded from interpretive work. The reconstruction of the past, for Freud a principal part of the analysis, is thus replaced by the current interplay between analysand and analyst, between transference and countertransference [p. 258].

Dr. Loewenstein emphasizes a number of technical points in his successful analysis of Mme. N.'s obsessional symptomatology. Dr. Z.'s failure to give enough attention to the analysis of the transference had to be repaired by Dr. Loewenstein. Because of the severity of the symptomatology this connection was not made for the patient until the end of the third year of a three-and-a-half-year analysis. It was necessary to deal with the more recent conflicts first, and only in relation to these current problems could aspects of childhood be mentioned. Dr. Loewenstein noted: "It was not possible in the relatively short time at my disposal to elucidate this patient's early conflicts sufficiently, which accounts for the incomplete results of the analysis" (p. 43). The effective interpretations "were those which included her ego reactions as well as her aggressive and libidinal drives" (p. 43). Dr. Loewenstein's recognition that the patient's resistance was woven into the structure of the psychoanalytic situation provided an entrée for both understanding his patient and finally breaking up the ritual which had become part of the fabric of the analysis during the unsuccessful treatment with Dr. Z.

The way the obsessional illness of Mme. N. was shaped by the unanalyzed transference to Dr. Z. was particularly striking. That the fear of being contaminated by the "old maid's touch" was in fact related to fears about her "old maid" analyst displaced onto the servant was especially illuminating. That Mme. N. was able, with her symptom, to make a mockery of her treatment and wreak her own revenge on her analyst, who was sufficiently distressed to forgo any recompense for a six-year period, also dramatizes the extent of the unconscious countertransference involvement of analyst with patient. The importance, in terms of the patient's well-being, for the analyst to be able to recognize transference and countertransference reactions is very effectively documented. That unanalyzed transference reactions promote both libidinal and ego regression seems clear from this case presentation. It is also clear that when a previous treatment has led to the emergence of a more serious clinical picture, the new analyst's approach to treating his patient will require some modifications. A certain flexibility, openness, and tact is required of an analyst who needs to reanalyze a patient. The unrecognized transference reactions to the previous analyst need to be analyzed. This is especially true of the unrecognized negative transference.

Dr. Loewenstein's recognition and perceptive handling of the resistances he clarified led to the resolution of his patient's crippling symptom. It is also apparent that there were many questions raised during the discussion of this paper and specifically connected with this patient and her neurosis that, in the three-and-a-half-year period of her analysis, failed to be resolved. Thus, the resolution of a symptom is not synonymous with the cure of a neurosis, as Dr. Loewenstein himself noted.

It was, however, possible to get a sense of how Dr. Loewenstein worked and to appreciate the importance he attributed to *understanding* the structure of Mme. N.'s symptom. The significance of understanding (understand—literally to stand under) for the analyst is of particular importance, especially in this case study. Fleiss (1961) in an effort to define analytically the literal derivation of the word *understand* describes, "the original position of the sexually curious child of the second oral phase relative to the object of his curiosity: The Maternal Cloaca" (p. 330). Fleiss also indicates that *inhibitions* of this capacity to understand can lead from sublimatory comprehension back to the repressed meaning of the word. This could lead to the kind of failure to grasp the significance of Mme. N.'s symptom that was evidenced by her analyst Z.

It is interesting that once Dr. Loewenstein felt *he* understood the words of Mme. N.'s nursery rhyme, "I have good tobacco in my pouch . . . you shan't have any" (p. 33), he felt that his patient was analytically accessible to treatment. Mme. N. wanted certain goods which she did not want to share with her mother or sister. She felt guilty and anxious about her feelings. Dr. Loewenstein not only recognized her conflict, he could also face what her nursery rhyme unconsciously meant. "Good tobacco in her pouch" symbolized her view of her genital as a cloaca. With his *understanding,* he could help her acknowledge her genital and the fact that she did not need to share it with the other woman in her life. His acceptance of her as a sexual person became an important part of the analytic atmosphere and was in marked contrast to her previous therapeutic experiences. The new analytic ambience probably had a significant effect in altering the rigidity of her superego, which could provide a therapeutic thrust in the direction of therapeutic change.

This opportunity to review Dr. Loewenstein's case study was stimulating and challenging. His candor, dedication, and skill were apparent. It is difficult to add more than a few speculative comments about the analytic process and the symptomatic results. A case study like this does provide an opportunity to reflect upon the many factors influencing the therapeutic consequences of a patient's exposure to very different kinds of analytic treatment.

REFERENCES

Blos, P. (1979), The second individuation process of adolescence. In: *The Adolescent Passage.* New York: International Universities Press, pp. 141–170.

Fleiss, R. (1961), *Ego and Body Ego.* New York: Schulte.

Freud, A. (1977), A study guide to Freud's writings. In: *The Writings of Anna Freud,* Vol. 8. New York: International Universities Press, 1981, pp. 209–276.

Freud, S. (1909), Notes upon a case of obsessional neurosis. *Standard Edition,* 10:153–318. London: Hogarth Press, 1955.

Gill, M. M. (1979), The analysis of the transference. *J. Amer. Psychoanal. Assn.,* 27 (Suppl.): 265–288.

Loewald, H. (1980), On the therapeutic action of psychoanalysis. In: *Papers on Psychoanalysis.* New Haven, CT: Yale University Press.

A DISCUSSION OF "THE OLD WOMAN'S TOUCH: REFLECTIONS ON THE TREATMENT OF A CASE OF OBSESSIONAL NEUROSIS" BY RUDOLPH M. LOEWENSTEIN

Edward M. Weinshel, M.D.

Dr. Loewenstein's elegant paper turned out to be an unadulterated treat. My assignment coincided with the publication of some of his collected papers (1982); and the opportunity of reading and studying "The Old Woman's Touch," along with the rest of the exemplary contributions to the psychoanalytic literature, was a consoling reminder of the vigor and perceptivity of a colleague who has been so much missed and mourned since his death in April 1976. Further, this paper represented a multilayered treat, dealing as it does with psychoanalytic work and the problems of a number of psychoanalysts' psychoanalytic techniques.

First we learn, at least indirectly and from inference, about Dr. Z. who treated the patient for eleven years, essentially from about 1919 to the early 1930s. (Since I do not have precise dates available, those that I am using are somewhat arbitrary, and I trust reasonably correct.) Then we have the report on Loewenstein's analysis with Mme. N. which took place, let us say, from 1931 to 1934; Loewenstein's "Reflections" in 1956 on Dr.

Z.'s work and his own constitute the third layer; and my own observations will make up the fourth. The whole slice, therefore, encompasses about sixty-five years of psychoanalysis, a significant portion of our comparatively brief history. In spite of analysts' penchant for history, and in spite of a considerable body of work dealing with the evaluation of our theory and practice, we do not have a crystal-clear picture of how analysts in those successive periods of the development of our science actually worked with their patients, let alone how they thought about that work. The number of detailed case histories, especially those which feature the interchanges between the analyst and the analysand, are (as we know too well) limited; and even these are not altogether satisfactory or convincing. It has always been particularly difficult to correlate the analyst's theoretical understanding and orientation, his interventions, and the actual impact those interventions exerted on the patient and on the analytic process. These tasks remain significant and thorny challenges to both the psychoanalytic clinician and the psychoanalytic research worker.

The book *Practice and Percept in Psychoanalytic Technique* (1982) reflects quite eloquently the extent to which that interrelationship between theory and practice has been a controlling focus of Dr. Loewenstein's interest. It is a theme consistently discernible in his scientific papers spanning a period of fifty years (from 1923 to 1972). That focus became more extensive and explicit during the 1950s and 1960s with the emergence and efflorescence of ego psychology. Those writings overlapped, of course, with publication of the series of definitive theoretical papers written in conjunction with Heinz Hartmann and Ernst Kris. Those contributions provided a reasonably comprehensive theoretical exposition for the ego psychological and the structural perspectives of psychoanalysis. Although the papers of all three of these illustrious analysts contributed immeasurably toward our understanding of ego psychology and the potential applications which ego psychology and the structural point of view offered for psychoanalytic technique, it was Loewenstein who pursued this line of endeavor most persistently and most explicitly.

Loewenstein's position, however, has always been cautiously evolutionary rather than precipitously revolutionary. In "Ego Development and Psychoanalytic Technique" (Loewenstein, 1951) he stated, in his characteristically low-keyed style that "as a matter of fact . . . there has been no fundamental change in analytic technique. The increase in tolerance of the patient's ego to his unconscious drives has always been sought for. It is now, however, being achieved with greater security and greater ease" (p. 32). He describes:

> [A] shift of emphasis as compared to the past. Indeed the area of interest of the psychoanalyst is widened: it is not exclusively concerned with the uncovering of the earliest forms of pathogenic conflicts. The interest of the analyst dwells *for a long time* on all the intermediates between the original conflict and its present manifestations. That is actually no *fundamental* change in psychoanalytic technique either [p. 32; emphasis added].

He points out that "The analyst uses interpretations in order to produce those dynamic changes which we call insight. . . . Among other things, the patient must gain insight into the resistances that he opposes to his treatment" (p. 34).

A few years later in "Some Remarks on Defenses, Autonomous Ego, and Psychoanalytic Technique" (Loewenstein, 1954), Loewenstein extended and expanded his presentation of the ways in which Freud's contributions of the 1920s (Freud, 1921, 1923, 1926) and the more recent developments in the field of ego psychology (Loewenstein, 1954, p. 188) influenced and led to certain refinements in psychoanalytic technique, particularly "in that part of our work which we place under the heading of analysis of resistances" (Loewenstein, 1954, p. 189). Yet, he goes on to underline his belief that: "Important though this influence of ego psychology has been, it has brought about no fundamental change in psychoanalytic technique, but rather a shift of emphasis which, however, has had significant consequences" (1956, p. 189).

Those shifts in emphasis have occurred most notably, Loewenstein asserts, in three areas:

> (1) As compared to the past, we now pay increased attention not only to early childhood but also to events and conflicts occurring in our patients in later life and in the present.

> (2) We dwell nowadays, more deliberately and more persistently than we might have done in the past, on the resistance and on the ego aspect of the patient's production.
> (3) We accord greater attention to the patient's autonomous ego functions and the role they exert on conflict solution, on the choice of pathways of gratification, and, possibly on the choice of defense . . . [1954, p. 189].

But in his next sentence, Loewenstein warns again that:

> [T]his shift of emphasis is but the systematic elaboration of Freud's advice that analysis of resistance should take precedence over analysis of id derivatives. We might suggest that what we call analysis of resistance inevitably ties in with analysis of the patient's way of reacting to his treatment in general as well as to specific interventions and interpretations [1954, p. 190].

I believe that this relatively long preface to my discussion of Dr. Loewenstein's paper (a much better and more thorough preparation would be a leisurely reading of *Practice and Percept in Psychoanalytic Technique* [1982], particularly Dr. Jacob Arlow's splendid introductory chapter) provides the reader with some conceptual signposts which indicate where Loewenstein is coming from in the "the old woman's touch" paper.

I do not intend to present an organized "discussion" of the case per se, offering my own formulations of Mme. N.'s psychological problems and/or psychoanalytic treatments. Such "reanalyses" pose numerous, and often treacherous, difficulties at best; and when the original analyst (and, in this instance, numerous analysts—and I'm not even certain if all the therapists were indeed analysts!) is unavailable for a dialogue that could clarify cloudy areas of confusion and difference, such an endeavor touches on the foolhardy. My own interest is on the historical developments in psychoanalysis, theoretical and technical, as they are reflected in Dr. Loewenstein's candid and penetrating discussion. In pursuing this focus, it is inevitable that I refer to the case material; and I will try to do so not so much as a "supervisor" but as an explorer trying to note changes in our thinking and in our analytic work.

In that vein, I would like to extract, quite arbitrarily, themes which impressed me as significant in both the patient's pathology and in the unfolding analysis. First, I was struck by the fact that the patient's psychoanalytic history is replete with instances of betrayal (not just disappointments) at the hands of her therapists. Dr. X., after two years of unsuccessful treatment, flagrantly broke professional confidence and related to her husband the facts of the patient's premarital affair. Dr. Y. peremptorily broke off the therapy when the patient confided to him her suicidal thoughts, an abandonment not easily justified *even* if the threats were primarily coercive and manipulative. Dr. Z.'s malfeasances were so egregious and so numerous that they hardly need detailing here. (I am mindful, of course, that it is not altogether clear in the paper whether Dr. Loewenstein's data came from the other analysts or from the patient. From the perspective of the analysis, the difference is not crucial. What is related reflects the patient's psychical reality.) I am not at all sure to what extent it was accepted procedure at that time to work out an analytic contract with a patient's spouse; but, in effect, this is how Dr. Loewenstein began his treatment with Mme. N. via his conversations with her husband. I realize that the situation was far more intricate and delicate than my truncated synopsis might indicate, but it appears that Dr. Loewenstein flirted with the possibility of contaminating the analysis before it had barely begun. Such a sequence of catastrophes (real or potential) could hardly be understood, we would all acknowledge, *only* in terms of the analysts; and this is particularly striking in the light of comparable betrayals by her father, and indirectly by her mother. I would suggest that the patient herself played a significant role in the evolution of these events, that her contribution reflected significant elements in her character (as well as her neurosis). Whatever it was in the patient's character, demeanor, and general behavior which invited such betrayal constituted a critical resistance configuration which helped to destroy or (with Dr. Loewenstein threatened to disrupt) her analytic work. It hardly needs noting that the patient's "contribution" in no way justifies the analysts' abdication of their analytic positions.

Second, the patient's spiteful compliance, as evidenced by her "caricature" of what a psychoanalytic patient does with dreams and associations, was recognized and exposed by Dr.

Loewenstein (providing the crucial turning point in the analysis) as a pivotal and formidable resistance. I would suggest that comparable pieces of behavior could have been detected in her extra-analytic and preanalytic life and activities; and, in all likelihood, these patterns were also products of her character structure.

Third, the patient made efforts, both successful and otherwise, to control the analytic sessions and the analyst (i.e., her demands that the analyst repeat a number of times the last interpretation he made in the session; her importuning pleas for reassurance; her transformation of the physical appearance of the analyst's office with reams of tissue paper; that "her associations *compelled* interpretations in terms of childhood problems" [p. 308]; emphasis added). These efforts not only provided a vehicle for the discharge of a good deal of aggression but also served as potent resistances. I cannot be comfortably certain of this, but I would surmise that these efforts at control and manipulation also had their roots in the patient's character structure.

It may well be that my fourth "theme" should be considered as an addendum to the first; I am referring to the aura of "morality" that permeates the entire psychoanalytic narrative. It sounds like a Victorian melodrama with lies and deceptions, deceit and betrayal, fiscal chicanery, authoritarian "injustice" and paternal tyranny, with whiffs of infidelity and incest. The patient is searching frantically for incorruptible parental/authority figures while simultaneously exerting her not insubstantial resources to corrupt those very figures and expose them as fraudulent and dishonest. This same struggle *appears* to be carried on with equal vigor and violence internally. Again this "melodrama" constitutes a conspicuous if not altogether obvious resistance to the analytic work.

I am not suggesting that these four issues are necessarily the principal themes or problems in the case of Mme. N., and certainly each analyst will respond to the patient in his or her own way so that the consequent material evoked in the analysis might be quite different from that presented by Dr. Loewenstein. My selection has been influenced, furthermore, by my belief that they are issues which provide us with a vehicle for thinking about changes in psychoanalytic thinking and technique at different periods in the development of psychoanalysis. You will note that my emphasis is on resistances, character, countertransference, and the superego. I would also state my agreement with Loewenstein that although there had and have been a series of gradual shifts of emphasis and increasing refinements in analytic technique, the basic conceptual planks in that technique had already been constructed by Freud by the time Mme. N. began her psychoanalytic work. Since I cannot review here the entire history of Freud's thinking on this topic, I will suggest that in his papers on technique (Freud, 1911–1915), and especially in "On Beginning the Treatment" (Freud, 1913), Freud had already conceived and thought through his fundamental ideas on psychoanalytic therapy. His goal, I believe, virtually from the beginning, was "that of the resolving of existing repressions" (1913, p. 130); his subsequent contributions and those of other psychoanalysts (and certainly those associated with "ego psychology"[1] must be considered preeminent in this regard) led to a clarification, elaboration, and refinement of how an analyst might more effectively achieve that goal.

In my introductory remarks, I mentioned four "layers" in this historical survey; I have arbitrarily allocated the first period to the years 1919 to 1931; the second, 1931 to 1935, the time of Loewenstein's analysis with Mme. N.; the third from 1935 to 1956, the time between that analysis and Loewenstein's writing of his "Reflections" paper; the fourth, 1956 to 1983, essentially from the time that article was composed (and the beginnings of my own psychoanalytic experience) to the present. However, since the clinical data from the first period (1919 to 1931 and particularly the time of Dr. Z.'s work with the patient) is so sparse and so "second-hand," I will not deal with

[1]It is both inevitable and unfortunate that ego psychology was misunderstood as a special and segregated variety of psychoanalysis, as if then one could think and talk of ego analysis, id analysis, superego analysis, character analysis, or even defense analysis. I would suggest that this misconception has been confusing and has resulted in some delay and difficulties in recognizing and accepting that all of these "qualified" designations are all part of one entity, namely psychoanalysis. By the same token, so-called ego psychology did not begin with Anna Freud (1936) or Heinz Hartmann (1939). This is a topic that deserves further scrutiny.

it in any systematic way. From the material that is available from that work, I believe that many of us would dismiss it as wild analysis. More objectively and more charitably, it may be advisable and more appropriate to attribute what took place in Dr. Z.'s analysis as a consequence of an incomplete and inadequate understanding and absorption of what Freud had promulgated in the previous decade. I think that I can most effectively highlight at least some of the significant changes that have taken place, by comparing the thinking and technique that can be observed in the last three periods in six not altogether discrete categories. Where Loewenstein's data is not totally explicit, I have had to draw inferences as best I can.

1. I believe that our attitude toward diagnosis and the nosological diagnoses that we employ has changed in the past half-century. More emphasis and importance was then given to the "diagnosis," and the diagnosis was determined largely by the symptoms manifested by the patient. When Loewenstein first evaluated the patient he saw her primarily (on the basis of her presenting symptoms) as a severe obsessive–compulsive neurotic, but he noted "that she might be suffering either from one of those neuroses that are inaccessible to psychoanalysis or from a latent psychosis in the guise of obsessional neurosis" (1956, pp. 295–296). In his 1956 discussion he states that the patient's "main conflicts were expressed in a compulsive–obsessive form" (p. 312). Relatively little is stated or implied in regard to her overall personality or character, or regarding the strengths of her ego and the effectiveness of its functioning (Weinshel, 1970, pp. 694–695). I doubt that the majority of analysts today would come up with the same diagnosis (it is not unlikely that a significant segment would not even address themselves to the topic of diagnosis), and I would venture that a relatively wide variety of diagnostic formulations would be entertained. Further, those designations and formulations would tend to focus on character and on underlying ego structure: obsessive–compulsive character, masochistic character, narcissistic character, "borderline." I am not raising the question of the "correct" diagnosis per se, but rather the ways in which those labels reflect changes in our thinking about a patient and his difficulties. Those changes indicate a decreased interest in the symptom and an increased

focus on development and the developmental level of the central conflicts as well as an attempt to assess the overall personality structure and its "strength." Those changes in how the patient is "viewed" do play a part in how the analyst approaches his patient and the nature of his interventions.

2. In the early thirties it would appear that the vicissitudes of the oedipal phase were considered, without much questioning, to be responsible for the nuclear conflict in the neurosis; and the presence of pregenital conflicts were seen as a product of regression. In his paper, Loewenstein states:

> One might say that the old conflict centering around sexual temptation had regressed into a conflict centering around money, aggression, defilement, and guilt connected with a woman. This change clearly confirms the distinction Freud made between anxiety hysteria (phobia) and obsessional neurosis. Her former neurosis, a phobia, had been based predominately on conflicts of the phallic stage, but it had regressed into a neurosis based on the anal–sadistic stage of libidinal development . . . a regression from the oedipal to the preoedipal stage: from interest focused on the man in the phobic phase of the patient's neurosis to absorption in the woman in the obsessional phase [1956, pp. 305–306].

Again, it can be seen how the diagnostic label and the symptom determine the formulation of what goes on in the course of the analytic work; and, although this is not altogether clear, Loewenstein talks about two different neuroses, one phobic and one obsessional, rather than different phases of the same neurotic process. Further, the aggressive manifestations of the patient are tied in with the "obsessional period" without consideration for the aggressive components of her behavior and character throughout her life and in the analysis. Little interest is evidenced in connecting (as I think would be the case today) the source, meaning, and impact of the pregenital problems, especially as those conflicts would influence the oedipal phase experience (or with character formation and structure). Today, more analysts are more prone to see the oedipal phase conflicts as being less central, less *the* nuclear conflict, and to look to the preoedipal difficulties as the principal source of the disturbance. Parallel with this shift many analysts today are more likely to see the basic psychopathology (or to describe that pathology) not as "psychoneurotic"; and, as a consequence, the concepts of fixation and especially of regression (from the oedipal phase) are invoked much less frequently than they have been in the past.

3. The *goal* of analysis has remained essentially constant, namely, the undoing of the pathological regression; but the concept of how that goal might be achieved has altered considerably. The way that conceptualization has altered is the principal thrust of Loewenstein's paper. Dr. Z., as far as can be determined, paid little attention to the resistances or the defenses; and her interventions were directed at the derivatives of the instinctual drives without much concern for the defenses or "the specific problems of this patient [which] made her recognizable as an individual" (1956, p. 296). In 1931, Loewenstein was aware of the significance of the resistances and the need to analyze those resistances, and there is copious evidence that he did so. Certainly, his dealing with the patient's dream association "routine" as a resistance permitted the analytic work to proceed. It does not appear that work on the resistances was central to his approach or that he was as attuned to their clinical manifestations (1956, p. 314). By the fifties, with "a deeper and more refined insight into the psychology of the ego" (1956), Loewenstein was thinking more in terms of helping the patient "gain insight into the resistances that he opposes to his treatment" (Loewenstein, 1951, p. 34) rather than merely "overcoming them." I would suggest that this shift in conceptualization which called for patient and tactful *work* with the resistances and the *gradual* emergence of insight in small increments (Strachey, 1934, p. 283) is closely related to the current goals of structural change and modification of the ego. At the same time, there has been a *relative* decrease in the emphasis on the uncovering of the "content" of the repressed conflicts.

4. These changes in the goals of analysis are correlated with changes in the emphasis (as has already been pointed out) in *psychoanalytic technique*. Before 1931, the focus was on the exposure of the repressed content (rather than a gradual analysis of the resistances associated with that content), the construction of the infantile history, and a search for sexual

problems and trauma. By 1931, the work with resistances had become more common and better understood; the role of the transferences was grasped more comprehensively, and the analysis of the transferences had become more effective; the old dictum of analyzing from the surface began to be better appreciated and applied. When Loewenstein wrote in 1956, the increased understanding of ego psychology permitted a more sophisticated analysis of both transference and resistance and an ever-increasing clarification of the need to connect the past and the present, the patient's external and internal worlds, and of the interplay within the three constituents of the tripartite psychic apparatus. In addition, analysts have demonstrated renewed curiosity in the intricacies of the development of character, its role in the overall psychic structure, and in the problems of character in clinical analysis.

The situation in 1983 is, in a sense, much more complex. In part this is due to our accruing experience and knowledge with a concurrent increased appreciation of the complexity of the human psyche and of psychological conflict. In part, and in a way related to the above, "we, as psychoanalysts, have become more diverse in our theoretical orientation; and therefore, since to some extent our practice reflects our theoretical frame of reference, there is a greater diversity in our technical approach" (Weinshel, 1976, p. 458). For many the direction and emphasis in the development of psychoanalytic technique enunciated by Freud and elaborated by Loewenstein have continued and have become more refined and more important in their analytic work. The increasing interest in the psychoanalytic process has broadened the theoretical base for our work and has provided a better framework for correlating theory and technique (Weinshel, 1984). On the other hand, with this greater diversity, the focus on the exploration and the "handling" of the resistances has been superseded by other technical approaches. This thorny topic deserves a more extensive discussion. However, some preliminary observations can be found in Weinshel (1976, pp. 456–458) and in Calef and Weinshel (1979, pp. 487–489). Paul Gray in his elegant and eloquent paper " 'Developmental Lag' in the Evolution of Technique for Psychoanalysis of Neurotic Conflict" (Gray, 1983) argues that there has *always* been a resistance among psychoanalysts (including Freud himself) to uncovering resistance. It is a sobering dissertation on the obstacles in this area of our technical efforts; it warrants careful, open-minded study. As one colleague remarked, in a discussion from the floor at the London International Psycho-Analytical Association Congress in 1975, "There is no consensus among us as to what the classical Analysis of the Future will be!"

5. The appropriate handling of transference was already recognized as one of the crucial aspects of analytic technique well before Loewenstein undertook Mme. N.'s analysis. Dr. Z., however, either neglected this element or dealt with it in a haphazard or global fashion. Loewenstein's analysis of Mme. N. demonstrated his appreciation of the importance of transference and his skill in analyzing it. It is my impression that by 1956, he was more cognizant of the subtleties of the virtually infinite permutations of transference, especially when it is manifested as a resistance. Today the importance of transference is recognized, almost universally, as the arena where so much of the analytic work must take place. There is, however, less consensus as to how (and when) that work should be carried out. Gill's emphasis on the transference in the here and now and in the early phases of the analysis (Gill, 1982) and Kohut's (1971) delineation of special archaic "self" transferences are perhaps the most conspicuous examples of those controversies.

I will mention only briefly the changing role of countertransference in analytic work. Loewenstein deals with it very little, at least explicitly, in his analysis of Mme. N. but does point out its significance (even if not by name) in regard to Dr. Z.'s mishandling of the patient (1956, pp. 301, 304, 308, 309). Although extensive material is lacking, it seems evident that Dr. X.'s and Dr. Y.'s behavior in regard to the patient must have been, at least in part, determined by countertransference elements. Finally, when Loewenstein "asks" whether it "was necessary to apply the 'rule of abstinence' in the way described" (p. 312), it may well be that his question reflects some concern and remorse about some countertransference feeling. The countertransference aspects of the case are not treated at length or in depth; and it seems difficult to imagine that someone writing in the 1980s would not have made those aspects more prominent. In the eighties, however, the emphasis on countertransference (or its cousin, empathic failure) has, in some quarters become so extreme that at times it would appear that the patient and his problems are considered to be a superfluous complication. It is my impression that psychoanalysts today are more aware of the countertransference issues, and still experience them! In spite of all the recent work done in this area, the statement in regard to countertransference that I have found most helpful is the one made by Fenichel in 1938 on the goal of the training analysis: "the capacity to avoid the possibilities of the analyst [using] 'analyzing' for some purpose other than analysis" (Fenichel, 1938, p. 27).

6. It seems to me that the "analysis" of the superego and of superego conflicts has not developed a great deal in the past fifty years. I mentioned the whole question of the "Morality" atmosphere at least in part because so little was said by Loewenstein about these egregious issues either in his description of his analytic work with Mme. N. or in his overall discussion of the case. Problems of morality, integrity, responsibility come up in every analysis; and, yet, nothing close to an integrated study of these problems has been presented. Rangell's work on "A Psychoanalytic Perspective Leading Currently to the Syndrome of the Compromise of Integrity" (1974) is a landmark contribution which indicates both many of the issues on this subject and the direction further investigations might take.

These remarks are not intended as a comprehensive critique of Dr. Loewenstein's paper. They represent an attempt to convey some of the thoughts, reactions, and concerns stimulated by this extraordinary case. I hope that I have communicated my respect and affection for Rudi Loewenstein and my admiration for the heritage he has bequeathed to us.

REFERENCES

Arlow, J. (1982), Introduction. In: Loewenstein, R. M., *Practice and Precept in Psychoanalytic Technique*. New Haven, CT: Yale University Press.

Calef, V., & Weinshel, E. M. (1979), The new psychoanalysis and psychoanalytic revisionism. *Psychoanal. Quart.*, 48:470–491.

Fenichel, O. (1938), The theoretical implications of the training analysis. *The Annual of Psychoanalysis,* 8:21–34. New York: International Universities Press, 1981.

Freud, A. (1936), *The Ego and the Mechanisms of Defense.* New York: International Universities Press, 1965.

Freud, S. (1911–1915), Papers on technique. *Standard Edition,* 12:85–173. London: Hogarth Press, 1958.

——— (1913), On beginning the treatment. *Standard Edition,* 12:122–144. London: Hogarth Press, 1958.

——— (1921), Group psychology and the analysis of the ego. *Standard Edition,* 18:67–143. London: Hogarth Press, 1955.

——— (1923), The ego and the id. *Standard Edition,* 19:3–66. London: Hogarth Press, 1961.

——— (1926), Inhibitions, symptoms, and anxiety. *Standard Edition,* 20:87–175. London: Hogarth Press, 1959.

Gill, M. M. (1982), *Analysis of Transference,* Vol. 1. New York: International Universities Press.

Gray, P. (1983), "Developmental lag" in the evolution of technique for psychoanalysis of neurotic conflict. *J. Amer. Psychoanal. Assn.,* 30:621–655.

Hartmann, H. (1939), *Ego Psychology and the Problem of Adaptation.* New York: International Universities Press, 1958.

Kohut, H. (1971), *The Analysis of the Self.* New York: International Universities Press.

Loewenstein, R. M. (1951), Ego development and psychoanalytic technique. In: *Practice and Precept in Psychoanalytic Technique.* New Haven, CT: Yale University Press, 1982, pp. 30–39.

——— (1954), Some remarks on defenses, autonomous ego, and psychoanalytic technique. *Internat. J. Psycho-Anal.,* 35:188–193.

——— (1956), Reflections on the treatment of a case of obsessional neurosis. In: *Troubled Women,* ed. L. Freeman. Cleveland and New York: World Publishing, 1959, pp. 295–316.

——— (1982), *Practice and Percept in Psychoanalytic Technique,* Introduction by Jacob A. Arlow. New Haven, CT: Yale University Press.

Rangell, L. (1974), A psychoanalytic perspective leading currently to the syndrome of the compromise of integrity. *Internat. J. Psycho-Anal.,* 55:3–12.

Strachey, J. (1934), The nature of the therapeutic action of psychoanalysis. *Internat. J. Psycho-Anal.,* 50:275–292, 1969.

Weinshel, E. M. (1970), The ego in health and normality. *J. Amer. Psychoanal. Assn.,* 18:682–735.

——— (1976), Concluding comments on the congress topic. *Internat. J. Psycho-Anal.,* 57:451–460.

——— (1984), Some observations on the psychoanalytic process. *Psychoanal. Quart.,* 53:63–92.

2. THE ANALYSIS OF A DOLL PHOBIA

Introduction

The analysis of a doll phobia exhibits an exemplary focus on analyzing symptoms, an asset which unfortunately has lost part of its significance in recent years. It describes the importance of analyzing masturbatory fantasies in understanding and construction of the patient's infantile neurosis. The analytic report also illustrates attention to a variety of nonsymptomatic phenomena, character traits, perverse acts, and fantasies.

Dr. Rangell describes the analysis of a thirty-eight year old man with intense and prolonged fear of dolls dating back to his childhood. A wide range of dolls and icons produced fear of different intensities in the patient. In addition to phobia, the patient's extensive maturbatory fantasies and practices, which served as his central sexual activity, occupied an important position in his psychic life. The patient had severe marital problems and had been involved in a variety of extramarital affairs.

Using the metaphor of a wheel, Rangell places the doll at the hub of the wheel with multiple determinants of doll phobia serving as spokes leading away from and into the hub. Rangell describes graphically how different aspects of the doll represented for the patient multiple meanings from different historical levels. The doll was equated with the patient's penis, human body, phallic mother, the woman's phallus, and so on.

The patient's phallic–oedipal conflicts were highly intermeshed with many anal components rooted in his constipation, and maternal administration of daily enemas dating back to the age of three. The relationship with the mother was revived graphically in the transference toward the analyst. The analysis of the patient's extensive resistances, transference reaction, and vivid masturbation fantasies provided ample ground for the reconstruction of his infantile neurosis in the phallic–oedipal and anal periods and the extensive interconnections between these developmental levels.

Dr. Spruiell uses the detailed descriptions of Rangell to propose a parallel and interdigitating dynamic for the patient's symptomatology; perversion rather than phobia in the patient with narcissistic, in addition to obsessional, personality structure. He focuses on the patient's denial of the existence of the genital universe and a certain type of supporting ego and superego structure permitting such a state of denial; denial of difference in the genitals of the two sexes, and the generational differences between parents and children. Dr. Spruiell suggests that the patient can be better described as having a perversion with atypical phobia; a formulation which emphasizes the pleasurable rather than the fearful component of the patient's encounter with the fetishistic–phobic object. He described the special split in the patient's ego which allows him to be simultaneously overwhelmed and deny castration anxiety; an anal–sadistic ego organization seen in patients with fetishism. The "phobic" object is seen as a concealed fetish exhibiting the characteristics of fetish and phobic objects. Dr. Spruiell proposes that symptoms, character traits, and perverse acts can be placed at the rim of the wheel. The patient views the oedipal conflict as unresolvable, but he simultaneously seeks oedipal victory. Dr. Spruiell applauds Rangell's success in the analysis of phobic symptoms and negative oedipal conflicts but wonders about the absence of an intense negative transference reaction characteristic of such patients. He also emphasizes the importance of the alteration of the "organizational split" of the ego as a goal of the analysis for the patient with doll phobia to allow him to move toward a satisfactory genitality.

Dr. Spruiell proposes that this patient would be considered a patient with a narcissistic personality by some contemporary analysts who would "sanitize" the patient's preoedipal and oedipal organizations from its sexual and aggressive drive implications.

Describing the differences between products, process, and procedures, Dr. Abrams provides a complementary perspective on Rangell's analysis of the patient's intense fear of dolls and his masturbation fantasy. He points out the patient's serious and disabling character with shallow relationships, compliant but covertly superior attitude, and obsessional traits. The patient exhibits difficulty with the establishment of a stable libidinal phase organization, denial of anatomical differences between the sexes, phallocentricity, conflictual relationships with both parents, and the danger of loss of his manhood due to severe castration and infantile ties with both parents. Abrams points out that in addition to the analysis of phobia and secret masturbation which has been the focus of the report by Rangell, the characteristics of the analytic situation have played an equally revealing arena for the patient's infantile conflicts and search for gratification rather than insight. The patient saw the admission of improvement in analysis as a sexual submission to the analyst and therefore a castrating experience. The analyst was equated with impulses. Abrams also agrees that the patient's masturbatory habits and personality traits can be placed at the rim of the wheel.

THE ANALYSIS OF A DOLL PHOBIA

Leo Rangell, M.D.

I

From the complex fabric of a case, only material relevant to the patient's phobia for dolls will be extracted. This too will, of necessity, be much condensed, and only the main streams indicated. The phobic symptom was greatly overdetermined, which accounted for its tenacity and long duration. The doll can be pictured as the hub of a wheel. From the hub there radiate outwards numerous spokes, each representing an origin, a motive, a cause, or a historical determinant feeding into the hub doll. The various spokes also have interconnecting links, in irregular fashion, joining the various parts together into a network.

The phobia had existed for as long as the patient could remember, at least from his fifth year. What finally brought him into analysis, at the age of thirty-eight, was an article in *Life* magazine to the effect that the age for analysis was up to forty. The patient, who had considered treatment on and off for many years, was finally confronted with a deadline. At thirty-eight, figuring a few years for the analysis, he could just make

Reprinted by permission, *International Journal of Psycho-Analysis,* Vol. 33, 1952.

it. This turned out, as could be predicted, to be a deep-rooted character trait of his.

It was interesting, through the eyes of a man who feared them, to discover how ubiquitous dolls are in our culture. When one chooses an object for a phobia, he in a sense becomes married to the object. In order to avoid it, his eyes seek it out. He finds it in obscure places, he sees it with his peripheral vision. The patient was afraid of any kind of three-dimensional figure, of dolls with which children play, of mannequins, of window dummies used for display purposes, of puppets, of pieces of sculpture, of various objects d'art in the form of figurines. An ashtray or a lamp base might be carved as a figure, a bar of soap might be fashioned in the form of a little animal. Any such object was a threat, was his enemy, and provoked anxiety.

Gradually certain conditions or qualifying characteristics emerged which were of special importance, and which determined where in the scale of its ability to frighten a certain object stood. Some of these qualities or attributes were known to the patient from the start, while others crystallized out as the analysis progressed, so that even the symptom became clearer and more defined. Each condition had its specific dynamic meaning and history and became an integral part of the phobia to fulfill an unconscious requirement. To understand each prerequisite was to decipher a code which then acted as an accurate road sign pointing the way back to specific aspects of the infantile past.

Thus, the material of which the figure was made was important. Porcelain, plaster, china were bad; metal, steel, tin, not so bad. Why? Because the former could break easily, were delicate, fragile, could shatter into small pieces. Metal was less likely to do this; it could dent, or bend, but not so readily break off. Something sticking out from a figure made it especially fearful. An arm or a leg outstretched, or separate little fingers, were bad, because a slight accident could break them off. The more lifelike a figure was, the worse it was; and it was particularly the moment of a figure "coming to life" or simulating movement which was the most frightening. From this standpoint rubber was bad, since it was smooth-flowing, regular, lifelike. Celluloid was very bad; it was also lifelike, and when wet it could curl and almost move. Wax figures, which could melt, or soap forms, which could actually change in shape and even disappear, could not be tolerated. A doll with a hollow inside, particularly a hollow head, was worse than a stuffed doll. For if it were shattered, there would be nothing left, just air, just a gaping hole. Maimed, broken, or melted dolls were especially frightening. Surprise was an undesirable element. If he saw what was coming, he could steel himself and meet the emergency. If he came upon a figure suddenly, he was unnerved. A window between him and a display figure was a protecting screen. To find the same figure in the open, as on the floor of a store, made him feel defenseless. To look at the doll was bad enough; to touch or be touched by it was frightening to conceive; to have it rub against his arm, even in thought, was enough to cause sweating and near panic. Human dolls were worse than animal ones; female ones worse than males; juvenile ones worse than adult; nude dolls worse than clothed ones.

Some of the recent technologically successful doll creations, such as the Baby Coo, Di-Dee-Doll (you feed it water and it wets), Betsy-Wetsy, were anathema to him. Once, shortly after his marriage, while shopping with his wife in a department store, he stepped out of an elevator into the toy department, where he was suddenly confronted by what seemed to him row after row of toy models, masks, grimacing faces, moving and pointing figures and so on. He felt weak and sick, grabbed his wife's arm and fortunately was able to make a hasty exit.

There will now be given some brief pertinent background data for a general orientation, following which the various individual etiological streams or spokes will be traced longitudinally through the life history of the patient. Both parents are now in their eighties, and live in an Eastern city where the patient was born. The mother is American-born, always spoke well, was beautiful, red-headed, refined, calm, sweet; the patient was always proud of her. The father is foreign-born, spoke with a foreign accent, was always sentimental and sloppy; his eyes watered in the movies or when he swelled with pride; he was explosive, outspoken, unrefined; the patient was always ashamed of and guilty toward him. Only in recent years did the patient's opinion of his parents reverse; he then considered his mother empty, vacuous, shallow, ignorant; and his father shrewd, intelligent, and a good judge. There is a sister, seven years his senior, the only living sibling. In addition, before the patient was born, the parents lost a little girl, aged three, of meningitis. The mother is said never to have smiled during her pregnancy with the patient. The birth of a boy was a disappointment to her; but the father cried at the birth of his son, and announced, "All Philadelphia is mine." The mother kept him in long curls and frocks until three-and-a-half to four. At four-and-a-half his father went bankrupt and their economic condition took a deep decline.

At the time he began analysis the patient was thirty-eight, married, and had one son aged seven. In addition to the phobia, another presenting complaint was the existence of chronic severe marital difficulties; the couple had separated four to five times, had talked of divorce; the patient had a long series of extramarital involvements. Since their marriage they had lived with the patient's mother-in-law, in a house owned by the latter. This arrangement made for much friction and irritation to the patient, but in spite of his constant complaints he always found excuses for not altering the situation. A brief description of the patient: he is personable, affable, and in appearance makes a favorable impression. He speaks in a deep, resonant voice which often provokes comments about its very masculine quality. He is fluent, witty, superficially aggressive and forward. His occupation: statistical analyst; he works at "figures," at which he is considered unusually proficient. He has always been adept with figures, was always first in mathematics at school, and has numerous systems with which to perform complicated figuring instantaneously in his head.

The patient is now finishing his third year of analysis, with consistent attendance except for the usual vacations, for a total of somewhat over 700 hours. The results and changes up to this time will be given below.

II

The dynamic meanings of the phobia and the substructure from which the symptom sprang and into which its roots extended, gradually evolved during the course of the analysis. Pieces of this structure were forthcoming from many different directions, such as the content of the free associations, the patient's daily activities, his character structure, his dreams, his fantasies, the transference, even his motor activities on the couch. It is understood that what follows is a composite picture.

Very early there poured out his enormous guilt and conflict regarding masturbation, which always was and still is his chief form of sexual activity and gratification. Along with the phobia, this had always been his most carefully guarded secret. Any reference to the subject in his presence, in company or when "out with the boys," created severe anxiety, the same as that produced by the phobia, so that he would quickly and deftly change the subject. One of his earliest memories was at the age of four, his mother and his aunt telling him to take his hands out of his pockets. This aunt was gentle, delicate, soft-spoken, pretty, looked "like a doll." At age four to five, a very significant and oft-repeated memory related to a glass curio cabinet which contained their good Dresden china, fragile and breakable: his mother would warn him, "Don't touch, it will break." At about the same period, his father, holding the boy in his arms, would playfully bring the patient's hand toward a bas-relief hanging on the wall, then snap it back with "Cootchi-coo—mustn't touch." The path for displacement was thus laid down, and the nuclear idea for the phobia was born. "Don't touch" was projected outward, displaced from the body to the external world. Instead of not touching the penis, he would not touch the china, the bas-relief, eventually the doll. The return of the repressed is seen in the choice of object. The doll, though inanimate, is again the human body. The doll is his penis, not to be touched.

The patient prided himself on being a stickler for authority, particularly toward scientists and doctors. If it were prescribed that he take a medicine at 10-2-4-6, he would not deviate a minute from the prescribed time, since that would nullify its effectiveness; he ascribed magical power to the dictates and advice of "big people." But this seeming obedience was a sham; he obeyed in small things strictly, in order to break the big rule brashly. "I will carry out conscientiously all your edicts, except, please, I will masturbate." The reaction-formation nature of this character trait was demonstrated by his consistent breaking of the analytic rules.

The glass protecting the Dresden china makes its appearance later in its derivative, the store window between him and the display dummy.

The "it will break" half of these early warnings usher in a very central chapter in the entire analysis, that of castration, the punishment feared for the forbidden act. The castration theme made its appearance on every front, but insight into it, and still more emotional acceptance of it and working through, was a slow, deliberate, and plodding process, beset with resistances of the strongest type. A remark was made to the patient, aged about six, that someone, in taking a handkerchief out of his pocket, dropped a dollar bill. The patient, since then, looks behind him whenever he takes something out of his pocket, to make sure nothing has dropped out. He cannot leave anything incomplete or dangling. When, in reading, he comes to the end of a sentence, or paragraph, or page, he must say to himself "period, end, finish," before he can go on, to make sure he has left nothing out, or left no opening, or that it's all there, rounded, closed, and smooth. One of the earliest remembered instances of his present phobia occurred at age five. Sitting in the bathtub he was playing in the water with a small celluloid toy fish, when the latter suddenly suffered a hole in it, swung around and hissed in the water. The little boy was frightened. In recalling this, the patient first tried to pass it off as a meaningless, normal childhood fear, but soon saw its connections with his present symptom. The following events were temporally related to this incident and made its meaning clear:

1. Being told, "Don't play with fire or you will pee in bed."
2. Standing outdoors at night with his mother and father watching a huge fire at a nearby celluloid factory. He remembered the general tension and anxiety, but more specifically recalled his parents' fears, and then of course his own, that the factory might explode. These background events enable us to translate his bathtub experience. He had not heeded the warning, he did play with fire, that is, sexual heat and excitement (the identity of fire, heat, sexual excitement was

clearly brought out in a number of dreams); the penis on fire did explode, castration did occur. The swishing fish, forerunner of the doll, was the peeing penis, detached from the boy and floating away. Note the quality celluloid, in both factory and figure. The sudden movement, the swish, and the lifelike quality reversed the process of projection. By threatening to bring the mechanical figure back to life, it stripped the symbol of its disguise, thereby provoking anxiety. Connected with this is the following dream:

"I am in a bathtub. I have an erection and touch it. I show it to my wife, who wants to take a picture of it. Then my penis is detached, floating around. But I tell myself it is nothing, as this always happens." The wife-mother has seen the forbidden erection, and castration has resulted. But the patient reassures himself, "It is nothing." The doll which is avoided is the detached penis, an unwelcome reminder of castration.

The presence of a strong anal component may already be suspected (reference to money above, the dollar bill, the compulsive ritual, the water, etc.). The patient looks at the toilet water compulsively to examine what flushed down. In fact, the following additional historical segment formed another sturdy base for the developing neurotic structure to lean upon. At the age of three, the patient had a convulsion, which was diagnosed by the doctor who "saved his life" as having been due to constipation from eating too many biscuits. There is a vague memory, or perhaps he was told this later, of awakening from this convulsion on a rubber pad; he connected this rubber with the element of rubber in his phobia. To prevent a recurrence, his mother, on the doctor's advice, instituted treatment by enemas. From age three to four-and-a-half, the patient received a daily enema from his mother. For a long time in the analysis he recalled only the discomfort and pain of this period, but then, after analysis of certain recurring anal behavior and characteristics, he remembered how, in the latency period, he had purposely "held it in," in order to induce his mother to administer an enema. He remembered and realized the pleasure of the retention, of the manipulation and attention by his mother, of the increasing tension by the water almost to the bursting point, and then the explosive expulsion. The phallic mother, the mother with the enema tip, the castrating woman, the woman who came in and took it out of him, became a dominant point of fixation in his sexual life. She became the ambivalently loved and hated object, the one most feared, and yet, by the repetition compulsion, a sine qua non of his sexual attainment. Anal eroticism and anal threat became blended and highly developed. The possibility of real damage during this period was reinforced when one day the mother, in her haste to get the patient to the bathroom, fell and broke her ankle. The patient considered it his fault and feared retaliation. Some years later, he had a wish that his sister should be permanently crippled. A few hours later, he fell and broke his arm. He considered this a direct punishment for his hostile wish. In later years, he stubbed his toes and injured his fingers at every turn. He did it to himself, to prevent an outside person from doing it to him.

Through most of his adult years, and until analysis, the patient suffered from recurrent alternating diarrhea and constipation, and carefully correlated every vagary in his bowel habits with what he had eaten. His senior business partner, with whom there existed a close and telling relationship throughout the entire analysis, a relationship which served as a barometer of what was happening to the patient, was a man with chronic ulcerative colitis. An "extra long good bowel movement" often made the patient late, and sometimes he would "please" the analyst by giving it up at home, coming on time, and doing it verbally, on the couch. Money, and time, were subjects of great preoccupation; they were treated as erratically, and with as much alternation in attitudes, as were his fecal contents. The connection between the two became clear to him by such associations as his concern over the "gold dust" on his shorts. He constantly argued about the fee, and about wanting time off for various reasons. He would frequently estimate what his annual income was going to be, and would "warn" the analyst of impending disaster. He was chagrined when his income doubled after the first year of analysis. He pictured the analyst as an extractor, and in this way he again enjoyed the mother with the enema tip. He counted the change in his pocket every morning and evening, and had to go over his daily transactions to the penny. Gnawing anxiety ensued when anything was missing, and he would spend hours trying to recover the error. When he added long columns of figures or money, he checked them three ways, up, down, and diagonally. Yet he threw away large chunks of analytic time by repeated lateness, and one day impulsively bought a big new convertible. There were certain daily obsessive–compulsive thoughts and actions, a habit of "getting stuck" on thoughts and being unable to let go, a tendency to procrastination, numerous perfectionistic traits, and yet a piling-up and messiness on his desk.

Castration anxiety caused a regression to a previously strong point of anal fixation and regressively colored the latter. Each then confirmed and lent strength to the other. The earlier anal experiences made the later phallic castration possibilities more real, and the phallic dangers in turn revived and reinforced the earlier anal threats. The phallus, like the stool earlier, could be removed and broken off. The doll was both. In one dream the doll was associatively connected with ears of corn covered with brown gravy. In another dream, the patient was trapped in City Hall, to which he associated "shitty hall," and which he had entered by the back end. He once, in his work, had visited a window trim company, and was much afraid that in walking through the building toward the office he might suddenly come across a row of mannequins lined up in some long dark hallway. The mannequins equal the stool; lined up in the hallway equals the rectum.

But the patient too was trapped, and he himself seemed to be equated to the doll. The connection between patient equaling his own phallus, and in turn equaling the doll, came out convincingly from many angles. On the couch he engaged in repeated automatic actions of lovingly stroking and fondling his abdomen, rubbing his hands regularly and rhythmically over the top of his head, stretching and then relaxing his entire body, and accompanying this with a rising crescendo of voice, ending in a violent yawn or sigh and then receding. While this was in part a resistance and a defiance of the analyst, there could be no mistaking its character as a maturbatory substitute and an avenue of libidinal gratification. Interpretation of this to the patient was, after some time, accepted and the behavior modified. He was using his whole body as a phallus. He would play ten to fifteen sets of tennis a day, then come in and complain that his body was stiff, and "My head feels as if it is bloated and swelling up from within." When a pretty girl passed their office window, all the boys would stand up at attention. This equation, this interchangeability of the whole for one of its parts, is also seen in the symptom: the doll, a whole body, also stands for the penis. The patient equaled the doll equaled the penis equaled the stool.

The doll is a retreat into the mechanical. Reversal of this process, with the mechanical threatening to come to life again, threatens to undo this defense and provokes anxiety. The moment of its coming to life, the most feared, is also the most enjoyed; it is the beginning of the forbidden erection. The patient remembers lying on a couch and bringing about repeated erection and relaxation; it was the start of the erection which gave him the greatest pleasure. In his masturbation he employs "mechanical contrivances." The act is a production, lasting one to two hours, usually in the small hours of the morning, while the family is asleep. It takes place in the bathtub (compare the fish episode above), where the water washes away the guilt. With a wet towel he binds himself tightly like a diaper, sometimes imagining his genital to disappear. He rubs soap bubbles around his anus (mother's soapsuds enema), and with a rubber hose plays a stream of water around his anus or anteriorly. All this is accompanied by looking at pornographic picture books which he has carefully bought and prepared; plus the accompaniment of vivid detailed fantasies.

These fantasies, taken together, are in significance like a crucial repetitive dream; they are condensed, symbolic, and reveal which pregenital and partial impulses are receiving expression. The recurring and fairly constant features are these: the patient is picked up and taken in tow by a dominant, aggressive woman, "The Queen," or "Her Highness," who then seductively exhibits herself to him. Variable forms of domination are practiced on the patient; sometimes he is bound, or blindfolded, or beaten with a whip. His clothes might then be cut off, and he is usually dressed up as a female. The leading lady, or else some of her assistants, then demonstrate to the patient how to seduce a man; oral practices are employed; the patient is supposed to follow suit. Finally fellatio and cunnilingus are performed on each other between the patient and the woman.

The oedipal character of his phallic strivings is evident. The women he chooses, in reality as well as in pictures, are all redheads. One of his favorite burlesque queens had a name very akin to his mother's. He recalled an early memory of being held in his mother's arms; she had a black lacy veil over her face and smelt of perfume. The patient now will sometimes wear his mother-in-law's black silk panties as a prelude to masturbation. His mother-in-law, from whose roof he cannot move away despite his protestations, occupies a prominent position in his sexual fantasies. He married a second cousin. Many of his fantasies, and a number of his "affairs," are within the family. An early sexual fantasy is of a woman completely covered with a tight black garment, with only the genitals and nipple areas exposed. He was strongly impressed and early stimulated sexually by the story of Circe who turned Ulysses' companions into pigs—or by a fairy with a wand who could do magical things. She could make inanimate things come alive, and turn people into inanimate things. (This equals mother with the enema tip, who can make his erection come to life, but can also turn his penis or stool into a doll; desired and exciting, yet feared and threatening at the same time.)

A doll is something which is looked at as well as played with; behind the display window it is an object for exhibition. As such it played a part in connection with the patient's strong scoptophilic impulses. Looking at the lewd pictures comprised a prominent part of the masturbatory foreplay. These pictures were carried in a "dummy" folder, one which presumably contained his work papers. He treated it as a "hot cargo," as evidence for a crime; he felt anxiety in driving past a policeman when this folder was in the car. What if he should die and this be found among his possessions? His scoptophilic impulses were served in his daily routine; he had arranged his desk near a window where he watched women's legs pass by; he created elaborate fantasies concerning certain "regulars" in this passing parade, who subsequently found a way into his masturbatory fantasies as well. This office arrangement ceased during the analysis, cutting down his workday by several hours. (Note his position behind the window, in the place of the usual mannequin. The latter is feared because she is looking back.)

When finished with a picture, he has sometimes thrown it down the toilet. Here it might curl when wet and begin to assume a three-dimensional look, provoking a great anxiety in the patient. Thus up to a point, an object satisfies impulses, but when depth is added, the same object becomes phobic. Among the visual pictures which early attracted him sexually and with which he masturbated were cut-out paper dolls, which his sister, and later he himself, made and played with. Sometimes these too would wave and become lifelike, and would then frighten him. These are a transition between impulse satisfaction and phobia. This connection, that the feared object is at another level desired, was understood in the reverse direction by the patient when, during the course of the analysis, in looking at a mannequin one day from afar, he developed an erection.

His voyeurism was an attempt to deny castration. He remembered how once he saw his mother bending over after she had finished on the toilet, and that afterwards he told his grandfather that mother had hair around her behind. The pubic hair was displaced posteriorly, a falsification designed to maintain the illusion that in front there was still something, or that it was hidden under the hair. The patient spoke with warmth and affection of an aunt who, when scolded by his mother for appearing nude in front of the patient, replied casually, "Oh, it's nothing. All bodies are the same. It's all just skin." The patient repeated this statement with pride and as authority a number of times. When one day the analyst remarked, "But it isn't true," the patient reacted with sincere surprise, and realized why he had never wanted to question the accuracy of this statement.

He looked but he did not allow himself to see. With cunnilingus, in fact and in fantasy, he stopped short of seeing. He was ignorant of the anatomy of the vulva, and had the idea, even into the analysis, that the clitoris was large and was inside, somewhere near the cervix. If there was no penis sticking out, there was still one inside. The analyst remarked how odd it was that the patient, who was a scholarly type and who, being related to doctors, had medical books available, and never looked at a picture in these books to satisfy his unanswered questions. He reacted with astonishment. "My God. I would move heaven and earth to find a misplaced comma, but would never lift a finger to find out where the clitoris was." He recalled as a boy, lying on the ground under a woman's skirt, how he had shut his eyes. He had always told himself that this was because he "was a gentleman," as compared with his friends. He had almost a fetishlike attitude toward a black silk stocking and a high heel, which was almost equated to woman for him. He would speak of seeing "a beautiful silk-stockinged leg with a high heel" walking down the street. He displaced downwards (as well as in other connections upwards); woman was not a castrated being; the high heel was a penis, mechanical again; and under the stocking on the thigh could be hidden a penis. In his sexual fantasies a woman would put her high heel in his face. One day the sudden sight of a man's completely bald head frightened him; it was like the "sheer nudity" which he most feared in the doll. Here was the perineum, from front to back, unequivocally exposed, and it was smooth; nothing was sticking out. His eyes were strongly libidinized. On the couch, he rubbed them constantly, with a regular, rhythmical, almost ticlike pattern, which had an automatic and irresistible quality to it. Often the itching of his eyes alternated with itching of the testicles.

The doll was his mother, it was woman, it was the being without a penis. Dolls have no genitals. Female dolls scared him worse than male ones. Hollow dolls were empty, were holes. When a doll was shattered, it was air, it was nothing, it was castrated; it was the female genital. He could not contemplate seeing it; clothing on the doll made it easier.

Exhibitionistic tendencies, the counterpart of his scoptophilia, were also active, and were demonstrable in his general behavior, his Don Juan attitude toward women, his manner of speaking, his aggressive superiority toward his colleagues, and often a haughty and self-satisfied manner in the analysis. As a corollary to his avoidance of anything associatively connected with castration, there existed, and for the same reason, his need to exhibit in a positive way his still present and undamaged phallus. This too was achieved, characteristically, by displacement, and by the use of his entire body and performance as a substitute for the genital.

In addition to the roles played by the doll in the service of auto- and heterosexuality, it also served a function to the patient in relation to a strong unresolved homosexual conflict. The latter had been able to emerge into consciousness only recently, having previously been kept rigidly repressed, and any allusions to the subject were attended with severe anxiety. A brief and transitory reference to his homosexual impulses occurred early in the analysis in conjunction with a dream in which he was chased by a number of men and turned and threw milk into their faces. His associating milk to semen provoked denial and fear on his part, following which the subject disappeared for a long time. Only in recent months, following analysis of his ambivalent relationship to his phallic mother, and in conjunction with a strong positive father transference, have his homosexual impulses and his deep attachment to his sentimental father come into their full light and been faced. From the age of six to eleven, following economic reverses which forced them to move into a smaller apartment, the patient slept with his father, the latter hugging him close from behind. The patient remembered first his shame and guilt regarding this, his reluctance to admit it to his friends, and finally the pleasure he obtained from it. During late latency and early adolescence, there was mutual masturbation and "touching penises" with the boys. Much of his present-day behavior became understandable with the liberation of this phase of his repressed sexuality, which is still taking place and being worked through: such as his proclivity for working late with the boys, his long tennis sessions, his relation to his senior partner, his interest in stag parties, burlesque, and so on. Many of his "heterosexual" interests and exploits were thinly veiled reactive defenses against homosexual impulses. In his sexual fantasies he fought, against obvious pressure, to prevent the appearance of homosexual object choices, which finally did break through on a few occasions. He was afraid that if he allowed them in fantasy they might also occur in fact, as happened with cunnilingus and other fantasies. Belonging in this connection are the following, which can only be briefly mentioned: his strong feminine identification, transvestist tendencies in masturbation and fantasies, oral receptive inclinations, and erotic practices, and his passive masochistic impulses.

Just as his relationship to the phallic mother was a blend of desire and threat, so too was it in his relation with his father. The feared castrator, heretofore the mother, was now brought out to be the father, in a dream in which "the patient is playing in a deep valley. A giant, with whiskers like his father, comes threateningly down, chopping trees as he comes."

The patient's position, rooted in anal ambivalence, poised between hetero- and homosexuality, between active desires for his mother and passive desires for his father (and aggressive mother), and with corresponding inhibitions and fears in both directions, is expressed in the following dream (the detailed associations cannot be gone into):

"My son has a .22 rifle which he is shooting at his mother. It is just a game. I have a .30-30 rifle, am behind him, and am also going to shoot it at her. She wants it but I think the shock will be too great. I go to the back door. A man is behind the glass door, and he scares me. I shoot at him. Is he friend or foe? I shouldn't have shot so quickly. But the bullet bounces off the glass and floats lazily away. I want to hit the man with the gun. I awake screaming with fear."

Here the doll behind the glass is a man, the homosexually desired father. The doll is not only his own penis, it is also another man's penis, his father's penis, the penis homosexually desired and therefore feared.

Connected with this is the fact: girls, not boys, play with dolls. His interest in the phobic object betrays, and his avoidance of the doll denies, his passive feminine orientation. "Why can I not stand to see a little girl's doll melt away?" he once asked. Because the little girl's fantasied penis must remain intact. In this connection we recall the sister who died before the patient was born and whom he replaced. She was always said to have looked "like a little wax doll." If she had lived, said the doctor, she would have been damaged. The patient heard this repeatedly during his early years. The possibility of damage, of castration, even of death, existed then on a "real" base. The patient was living in her stead; the same could happen to him; he too could become inanimate, dead, a wax doll, and melt away (his convulsions, age three). Or, he could live, and be, like her, feminine, damaged, castrated. His mother furthered this by keeping him in curls and dresses until four.

To recapitulate, this section has described the following main etiological spokes feeding into the central doll at the hub of the wheel: the doll represents, in turn and simultaneously, the patient's own penis, his stool, he himself in toto, his mother, woman in general, the female genital, another man's (father's) penis, the sister who died, the little girl's fantasied penis. There are other smaller secondary spokes; and all the spokes interconnect.

III

It is necessary to reaffirm at this time that the preceding material and content did not flow forth in an uninterrupted stream, but rather that the sequence and rate were determined by the specific resistances and defenses and how they were dissolved. It is interesting in this connection to note that Breuer and Freud, in *The Studies in Hysteria* (1893–1895), used an analogy very similar to the main structural analogy of the wheel used in this presentation. Regarding the pathogenic material as stratified in layers of different resistance potential, with the pathogenic nucleus at the core, Freud states that "the analyst should himself undertake the opening of the inner strata and the advancement in the radial direction, while the patient should take care of the peripheral extension" (p. 292).

While the phobic symptom, the high degree of symbolic representation, the hypersexualization of all activity, and the phallic exhibitionism all point to a predominantly hysterical level, the analysis was nevertheless in most respects the analysis of a compulsive character. In line with this, the chief defenses were isolation and related mechanisms. The pathogenic early memories and infantile traumata were not long in being remembered, but they were stripped of emotional import, and their intimate connections with the main streams of symptom and character formation were obscured and denied for long periods of time. The patient intellectualized and rationalized freely; he "knew" things and adopted them readily, but they applied chiefly to others, or to himself in theory only, not to be seriously entertained or to be really translated into action. Thinking itself was highly libidinized, and his newfound insights were at first used exhibitionistically and aggressively both in the analysis and in his daily life. He translated into slogans, which on the one hand expressed the point but on the other kept him from getting too close to it. Thus, though he went with a procession of women, his behavior with them led him to see that "I am not an intercourser," a phrase which he then wore out until it lost its meaning. He defended by flippancy, by playing games: "the oedipus edifice which stands in my way," or, with reference to the body equals phallus material which had been under discussion for some time, he once said, "If anyone else ever called me a prick as often as you do, I'd get mad."

Other defenses employed by him in his character makeup, as in his analysis, were reaction formation, displacement, and acting out. Even his deep and masculine voice was studied and cultivated; during moments of emotional excitement he would feel that his voice became high-pitched and shrill, which to him was feminine, Jewish, castrated. During one phase of the analysis, much of the libidinal energy was diffused out in rhythmical, automatic, muscular activities on the couch. When this was analyzed and worked through, and its substitute character appreciated, it was followed by a more detailed verbalization of the vivid sexual fantasy life. Many of his resistances were intended for impulse gratification as well. He "did" his analysis as he treated his impulses. The flow of material was alternately profuse and begrudging, in line with his bowel habits. At times it flooded the analysis, with a torrent of dreams, associations, and recollections; and at other times it was almost completely blocked, by lateness, a few missed hours, or by stretching and yawning on the couch. The significant material tended to be obscured in a flood of detail. In his masturbation, he liked to go "past the optimum point"; that is, beyond the point when he should have had orgasm, then recede, then come up again, and so on many times. He attempted to make the same use of analytic insight and interpretations—accumulate them past the optimum point, beyond the point where they should have been effective, then let them recede into the background, and then he would be ready for more. This tendency to convert every activity and procedure into an instrument for pregenital impulse satisfaction was a maneuver which had to be attacked repeatedly to further the analytic work.

Just as a perversion, during the course of analytic therapy, is often first converted into a neurosis, so this patient's neurosis, during the course of therapy, took a temporary turn in the direction of perversion. That is, when, as a result of the analytic process, the strength of his punitive superego was diminished, the repressed polymorphous perverse impulses were able to come forth stronger and more openly. The patient repeatedly expressed the hope to be able to get rid of the phobia but to keep his "delicious" masturbation. The quest for satisfaction was seen too in the resistance of seeking transference gratification instead of insight.

The transference had a multiple character, varied in its manifestations, and served both to further insight and to defend against it. It was, as previously described, alternately a mother and a father transference, with ambivalent negative and positive aspects to each. Much of the advancement in the radial direction was achieved by analysis of the vicissitudes of the labile transference relationship. The analyst was reacted to mainly as the phallic mother or the sentimental father. One phase of the transference was a type of cross-identification, where the analyst became the patient and the patient became his own father. Thus, when the patient felt that the analyst was making a particularly poignant or discerning remark or interpretation, his eyes would moisten with pride instead of his absorbing what was being said. He became his father, beaming at his son.

The patient's present status is as follows. The general features, which lie outside the field of our special interest, will just be mentioned. The bowel symptoms cleared up very early, his ritualistic obsessive–compulsive behavior and symptoms have been greatly modified. His work habits, interpersonal relationships, and use of his time have shown considerable change in the direction of improvement. His marriage is on the road to being solidified. However, genital sexuality has by no means as yet been achieved. While the old neurotic defenses and solutions have been altered, pregenitality still predominates in many respects, and progression forward, through an adequate oedipal solution, to genital attainment remains as the work yet to be done.

References to the status of the phobia have been indirect, but for months now all indications point to the fact that the substructure has crumbled and that in large part it is the memory of the phobia which remains. Again and again the patient will allude to what should have been a phobic situation, and will confess to the absence or only minimal presence of anxiety or fear. But he hastens to find an excuse. There was not enough of a surprise element, or the material of this particular doll was not bad enough, or maybe this one never would have frightened him, etc. He is, in actuality, being conservative, and is only gradually feeling his way into the new world of figures. Once he went with his wife into a fur salon to buy her a fur coat (also a manifestation of the analysis); the only empty seat left for him was one immediately next to and under a mannequin standing on the floor. He sat down. But, to the analyst: "Don't take any credit. It was the only seat I could find." His mother-in-law has a sewing dummy hanging in her closet. When nobody was looking, the patient went in and stroked it in the dark closet. His wife has saved the bride-and-groom figures from their wedding cake, and recently put them under a glass top in their bedroom; the patient tested himself, touched them, passed the test. At a bar, a prankster bartender bent down and came up suddenly with an artificial rubber hand attached over his own, and shook the patient's hand with it. This had all the worst elements in it; the patient was able to laugh it off. He has visited homes with little girls in them, and has allowed himself to be exposed with impunity to their dolls. He recently visited the County Museum. There was a statue of Charles Chaplin, with hands outstretched, and a finger broken off. The patient shook hands with him. There have been numerous other such incidents. Last Halloween, hideous-looking rubber face masks appeared in every drug and toy store. The patient expected nightmares of trouble; instead he went through the season quite indifferent.

Phobic patients characteristically are reluctant to put to the test the results of their therapeutic labor, after having long been conditioned to the relationship between phobic object and the outbreak of anxiety. Particularly is this true where the phobia has existed, as in this patient, for virtually a lifetime. Years of such incrustation cannot be shaken off lightly. The patient is now in the process of working through his liberation from the phobic object.

As a final addition, the following bit of clinical data will be offered as pertinent to and an interesting variation of the case under discussion. It has in common with our patient a use of the same object, but for quite different psychic purposes. The same qualities which make the doll suitable to our patient for phobic avoidance, serve in this next example to qualify it as a means of sublimation. A well-known puppeteer makes his living and also satisfies deep inner psychic needs by dolls and puppets. This man is an overt homosexual. The puppet represents his narcissistically highly overvalued penis. His entire life is devoted to making them, dressing them, playing with them, and exhibiting them. He lives in a room next to his prized and successful collection. He can make them male or female, at will; he is enraptured by them. After a performance, the audience is invited backstage to admire them, at which time this man sits on a chair nervously biting his nails, a study in mixed feelings. In him mingle great pride and satisfaction plus gnawing anxiety lest someone cause the slightest damage to his prized possession.

The doll in both these cases is the concentrate of strong feelings and values emanating from the person's unconscious. In the one case, equilibrium is maintained by shunning this concentrated symbol; in the other, he is able to embrace and enjoy it.

A search of the literature failed to reveal any reports of a similar doll or related phobia. However, very relevant to this discussion is the material relating to the doll Olympia, in Hoffman's story "The Sand Man," which reappears again in Offenbach's opera *Tales of Hoffmann* and which is described by Freud in his paper, "The Uncanny" (1919). The following features of the story and Freud's interpretation of it form a bridge to our case: the student Nathaniel is identified with the doll Olympia, whom he loves, and who represents his own feminine counterpart; his love for her is thus a narcissistic one. Nathaniel's father is ambivalently loved and feared; he is the potential castrator. The uncanny effect is considered to be due primarily to the dread of castration. The attention is shifted chiefly to the eyes, to which are displaced the genital interests and fears. The "Sand Man" removes the eyes of bad little children. The father is in part a mechanician; much of the emotional tone of the story is created by the intellectual uncertainty as to whether the doll is alive or not, whether the inanimate has become animate. The father dies in a chemical explosion. The many similarities with our patient's relation to dolls occur at once. The conflicts within Nathaniel, however, lead not to phobia, but to madness.

POSTSCRIPT

It would be of interest to add a brief note to describe the final course and termination of the above analysis. This took place in roughly another year of treatment, at a slightly diminished intensity and frequency. The final work consisted not so much in the discovery or elucidation of new psychodynamic insights, of new spokes in the already complex wheel of causality, but rather in the digestion and working through of those which had already been uncovered, and the addition and delineation of the interconnecting links between the spokes, in a circular rather than in a radial direction.

Thus as an example, the patient associated one day to the fact that Raggedy Andy dolls were not as bad to him as were stiff ones. He had awakened that morning with a "stiff erection"; he realized then again, as though for the first time and with sudden conviction, that the doll was equated to an erection. We had been talking for days about the constant and energetic stretching, stiffening, and then relaxing of his body which went on during the analytic hours. So the doll, the erection, was his whole body as well. He loved it, he rubbed and fondled it, he was narcissistically attached to it. Why was it endangered, why did he have to concentrate so on preserving it? A veritable orgy of current masturbatory fantasies and actions provided the links and the answers, for they emphasized and brought out into clear focus the strong tendencies to feminine identification. In these fantasies, the patient would be transformed into and dressed as a woman, and would then be forced into oral practices on both men and women. It was the strength of these bisexual impulses which made it so necessary to guard the integrity of the erect phallus, to prevent it from becoming hollow, as the inside of the doll. The homosexual object choice was narcissistically determined, and was a projection of the self. Thus did the movement proceed, with the ego wending its way in irregular circular fashion along the intercommunicating paths from one radial grouping to another, from phallus to body, to woman, to female genital, to homosexual object, back and forth and in all directions. Just as each lent support to the other, so did insight into one lead to a diffusion of the process of understanding into the other, thus facilitating the working through and eventual dissolution of all the various etiological spokes.

During this final phase, every reference to and contact with dolls was notoriously without anxiety or phobic reaction, so that by the end he had a number of times picked up and handled the previously phobic object with impunity. Thus, on one occasion he picked up a rubber figure quite casually and squeezed it so that it whistled and its tongue came out. Parallel to this development in the realm of the symptom, there was a steady and impressive progress in the underlying character structure toward increased solidity and maturity, showing itself clearly in his marriage, his work, and in his general life.

However, the final complete extrusion from the ego of even the outlines of the ego-alien phobic structure, as well as the process of termination of the analysis itself, was colored again by the remnants of all his well-known pregenital impulses and defense mechanisms, as though they were making a last stand. He "hung on" orally as long as he could, retaining the memory and threat of symptoms, trying "to get as much as he could" and to "suck the treatment dry." He compared himself in the last months with a drug addict being taken off the drug.

New oral material emerged. His mother, mourning over her lost daughter when the patient was born, had been unable to give him the breast, and instead fed him by bottle. This, he observed, was the first "mechanical contrivance," the first substitute of the inanimate for the animate. Further dietary restrictions came about a few years later following the "constipation and convulsions." His anal desires to retain were also again at work, causing a prolongation of transference gratification and a resistance to its removal. Just as he had to tear up and destroy an envelope or piece of paper into many small pieces before discarding it, to make sure that he did not miss anything, so he clung to the analyst, and had to wring him out before letting go. And finally it was again castration fear which motivated his last grip on the symptoms and the analyst, for to let even them go would mean a revival of the sense of loss, a feeling of having dropped something, or of something having been torn away.

The final resolution, following the analysis of these lingering pregenital influences, came with the working through and solution of the oedipal conflict. This took place both on the levels of the transference and in his relationship with his senior partner, with primarily an identification with the father figure and the patient's rising to a new role of maturity. His final liberation from castration fear is emphasized in the following dream, which occurred in the last week of analysis: "I am driving a big long truck, with a supply of long steel bars sticking way out in the back. One short bar falls off—but I keep going and don't care in the least. My father is with me and he seems to be worried about it—but I am not worried and I have a 'So what?' feeling."

Indicative of his changed attitude and his new focus of attention was the following bit of material, brought out in the last few days of treatment. In associating to the item of "circles" which had appeared in a dream, the patient commented that the circle was the perfect symbol of completeness, as exemplified in a wedding ring. But, he was reminded, this very symbol had until now been to him the perfect symbol of incompleteness, representing as it did the vagina, anus, or mouth, from which something, the penis or stool or breast, like the steel bar in the dream above, had been forcibly removed. But now his gaze had shifted from the opening in the circle to the periphery, the closed line. His point of view had changed, literally. And similarly the doll to him was now not the hollow inside but rather the complete and intact and therefore safe skin covering the body wall.

REFERENCES

Breuer, J., & Freud, S. (1893–1895), Studies in Hysteria. *Standard Edition,* 2. London: Hogarth Press, 1955.

Freud, S. (1919), The uncanny. *Standard Edition,* 17:217–256. London: Hogarth Press, 1955.

A DISCUSSION OF "THE ANALYSIS OF A DOLL PHOBIA" BY LEO RANGELL

Vann Spruiell, M.D.

I

The analyst–reader, as he contemplates a prize-winning clinical paper, written thirty years ago by one of his heroes, experiences a certain timidity. He would like to say, "Fine paper! That's all that needs to be said." Not being able to get away with that, he consoles himself: the mature Leo Rangell, after so many years of experience, might well have emendations and new formulations of his own to make. He might place different emphases on the underlying context of his patient's symptoms, might describe the occasions for intrapsychic change differently; surely he would be inclined to utilize the clinical account of this patient as an example of the structural pathology he has subsequently written about so well, in particular, disorders of the superego.

Rangell's paper was to demonstrate the complicated origins, more astonishing than any spider's web, of a man's phobia for dolls—more than dolls, a phobia for icons of all sorts. To do this, he had to focus on the complex nature of the varied symptoms themselves, even then condensing them greatly. He pictured them as the spokes of a wheel.

The use of this organizing device, coupled with a rich descriptive ability, coupled also with a spare, often witty prose, results in a superb clinical account, the likes of which are seldom seen nowadays. The reader is reminded of Freud's early interest in understanding dreams; the patient's fear of, and enchantment by, icons is traced to multiple historical levels, shown to demonstrate multiple motivations. At the same time, the author is able to *in part* describe a successful analytic process, with the analysis of resistances and the development and subsequent resolution of the transferences. He also is able to describe a variety of phenomena which are not exactly symptomatic; some are character traits, some, in fact, perverse acts and fantasies.

II

The mournful fact is that it is impossible to write a clinical paper that can satisfy all of one's peers. It is probably impossible even to write a book about a psychoanalysis without some readers wishing for more discussion here, less there, differing with this intervention or that interpretation, finding themselves making different formulations. Even if a reader respects the author's wish to confine himself to certain areas or dimensions, leaving out others, he can hardly resist his vocation: to see and try to understand the wholeness of human beings. A clinical paper or book becomes a projective device.

If it is impossible to write a totally satisfying clinical paper, it is similarly impossible to compose a response that is more than subjective, better than impressionistic. Much depends on the reader's clinical experience, his age, his current interests. Even the intellectual climate of a time influences the way a given paper is read. The general interests, perhaps it would be better to say fads, of our contemporaries may stir connotations and inferences that were far from the author's original intentions.

It is characteristic of our present time that there is insufficient interest in the analysis of symptoms. For this reason alone, Rangell's paper should be required reading for candidates. Since I have little to add to *this* focus of his, I will discuss what was not his focus, namely the dynamics which so fascinatingly parallel and, at the same time, interdigitate with the dynamics of the phobias for icons. These are the dynamics of a perverse solution to the oedipal dilemmas. They are also the dynamics resulting in what many would term the *narcissistic* solution to those dilemmas. However named, they are the same.

III

To change focus, it might be useful to take Rangell's device of the wheel with spokes and hub and turn it inside out so to speak. Instead of the hub, let us make the phobias parts of the *rim.* As constituent parts of that rim—perhaps we should say laminated to it—would be other symptoms, character traits, fantasies, and other psychic acts. The causally and interconnected spokes, unveiled during a long analysis, would lead to a hub: *a small number of important unconscious fantasies.*

A patient is described for us, a personable, rather charming man of thirty-eight, a statistical analyst who comes for analysis because for years he has been preoccupied by fears of encounters with dolls. Any icon serves. But there are great variations in the reactions to qualitative differences in the figures: size, sex, composition, relative nudity, and so on. (These variations, and their historical connections, are brilliantly illustrated during the subsequent analysis.)

The man, otherwise intelligent, comes at this particular date for the rather silly reason that he read in a popular magazine that psychoanalysis was most useful for those under forty; according to his conscious reasoning, he has two years to go. (The deeper meanings of this play on numbers are not described, and the reader wonders if they represent anniversary reactions of some sort, and if the patient, when he actually arrives at the dreaded age of forty, creates a crisis in the treatment.) It quickly becomes obvious that this is not the only example of magical thinking which plays an actual part in the patient's life. In fact, he is filled with obsessions, which he acts upon, having to do with time, money, figures, bowels, and so on. In his other behavior, or at least much of it, he demonstrates characteristics which we conventionally associate with obsessive–compulsive individuals, and with more than the narrowly defined compulsive character. He and his wife are miserable with each other and have separated several times; he lives in a putatively unsatisfactory way with his mother-in-law; but we are told of no effort of his to move; he has many extramarital affairs; he is highly exhibitionistic and scopophilic. Most to the point of this discussion, he soon reveals in his analysis the most cherished secret of all: the fact that the only delicious sexual satisfactions of his life occur in the midst of wonderfully contrived masturbation scenarios; the accompanying fantasies are vivid sadomasochistic encounters.

IV

Rangell describes the most important of the etiological spokes which feed, in his model, into the central doll at the hub; he summarizes:

> [T]he doll represents, in turn and simultaneously, the patient's own penis, his stool, he himself in toto, his mother, women in general, the female genital, another man's (father's) penis, the sister who died, the little girl's fantasied penis. There are other smaller secondary spokes; and all the spokes interconnect [p. 92].

The interweaving of family myth, infantile and childhood history, and preoedipal and oedipal developmental issues in the construction of the basic phobia, along with its many variations, is almost awe inspiring. An older, highly idealized sister had died as a little girl before the patient's birth; the mother was alleged to have been depressed throughout her pregnancy with the patient himself; she had been unable to nurse him. Multiple prohibitions were given about masturbation; these were reinforced by threats of explosions. The toddler was, it seems quite sadistically, exposed to objects precious to the family, Dresden china, a bas-relief on the wall, and "playfully" snapped back with warnings. (Rangell, generalizing perhaps a bit overconfidently, says the path for displacement was thus laid down; the nuclear idea of the phobia was born.) At the age of three a convulsion exploded; a doctor is said to have saved his life by diagnosing the condition as a reaction to constipation. Thereupon, the mother instituted daily enemas for the next year and a half. An illustration of her involvement with the child is the fact that she kept him in curls and dresses until the age of four. At the height of the phallic–oedipal period, the father became bankrupt. Even though he was degraded in the patient's eyes, in comparison to the "refined" and beautiful mother, the boy slept with his father between the ages of six and eleven; subsequently, during his analysis, he was able to remember the strong erotic stimulation that resulted.

In summary, the author emphasizes the particularly intense castration anxiety before and during the oedipal period which initiated a regression to a previously strong anal fixation.

> Each then confirmed and lent strength to the other. The earlier anal experiences made the later phallic castration possibilities more real, and the phallic dangers in turn revived and reinforced the earlier anal threats. The phallus, like the stool earlier, could be removed and broken off. The doll was both [p. 85].

In addition, a very strong negative oedipal component existed, and was later analyzed.

V

Rangell mentions, but does not emphasize, the barely concealed charm that emanated from the icons to the patient. It was far easier for the patient to dramatize his fears in relation to them than to recognize that they were lovingly constructed in order to transfix. If the doll were both idealized phallus and stool, among so many other things, these were not only subject to damage, they were subject to the most exquisite pleasures. And the little boy and the later man were not about to give them up. If the complex phobias, and the reactions to them, could be likened to an inner, idiosyncratic set of rules—small rules to be always observed—it can be said that the patient had *another,* ultimately more important set of secret rules. These latter rules allowed and governed the masturbatory acts and the fantasies that accompanied them. They were manifested in the covert masturbation accompanying much of his apparently ordinary behavior. The former rules showed in the exaggerated (and, to the observer, almost mocking) submission to authority.

As Rangell points out, "this seeming obedience was a sham; he obeyed in small things strictly, in order to break the big rule brashly. 'I will carry out conscientiously all your edicts, except, please, I will masturbate' " (p. 81). The reader suspects that breaking the "big rule" was generalized in other secret respects in the patient's general behavior.

The big rules obviously had not only to do with the motor facts of his private masturbation; they had to do with the fantasies that accompanied them. Rangell comments that, just as a perversion is often converted into a neurosis in an analysis, this patient took a "temporary" turn in the direction of a perversion. The observer has to be skeptical; there is rich material to suggest that a perversion had been present overtly and covertly all along. It existed simultaneously with the clear-cut psychoneurotic organization. The perversion *emerged* as analytic data.

VI

Let us examine this material. Before doing so, however, it is important to reiterate some truths which to practicing analysts are self-evident. The lure of possible gratification of infantile wishes remains unending. It is never "given up," though the lure may be transcended by a higher organization, namely genital sexuality, which incorporates and indirectly gratifies certain features of the more infantile forms. In all people regressions occur from genital sexuality, triggered by anxiety. Sometimes aspects of a regression become enshrined, sculpted, as it were, in the form of character traits, which as Calef (1983) has pointed out, represent a partial fusion, or at least lack of conflict, between ego and ego ideal. Sometimes the infantile impulses are simultaneously repelled and secretly gratified, as in the case of psychoneurotic symptoms. Sometimes the infantile wishes are gratified directly in behavior, in which case we are apt to call the behavior "perverse." Sometimes all *three* "solutions" may be found simultaneously in the same individual.

But if perverse behavior, overtly or covertly expressed, has occurred in all humans, this is not to say that all humans have been or are *perverse,* or suffer from perversions. Such a condition is not simply the reverse of the neurosis; a perversion is a highly organized system of behavior which mediates the core of sexual pleasure; other forms of sexuality must be denied if not in fact, at least in pleasure. Transitory perverse organizations are created intrapsychically by many individuals, especially during adolescence. They may be of little final importance; they may seem primarily experimental. Finally, it may be that most individuals, if not all, are capable, providing superego strictures are in some way at least temporarily relaxed, of adopting perverse organizations. Most recover from the regressions, and only some individuals make the next step of commitment to an actual perversion: the denial of either the existence of the genital universe or at least the denial of possibilities of pleasure in it. This genital universe, in contrast to the "realities" existing in preoedipal terms, includes the recognition of the existence and difference in the genitals of both sexes and includes the recognition of the differences between the generations: the world of adults and the world of children.

Thus, the pervert, if he is to be called such, frequently the euphemism, "narcissistic personality," is used instead, must deny certain aspects of oedipal and postoedipal reality, even if he *consciously* affirms that same reality. He must live in terms of certain illusions, and he must maintain certain supporting intrapsychic organizations, particularly in terms of the superego, to allow for the continuation of an active perversion; he must already have these structures or he must somehow acquire them.

Rangell had not so much a phobic patient with a peculiar sexuality as he had a perverse patient with atypical phobias. The text itself amply supports this statement. It must be remembered that the statistician was married (unhappily) and had many seemingly heterosexual affairs (the fact that there were many implies little satisfaction of any lasting nature). His primary sexual pleasure came in the course of masturbation *scenes* (for that is what they were).

> In his masturbation he employs "mechanical contrivances." The act is a production, lasting one to two hours, usually in the small

> hours of the morning, while the family is asleep. It takes place in the bathtub . . . where the water washes away the guilt. With a wet towel he binds himself tightly like a diaper, sometimes imagining his genital to disappear. He rubs soap bubbles around his anus (mother's soapsuds enema), and with a rubber hose plays a stream of water around his anus or anteriorly. All this is accompanied by looking at pornographic picture books which he has carefully bought and prepared; plus the accompaniment of vivid detailed fantasies.
>
> These fantasies, taken together, are in significance like a crucial repetitive dream; they are condensed, symbolic, and reveal which pregenital and partial impulses are receiving expression. The recurring and fairly constant features are these: The patient is picked up and taken in tow by a dominant, aggressive woman, "The Queen," or "Her Highness," who then seductively exhibits herself to him. Variable forms of domination are practiced on the patient; sometimes he is bound, or blindfolded, or beaten with a whip. His clothes might then be cut off, and he is usually dressed up as a female. The leading lady, or else some of her assistants, then demonstrate to the patient how to seduce a man; oral practices are employed; the patient is supposed to follow suit. Finally fellatio and cunnilingus are performed on each other between the patient and the woman [pp. 86–87].

In addition, the patient had elaborate voyeuristic enterprises. He dressed up in his mother-in-law's black silk panties as a prelude to masturbation. He looked on a black silk stocking and high heel in terms of fetishes; he spoke of "a beautiful silk-stockinged leg with a high heel" walking down the street, revealing the dehumanization of the woman as a whole entity, especially one bearing adult female genitalia. Other aspects of his behavior were analyzed as disguised equivalents of perverse fantasies, making him resemble the patients Arlow (1971) described in terms of character perversion. Thus, the analysand demonstrated features of homosexuality, fetishism, voyeurism, and sadomasochism, in both overtly sexual and disguised forms. Clearly, he had achieved what Chasseguet-Smirgel (1981) called the "perverse solution," accompanied by a denial of the world of genital reality, and the substitution for it of an "anal universe" which razes all differences between the sexes and the differences between the worlds of childhood and the worlds of parents.

VIII

This man, before the successful resolution of his analysis, lived in a universe which maintained the illusions that the stool was equal to if not better than the penis, that women possessed these anal penises (the most terrifying doll was one that was *empty*), or perhaps they had enema tips, that castration did not exist, that big people did not exist in contrast to little people, accordingly, that incest taboos did not exist, in short that "oedipal victory" is possible, and not only that, it is possible with either father or mother. Yet it must be remembered that the man was not crazy. In fact, he lived simultaneously in a different universe, a universe in which the exactly opposite precepts obtained: castration not only existed, it was imminent; the most awful oedipal and preoedipal punishments lurked around every corner. In summary, he lived in a world of ordinary reality, distorted by the illusions and necessary defensive operations of an obsessional psychoneurosis.

It was Freud (1927) who first pointed out such mysterious "splits" in the organization of the ego in fetishism and later, he became convinced that such splits were much more common, in fact, present in many psychoneuroses.

In one organization, the fetishist is overwhelmed by castration anxiety; in the other, castration is totally denied: the feminine penis exists somewhere, somehow. To some extent, the ego is organized according to these separate, conflicting hypotheses; at the same time, no conflict is experienced. Clinical analytic experience convinces one that such organizational ego "splits" indeed occur, that perhaps they are as universal as the other kind of "split," that between the conscious and unconscious organizations. In some "difficult" patients, the differing worlds of assumptions and defensive organizations can be clearly seen; however, the shifts between organizations, the "switchings," are not easy to understand. One comes to the conclusion that it is as difficult to understand, in dynamic terms, such shifts, as it is to understand a process of internalization as it is actually taking place, rather than after the fact. After the facts also, it is possible to observe the gradual undoing of such "splits" after successful psychoanalyses. One has the impression that such a healing took place in Rangell's patient.

The conditions governing the ego "splits," the way the "ego alters itself in the face of traumatic events," is not well understood. They occur preoedipally, and it is not difficult to find material in the analyses relating particularly to anal sadistic organizations—and by the same token, to the rapprochement subphases of separation–individuation (Mahler, Pine, and Bergman, 1975).

Primal scene memories or fantasies, which sometimes can be dated to approximately the age of two years, are common. Such patients almost always demonstrate a fundamental sadomasochistic organization, but other perverse behavior, particularly fetishistic, is almost always seen.

What occurs is repression on the one hand, and a continuation of infantile sexuality, only superficially altered, on the other. Rangell, in particular, has emphasized many times, in the years following the publication of this particular paper, the distortions that then ensue in oedipal dynamics result in one organization set up like other "normal" to psychoneurotic individuals, the other organization set up in such a way that the individual attempts to "negotiate" with reality, as Chasseguet-Smirgel (1981) puts it, in the form of illusions rather than in the form of acceptance. This is, of course, also a reflection of the impaired structuralization of the superego, as Rangell also has repeatedly emphasized (1972, 1974). It will be remembered that the patient scrupulously obeyed small rules in order to break big ones. Is it surprising that humans who become totally involved in the use of power over other humans are so often visitors to those prostitutes who are specialists in "bondage and discipline"?

IX

It has already been suggested that the doll phobias of this patient were atypical. In most patients, the phobias are for *situations,* not for classes of objects, although the phobic reaction to the female genital seen in some male homosexuals is an outstanding exception. Rangell's patient, however, paid such apparently loving attention to his icons that they represented only slightly concealed fetishes. In fact, after the analysis was well under way, the analysand got an erection viewing a mannekin from afar. The most horrible doll was the empty doll, the one without contents. The tie between fetish and phobic object was revealed in the equation: doll equals penis; doll equals stool.

Thus, to return to the notion of the symptoms, character traits, and perverse acts being equivalent to the rim of a wheel, the hub representing a small number of unconscious fantasies, it might be said that in some places the laminations of the rim were tightly glued; in others, the distance between phobic and perverse fantasies was strongly maintained. At the hub, however, were, I believe, two fantasies. In one, the conviction was that oedipal conflicts are absolutely insuperable, unresolvable. In the other, there was the magical illusion that oedipal victory, with either sex, is absolutely possible, if only in the bathtub, secretly, in the early hours of the morning.

The success of the analysis is described in terms, primarily, of the analysis of the phobic symptoms, with attention paid to the analysis of the negative oedipal conflicts as well as the positive. There is no mention of the expectable, intense negative transference reactions, of a primitive sort, so regularly seen in such patients. One has the impression that Rangell, thirty years ago, was more optimistic than most people are today about the possibilities of ultimate "resolutions" of the transference neurosis and oedipal conflicts. Nevertheless, it is quite believable that a successful analysis occurred, and that it was related to the analysis of conflicts which were primarily the results of a very peculiar oedipal compromise, with not only preoedipal regressive reactions, but alterations of the ego which could only be thought of in terms of organizational "splits." For whatever reasons, the "laminations" were joined, and the patient was able to discover a more satisfactory genital universe without the necessity of the twin illusions which were so paralyzing: the illusions pertaining to phobias on one side and perversions on the other.

We are all in Rangell's debt. He described work with a patient who nowadays might be diagnosed as a "narcissistic personality," with the truly psychoneurotic organizations denigrated, and the preoedipal organization—the other side of the "split" mentioned—carefully sanitized of all sexual and aggressive implications. Everything would have been explained in terms of a damaged "self," the victim of some "unempathic" mother. But Rangell's clinical data belies such simplistic notions.

REFERENCES

Arlow, J. A. (1971), Character perversion. In: *Currents in Psychoanalysis,* ed. I. M. Marcus. New York: International Universities Press, pp. 317–336.

Calef, V. (1983), Theory of character. *J. Amer. Psychoanal. Assn.,* 31:211–224.

Chasseguet-Smirgel, J. (1981), De Sade: Der Korper und der Mord an der Realitat. *Psyche* (Stuttg), 35/3:237–252.

Freud, S. (1927), Fetishism. *Standard Edition,* 21:149–157. London: Hogarth Press, 1961.

Mahler, M. S., Pine, F., & Bergman, A. (1975), *The Psychological Birth of the Human Infant: Symbiosis and Individuation.* New York: Basic Books.

Rangell, L. (1972), Aggression, Oedipus, and historical perspective. *Internat. J. Psycho-Anal.,* 53:3–11.

——— (1974), A psychoanalytic perspective leading currently to the syndrome of the compromise of integrity. *Internat. J. Psycho-Anal.,* 55:3–12.

A DISCUSSION OF "THE ANALYSIS OF A DOLL PHOBIA" BY LEO RANGELL

Samuel Abrams, M.D.

I

Every description of a psychoanalytic case history combines components of products, procedures, and process. When the primary component is products, the history's focus is generally on outcome, in concrete behavioral terms or conceptual metapsychological ones. When the primary component is procedures, the description is likely to attend to technical matters, such as the hierarchy of interventions, the differences between construction and interpretation, the analyst's commitment to the treatment setting in the face of all the forces at work that attempt to dislodge him. When process is the primary component, the case history tries to conceptualize what is most distinctive about clinical analysis; that is, the mode of newly integrating the pathogenic past. Of the three components, the most difficult to describe is the last. This is true chiefly because products and procedures are clamorous in the course of a treatment while the process moves silently.

Rangell's is an unusually well-written, highly condensed description of a four-year analysis. For more than three decades the patient has secretly suffered a specific phobia: he is deathly afraid of "dolls." Despite the intensity of his symptom and the degree of pain associated with it, he has insistently deferred treatment. The severe long-standing phobia is complemented by an equally persistent habit, about which he is even more secretive. He masturbates regularly. Masturbation is his main source of sexual pleasure by far. It is done ritually, often in a highly elaborate fashion. The patient has obvious attitudes toward the symptom and the habit: he wants to be rid of the first, to preserve the second.

The patient's character is also impaired. This disturbance is both more serious and more disabling than the symptom or the habit, especially because he is not aware of any impairment, although it pervades his personal and working life. His relationships to people are shallow, he often treats them as if they were merely things. At one point in his analysis he recalls a childhood story of a fairy who can convert people into inanimate objects by simply waving a wand. Unconsciously, he continually tries to achieve that bit of sorcery.

When he does relate to others as people, his feelings are characteristically distorted. He appears compliant, especially to figures in authority, but the compliance is a facade that conceals an aggressive feeling of superiority. In spite of considering himself better than others, he limits his professional achievements. He wastes unnecessarily long periods of time with "the boys." He has a Don Juan attitude toward women, partly acted out in frequent affairs with partners often chosen from within his extended family circle. He seems neat, but it is a neatness that covers over a proclivity for messiness and inefficiency. A stickler for rules, he strives to conserve yet is ultimately wasteful. He is meticulously cautious about money yet can impulsively be dollar foolish. He is also described as someone who can "look but not see," perhaps implying some inhibition in abstract thinking; certainly his everyday world preoccupies him with concrete "figures."

Rangell's initial description of the patient's past history is sparse, almost schematic. There are sparse comments and recollections about the mother, father, sister, and another sister who died at age three. It was believed that the deceased sister would have been permanently brain-damaged had she survived. Presumably, mother became depressed thereafter and was said to have never smiled throughout the pregnancy with the patient. The fact that he is male is a disappointment to her.

His health becomes an issue when at the age of three, he suffers a convulsion. The physician attributes it to constipation, a consequence of overeating biscuits. Daily enemas are prescribed and mother undertakes this task for at least a year-and-a-half. The patient is also said to have been kept in long curls and frocks by his mother during his earliest years. The family, initially well-to-do, suffers a major economic reversal when the patient is four-and-a-half. Substitute caretakers, numerous until then, decrease thereafter, although there is at least one aunt and possibly a second who are important mother-surrogates during the boy's childhood.

Once the analysis deepens, however, the historical details expand, especially within the narrow age period of three to six. The memories appear to coalesce about specific themes. Injunctions against touching are recalled. Potential dangers of careless touching are underscored: porcelain shatters, bas-relief sculptured pieces break, toys burst. In one dramatic childhood memory there is a fire in a cellulose factory; as it burns there is fear of a massive explosion. The enema experiences are newly revived as not entirely devoid of pleasure. The young boy learns to retain his stool in order to provoke his mother to action. The inward filling up is remembered. Recollections of his frequently sleeping with his father surface later; father's front is pressed against the patient's rear—these memories prove embarrassingly intimate.

The registration and organization of these age three to six "outside" childhood events are soon seen to be very much influenced by "inside" psychological sources. One is the emerging libidinal phase organization crystallizing at this time. Antecedent events appear to have colored this emerging organization, which, in turn, has ordered contemporary experiences and reordered the antecedent ones. Rangell gets a clear picture of the child's phallocentric universe and concomitant emerging sexual desire for both parents. The boy wants to use his penis on his mother (somehow), and experience his father's and his mother's penis (somehow). These expressions of ambiguous desires conflict with a sense of danger: realizing such pleasure would cost him his treasured penis. If he succeeds in possessing his mother there seems to be a whiskered giant prepared to seize him; if he succeeds in yielding to his father there is an implicit sacrifice of his manhood. The danger is tempered by a reassuring clinging to his phallocentric orientation, as if the belief in a penis-rich world will protect him against loss. This orientation is challenged by repeated confrontations with the reality of anatomic differences between males and females. The young boy reaches for a complex solution: desire and fear are shifted to a thing, the doll, while sexual pleasure is secured in secret acts and fantasies. This solution, however, requires that he disavow the fact of anatomic differences. He firmly plants the statement of an admired aunt into his mind: all naked bodies are the same since all is skin. Out of such compromise is formed a central character trait, secretiveness, and a compulsive, defense, disavowal. The ingenuousness of the solution is marred by its obvious shortcomings. Such childhood conceptions of the universe and such childhood gratifications when sustained into adult life interfere with the potential for knowing and the flexibility of action that comes with adult development. The infantile neurotic constellation provides secret pleasures and securities, but also unnecessary pain and sacrifice as well as inhibition.

The memories of the past that bear on the phobia are complemented by the analytic work on the habit of ritual masturbation. Masturbation turns out to be a counterpoint to the theme of the phobia, although gratification is more apparent in the one and anxiety in the other. Only the tension of the anxiety in the phobic state betrays its concealed sexuality.

The behavior and fantasies during the acts of masturbation reveal much of the past. Characteristically, the setting is a bathtub, water serving to wash away guilt. The patient binds himself with a wet towel tied tightly like a diaper. He *imagines* his penis disappearing in this process, but he *knows* it is still there, hidden. He rubs soap bubbles about his anus and plays a stream of water with a rubber hose about his genitals and backside. The ritual includes his viewing pornographic pictures "outside" and vivid fantasies "inside." Rangell explores the details of these fantasies as carefully as he does the historical details linked to the phobia. The visual elements are emphasized; for example, there is intense looking, the penis cannot be seen, the blindfolding. The disavowal of anatomical differences persists, despite the preoccupation with looking. He will look and not see. Rangell who is otherwise parsimonious in his reporting of his specific technical procedures describes himself as having been lured into a confrontation. He challenges the aunt's enshrined comment that men and women are alike since all is skin. Men and women *are* different, asserts the analyst. The patient is surprised when he realizes that he has never wanted to question the accuracy of the aunt's statement.

The phobia and the secret masturbation comprise the body of the case summary. Rangell tells us that the explanations, the dynamic meanings, the historical connections are all embedded in the analytic work surrounding these symptoms. The investigation of both symptom and habit, however, provides yet a third area of focus, the analytic situation itself. Within the setting, features of the patient's innermost being come sharply into view. Rangell shows how the patient's approach to the therapeutic task and the relationship he assumes toward the analyst comes under the influence of the same central pathogenic core that had led to the symptom, the habit, and the disturbance of character. For example, the patient's breaking of the analytic contract proves to be a masturbatory equivalent. His profusion of words during certain hours are unconsciously equated with the compliant bowel offerings of childhood; sometimes they seem to be a response to the symbolic enema offered by the analyst–mother through some intervention. Fee and schedule are structured by early anal preoccupations and correlate with a variety of personality features. In short, the patient attempts to deal with his analysis as he does with his hidden impulses. All aspects of this explored relationship are obviously not detailed; but Rangell notes that the relationship was most complex and that the patient tried to use the interaction to pursue infantile gratifications more often than to achieve insight. Even toward the end of the narrative, it is implied that the patient is reluctant to credit the analysis or the analyst for any of the clinical improvements; in this instance, he seems to have structured clinical improvement as sexual submission and must defend himself against such forbidden gratifications in fantasy.

With it all, there is a happy therapeutic ending to the tale: the marriage improves, his work relationships change, the phobia remits, the masturbatory behavior (probably) reduces significantly. The patient undergoes a change in point of view, literally and figuratively. He expresses this in his description of a circle. Initially, the patient had envisioned a circle as the perfect symbol of incompleteness, as if something had been removed leaving an empty interior. (Such is the perspective of a phallocentric universe.) At the end the enclosing line becomes a new area of interest; it, like a wedding ring, is a circle that reflects a perfect symbol of completeness. The patient's view of circles and wedding rings is mirrored by an overriding metaphor that Rangell uses to conceptualize all that has transpired—the metaphor of the wheel. Although the case history is rich in products (behavioral outcomes, psychological discoveries) and abounds with inferences about procedures, the process is expressed chiefly by way of this paradoxical and tantalizing metaphor. The paradox: spokes radiate *outwards,* each feeding *into* the hub. This paradoxical two-way direction is reinforced two paragraphs later when Rangell speaks of the necessity of deciphering a code in the course of analysis that functions as an accurate road-sign pointing *the way back* to the past. Thus, there is movement both outwards and inwards and into the future and back to childhood.

Yet the metaphor is tantalizingly incomplete. The hub, the spokes, and the novel interconnecting network are described, but what is at the rim of the wheel? Is it the masturbatory habit, the counterpoint of the inner hub doll; is it the disordered character toward which all radiates; the transference; the core phallic–oedipal phase organization; the anticipated termination of the analysis (i.e., the movement toward the end of the treatment)? And what of the spokes and their novel interconnecting network? Is that network *discovered* in the course of the analysis or is it *created;* is it a result of the necessary reductionism or is it a consequence of a new synthesis?

Outwards and inwards, past and future, old forces and new structures, taking apart and putting together, discovery and creation: all of this happens in a good analysis. What is the process that allows it all to happen? How can the process be conceptualized?

II

Clinical psychoanalysis addresses itself ultimately to the consequences of a disturbed childhood.[1] The infantile past is pathogenic whenever experiences required for development have failed to achieve sufficiently stable mental representations to provide the components for the naturally evolving phase organizations; or, having once achieved the requisite degree of stability are kept out of the later expected developmental transformations because of the actions of defense. Psychoanalytic treatment is particularly designed for disorders of the second kind, although it often proves useful for the former when the original deficiency did not exceed certain limits and the potential for optimal engagement has persisted despite pathology and the passage of time.

In treating disorders of the second kind, the aim is to permit the repressed (that excluded by defense) to be freed and newly integrated into the later psychological organization. Rangell's description clearly demonstrates this action. An additional goal of many analyses is to allow for the experiential engagement of those dispositional components that had been insufficiently represented during childhood so that they might further enrich mental life. Rangell's case history does not illustrate this form of therapeutic action.

Psychoanalytic technique is designed to cultivate a specific process. The process may be characterized as a successive sequence of intrinsically stable steps and disequilibrating periods of transition. The steps and the transitions have distinctive descriptive and conceptual features. The defended unconscious is carried forward along this evolving sequence, finally freed

[1] I have not been able to provide a detailed bibliography tracking the ideas to follow. In addition to Freud, I suspect the analysts who have provided stimulation for many of the proposals include Victor Calef, Edward Glover, Peter B. Neubauer, and Sidney Tarachow.

and integrated. I will describe what evolves in four steps: the opening phase, the transference neurosis, the termination phase, and the phase of postanalytic consolidation.

The Opening Phase

At the outset, a person arrives for treatment because of discomforts due to symptoms or, more typically, albeit less apparently, because of a newly encountered threat to the stability of his neurotic character structure. Rangell's patient, for example, had managed to endure several decades of suffering with the repressed and its returning fragments; however, the prospect of aging and the possible loss of the treasured analysis may have proved disequilibrating.

Once he accepts the therapeutic contact, a patient usually attempts to cooperate consciously with the requirements of the analytic situation, although he is inevitably driven to structure the analyst and the recommended procedures into his own system. Stated differently, he attempts to assimilate this fresh situation into his customary approach to ordering experiences. For example, he may view the analyst as yet another figure of authority or of contempt; he may see the procedures as "rules" to obey unhesitatingly or to challenge automatically. It is important that the analyst recognize that the patient's system of being and relating reflects a stabilized character organization useful for adaptive strategies, and considerably removed from the infantile past, no matter how much a part that past has played in its formation.

The opening phase may last for years. It is a time when the patient tries to place the analyst and the work into his preexisting ordering of people and events, while the analyst tries to remain merely an analyst. The analyst who elects to yield his customary professional stance and commitment may be forfeiting the opportunity to understand and help his patient optimally. This typical struggle between patient and analyst, between stability and disequilibration, can be an intense one. Despite the intensity it is still not yet a *transference* struggle. In fact, the opening phase might best be schematized as a period of resistance *to* the transference.

When this phase is effective, specific structural features designed for pathological adaptive strategies regressively transform back to infantile meanings and origins. For this to evolve during this period, patients must bring to the work a capacity for controlled regression. Some prove to be too fluid; their structures readily dissolve in the setting of abstinence. Others barely move at all; their structures are too rigidly entrenched. They are so distant from the original impressions that it is unlikely that the relevant representations can ever be retrieved in a form that is useful for analytic work. Such polar extremes in degrees of libidinal adhesiveness or pertinacity are always formidable obstacles to the analytic process. In fact, dangerously excessive fluidity constitutes the one condition that justifies an analyst's decision to yield his customary stance and convert the setting into some other kind of treatment situation.

The Transference Neurosis

The initial interval is probably called the opening phase in metaphoric link between the beginning of the analysis and the early moves in a chess game. As a label it is not very useful since it neither names nor implies the attention to structures that characterizes this first step in the process. In contrast, the second, the transference neurosis, more happily evokes the dominant feature of this next step, the organized repetition of part of the past. The first stage passes into the second once two conditions are met. (1) Sufficient structures have been regressively transformed back into childhood meanings and origins to provide the basis for a new cohesive organization; and (2) the ensuing organized dynamic and genetic tensions have come to rest upon the analytic situation as an essential waystation.

This *forward* movement in the process that is characterized by a controlled movement *backward* may be conceptualized as follows: as the experiential features of the originally impaired phase organization are freed from the network of character within which they have become embedded, they crystallize about the person of the analyst and the proceedings of the analytic situation. Thus, just as the analytic relationship was initially dominated by the patient's characteristic approach to a current situation, it is now influenced by the compulsion that he repeat the past, although still not yet recall it. Consequently, as the opening phase was viewed as a resistance *to* the transference, this second phase may be regarded as the resistance *of* the transference. This statement underscores that the transference invasion of the treatment relationship is an obstacle (inevitable and necessary) to the experiential actuality of the infantile neurosis, that is to say, to going on to the next step in the psychoanalytic process. In effect, the transference neurosis mutes the full affective impact of the reviving disordered childhood pressing for recall. At the same time it supplies a special perspective of immediacy to the study of mental life.

The transference neurosis may last for a shorter or longer period of time. Some patients try to abort it because the feelings that come alive seem too much to bear. Others try to prolong it interminably because the threat of a direct encounter with the experiential actuality of childhood is perceived as too awesome or because the sense of renewed parenting provides an illusory security and satisfaction. The phase can have its intervals of clinical improvement and of symptomatic excesses. As it goes on much of the understanding acquired during the first step is reinforced because the experience of immediacy provides further conviction. In Rangell's brief narrative, the organized transference neurosis is not described, although several transference *manifestations* are plainly evident.

An aspect worth emphasizing is that this second phase of the process that involves the repetition of pathologic childhood relationships also features an infantile approach to the *task* of analysis. This feature of pathological approach is particularly apparent in Rangell's patient who often frankly relates to the analysis as he did to his feces and his penis when he was a little boy; that is, as to an instrument serving gratification and mediating unconscious fantasy. Rangell avoids a frequent management mishap in this phase: the zealous focus upon the object-relationship aspect with the neglect of those distortions introduced by the patient's entrenched infantile perspectives about play and work.

The transference as obstacle and waystation is slowly recognized during this second phase of the expected sequence. In due course the representations of the distorted past are further freed so that the patient may encounter the experiential actualities of infantile life. As the childhood origins become more convincingly demonstrable, what has seemed to be immediate present is revealed as repetitive past, and the analysis passes its next critical transition to enter the termination phase. The transference neurosis phase and its transition do not usually proceed without complexities. Transference demands have a way of provoking countertransference replies. The analyst may have been drawn into the drama of the past. He may try unwittingly to "correct" old relationships, respond to them in the belief that they are contemporary ones, or he may foster and maintain the illusion of security induced by the revived parent–child alliance.

The Terminal Phase

If all goes well, which means a predominantly painful disequilibrating transition, a new shift in organization of the analysis develops. Recall and convincing reconstructions evolve, thus assuring a more direct engagement of the repressed along with a fresh evaluation of the original defenses. The termination phase, so labeled because it will conclude once the analysis is formally brought to a close, is chiefly characterized by a more direct reacquaintance with the realities of childhood wishes, fears, and strategies. The repression lifts; it is a time when the sense of understanding or conviction gradually changes to genuine insight.

The direct contact with the past often revives the intense anxieties that prompted the original defensive strategies. Consequently, this phase can be expected to have its trials and complexities as well. Some patients retreat to the transference or even call up old character postures in an attempt to deal with the fresh affective challenges. The fact that the treatment's end may also be in the air further accelerates such retreats.

Timing, tact, and stance remain as important as ever. A subtle mismanagement can occur, sometimes as the analyst may zealously hold his patient to the memories of the past and overlook the fact that the aim of the revival is to loosen the affective ties to childhood, not establish permanent residence there.

As the actuality of the approaching ending impinges, the no longer deniable fact usually creates some last minute psychological pyrotechnics. The struggles of every phase are joined afresh. Not unexpectedly, Rangell describes a "last stand" quality to his patient's final months. The formal good-byes provide a transitional border to the last phase of the analysis, the postanalytic consolidation.

The Phase of Postanalytic Consolidation

What is known of this step has been drawn from follow-ups or second analyses. It is ironic that despite its importance to the success of the analysis, this step occurs *after* its end when the patient is truly on his own. The exercise of newly experienced autonomy and the need to effect transformations upon the discovered unconscious are compelling tasks. Consequently, this phase of an analysis may also go on for years, and for some, there may be no definable end-point to the opportunities for new integrations. Follow-ups and second analyses suggest that the obstacles to the expected achievements of this final phase arise from several sources. The analyst may have elected (openly or tacitly) to discourage autonomy, holding out a tie that contained unanalyzed transference threads. Or, from the patient's side, the residual transformational capacities may have been so badly eroded by disease and time that new integrative opportunities proved all but impossible. Or, perhaps life's circumstances had imposed immovable constraints to change; a new organizational consolidation cannot take root unless there are continuing rewards for the evolving system.

III

The schematic model proposed, an alternative to Rangell's metaphoric wheel, has some advantages but the possible deficiencies should not be ignored. A succinct statement of the expected sequence of analytic phases that feature dominant characteristics, critical transitions, and expected complications has many practical uses. It is a summary statement to dispute and refine. Also, a view of the clinical setting using the dimension of time may provide a novel perspective of certain treatment obstacles, ones that transcend the ordinarily expected resistances. Resistance to an evolving process may prove a felicitous concept. The model has potential disadvantages as well. A facile formula can never replace the technical knowledge that can only be acquired by the actualities of clinical experience; and certainly no analysis could ever really proceed in such a literal organizational march with sharply drawn transitions. Consequently, the model's best use is as a stimulus to provoke further interest in trying to depict and clarify the most obscure feature of clinical analysis, the silent process.

3. THE ANALYSIS OF A RELIGIOUS MAN

Introduction

Dr. Rosen describes the analysis of a thirty-six-year-old man whose symptoms of procrastination at work and problematic relationships were deeply engrained in his obsessional character. The detailed description of the analytic process and Dr. Rosen's interventions illustrate the patient's defensiveness in the initial phase of analysis and the analyst's extreme caution in searching for the appropriate point of entry to confront the emerging transference reaction without enhancement of the patient's extreme level of intellectualization. In the initial transference paradigm, the analyst was viewed as a stern, sadistic, and punitive figure demanding submissiveness. The patient's extensive fantasy life then centered around Martin Luther and the patient's identification of Luther with his own anal rage. The transference paradigm then became relatively benign in contrast to the initial punitiveness. The analysis of the anal components of the patient's conflicts led to the discovery of his oral greed and the reconstruction of the patient's early childhood life when the maternal depression and hospitalization gave rise to the patient's fantasy and guilt feeling for having greedily impoverished his mother. The material then continued to express the patient's oral greed and anal rage, as well as phallic–oedipal derivatives requiring a type of "split level" intervention on the part of the analyst: addressing both the phallic–oedipal and preoedipal aspects of the patient's greed, ambition, and competitiveness. The analysis of the patient's guilt over his ambition and competitiveness and its preoedipal derivatives provided clues to the understanding of the patient's procrastination. The numerous dreams of the patient, such as the Goodyear blimp dream, provided a firm basis for the reconstruction of the patient's experiences during maternal depression and later on his passive wishes toward a phallic and enema-giving mother. Different aspects of this material emerged in the patient's sexual fantasies during intercourse colored by anality and the use of force. The working through of the anal and oral regressive derivatives enabled the analytic work to proceed toward examination of castration (circumcision dream) themes and reduction of the patient's fear of competitiveness and ambition.

The termination phase was planned in advance and provided the analyst and patient with the opportunity for cooperative and mutual planning while addressing significant issues, such as insufficient mourning of the death of both parents and completion of the analysis of the narcissistic roots of the patient's feelings of omnipotence and grandiosity.

Dr. Rosen's detailed notes, covering three months of analysis, provide an opportunity to attend to the detailed, sensitive, and painstaking course of clinical psychoanalysis and the analyst's interventions.

Dr. Eisnitz addresses a number of unusual features of the case described by Dr. Rosen. The atypical features could have presented serious problems in analysis, although Dr. Rosen's sensitive handling of the issues prevented complications. The major potential problems included the patient's preanalytic knowledge about analytic theory, his deep involvement with religion, and an abundance of clinical information obtained from extra-analytic sources. In the discussion of intellectual knowledge about analysis the significance of both intellectual and affective processes in the analysis is emphasized; the importance of the intellectual processes being frequently downgraded in psychoanalytic literature. The second issue is the patient's religiosity, the extent of the involvement of religion in the patient's central conflicts and defensive processes, and the level of ego syntonicity or ego dystonicity of the patient's religious beliefs. The relationship of the patient with his religion heralded the unfolding of the transference relationship to the analyst with the patient expecting a passive feminine and submissive masochistic stance toward the stern analyst.

Dr. Eisnitz follows in detail the unfolding of the analytic process and Dr. Rosen's handling of the process with typical periods of advancement, defensiveness, and regression. He emphasizes the advancement of a special split in the patient based on his observing ego but also identification with the analyzing function of the analyst.

The analysis of the initial resistances resulted in the emergence of transference, the patient's masochistic traits, and denial of pleasure. The denial of his own masochistic fantasies seemed to restrict his ability to identify with the pain and suffering of his clients. The patient attempted to keep his masochistic and perverse fantasies and feelings toward the analyst out of the analysis. The interpretation of the patient's anal sadistic impulses allowed him to reveal his ambitious and omnipotent fantasies. The analysis of the oedipal and preoedipal aspects of the patient's behavior provided a solid foundation for effective analytic gains. The interpretation of the patient's oral greediness resulted in the emergence of the dramatic dream of the Goodyear blimp, exhibiting his guilt feeling about the mother's depression, confusion about the timing of the death of the grandfather, and passive character traits in reaction formation to destructive fantasies. The anal regression in the transference revealed his submissive attitude toward both phallic father and mother and possibly toward religion. In the important duck dream, the two sides of the patient's anality and anal sadism as well as castration fears emerge. His subsequent wish to get close to the analyst seems to represent the wish to gain closeness with the omnipotent father and to gain distance from his penetrating, enema-giving mother. The wish for closeness to his father was a possible contributor to his intense religious involvement and wish to get close to God.

The analytic results were impressive, particularly in the areas of work and relationships with the patient's clients. This was based on satisfactory analysis of the patient's sadism, grandiosity, and masochism as it affected his functioning within the religious and professional spheres. The analysis of his masochistic and passive feminine wishes as well as sexual aspects of positive oedipal feeling was more limited.

Dr. Joseph describes the relationship of the painstaking and steady work with resistances and defenses inside and outside of the transference with the moments of insight formation in the patient. Such steady work with defenses is particularly relevant to this patient with his distant, aloof, unenthusiastic, procrastinating, and ineffectual personality structure. The painstaking work on the patient's oral greediness and anal sadism paved the way for the emergence and resolution of phallic–oedipal struggles in the transference.

Equally important was the analysis of the hierarchy of the fantasy life of the patient as it was reflected in the vicissitudes of his experiences under the influence of psychic differentiation and oedipal development. The successive levels of fantasy formation dealing with the patient's dependency needs, feelings of abandonment, and weakness (impotence) were uncovered in various phases of analysis. Different aspects of the patient's self representation as manifested in fantasies were uncovered and integrated as a cohesive whole. This included the integration of the admiring and positive relationship of the patient with the father in his own self representation made possible by the resolution of the patient's feeling of disappointment in him as illustrated in the screen memory of "the shell game."

THE ANALYSIS OF A RELIGIOUS MAN

Irwin C. Rosen, Ph.D.

Mr. Paul Fletcher, a thirty-six-year-old devout Episcopalian doctor of social work working as a full-time pastoral counselor in a rural Episcopalian church, came for psychoanalysis following an evaluation in an outpatient service. He had taken several courses in the extension school of a psychoanalytic institute and during his participation in that program several years ago, decided to have analysis himself. He was bothered by his lack of enthusiasm for his work, his procrastination in it, his limited effectiveness in counseling, and a chronically low mood state since the death of his father approximately eighteen months before, and his mother six months before, feeling that he had been unable to mourn adequately the death of either parent. His presenting symptom of procrastination as well as his intellectualizing character style were manifest in his manner and pace in seeking treatment. Two years prior to the evaluation which led to his entering analysis, he had consulted a psychiatrist about a vague array of "life dissatisfactions" but did not follow up on the consultant's recommendation for treatment until two years later, during which interval both his parents died.

Mr. Fletcher was married, a father of four young children, and financed his analysis in part through an inheritance which he received from his father. He had a sister four years his senior; he was the son of a moderately successful owner of a clothing store and a mother who appeared to have been so preoccupied by and disturbed by the illness and death of her own parents during Mr. Fletcher's childhood that she seemed to have been unable to provide him with very much maternal support and nurturance. The father was a man of great anger, inwardly directed, who withdrew from the family into long hours at his business or in his garden. For a number of years prior to his death he suffered from osteoarthritis.

In an outpatient examination Mr. Fletcher was diagnosed as, "Depressive reaction, mild, with an underlying obsessional compliant, passive–aggressive personality structure." The treatment recommendation was for psychoanalysis, which he accepted as a sacrifice of time and money that he was willing to invest in the pursuit of "the increased effectiveness of my counseling, a greater depth to my spirituality, a strengthening of the communion with my wife, and the freer development of my children." This quotation captures Mr. Fletcher's stilted, over-intellectualized initial manner of speaking in the analysis. He presented himself and his history in a highly abstract, sweepingly generalized way. Only slowly were we able to discern the details of his development, his life history, his family relationships, and the accumulation of intrapsychic and external stresses which had brought him to analysis.

Mr. Fletcher was born in a small city, the second of two children in his family. His mother was an only child, closely attached to her father. Her college education was interrupted by her mother's death from cancer. She returned to her father's home and a short time later married Mr. Fletcher's father. He was a college graduate who was said to be quite talented in mathematics and had been offered a position teaching mathematics in a boy's school, but instead accepted an offer to work in his father-in-law's clothing store in the city where Paul was born and grew up.

For the first ten years of Paul Fletcher's life his family lived in the maternal grandfather's home. Mr. Fletcher said that his grandfather displaced his father in the eyes of his mother, and that his father was never the head of the household in his own right until the grandfather's death. Even after the grandfather's death, the father apparently had some difficulty asserting his authority and, according to Mr. Fletcher, would withdraw in passive submission if there was any disagreement between himself and his wife.

Mr. Fletcher described his mother as being doting, solicitous, and affectionate toward him throughout her life. He said that even after he was grown she always still seemed to see him as a little boy who was unable to care properly for himself. He said that even after he was an adult and in the Army his mother used to worry about whether or not he was wearing his overshoes in wet weather.

Mr. Fletcher described his father as an upright, honest, honorable man who suffered from chronic feelings of frustration about his life situation and never derived much sense of satisfaction or fulfillment from his work as a merchant. Mr. Fletcher felt that his father was too passive, stoical, and too inclined to keep all of his feelings to himself. In later years his father developed severe osteoarthritis, which Mr. Fletcher, in his intellectualized fashion, described as "a turning of his aggression toward himself." He recalled that his father would sometimes get out of bed in the middle of the night, suffering from severe arthritic pains, and crawl to the bathtub on his hands and knees rather than ask anyone to assist him.

Paul Fletcher claimed a fairly close and affectionate relationship with his father during childhood, and recalled doing a great many things with his father. He spontaneously reported a particularly vivid memory of a time in which his father took him to a carnival sideshow where some seasoned manipulator was carrying on a "pea and shell" game. Mr. Fletcher observed that his father became so intrigued with this game that he momentarily cast aside his conventional frugality and conservatism and bet $5 that he could identify the shell under which the pea was hidden. The father was momentarily distracted by one of the manipulator's assistants, the shells were switched, and father lost his $5. This anecdote seemed to characterize neatly Paul's perception of his father as a man who was cheated and frustrated by life and the people around him. It also set the stage for the wary, suspicious, anally retentive transference paradigm that was characteristic of his approach to the analysis. Many times during the later unfolding of the transference, Paul presented himself as a waif, constantly in danger of being taken in by wily mountebanks. He was something of a haggler; dickering over the analytic fee, prices he paid for food, clothing, medical care, and appliances, and his manner during such episodes was one of tight, retentive, self-contained vigilance and guardedness.

Mr. Fletcher was able to report very little about his early development. He said that he learned in later years that his mother had some type of a "nervous breakdown" shortly after he was born. He said that he did not know the nature of her illness and was unsure if she was hospitalized for any length of time. Later, as the analysis progressed, much of the repressive vagueness surrounding mother's absence was dispelled.

Paul Fletcher reported a rather tranquil and unremarkable adjustment during his school years. He claimed to be a better than average student, and could not recall experiencing any academic or social difficulties. He did experience some emotional turmoil at puberty and in early adolescence. He said that he was mildly obese as an adolescent and had been extremely self-conscious about his physical appearance. He reported that he suffered from gynecomastia and because of this was the object of a great deal of ridicule from his peers. He recalled an incident which occurred one summer when he was at Boy Scout Camp, around the age of thirteen or fourteen. He said that one of the Scout leaders and a group of boys jumped on him, pinning him to the ground, and painted his nipples with Mercurochrome. He was overcome by shame and rage as a result of this experience and still feels angry and indignant when he thinks about it. He also recalled feeling highly sensitive as an adolescent about what he perceived as some discrepancy between the size of his genitals and the size of those of his peers. After graduating from high school, Mr. Fletcher attended a small liberal arts college, where he majored in religion. He said that he found the transition from high school to college somewhat difficult because he had done quite well in high school without a great deal of effort and had not developed habits of disciplined study. He said that he did not do very well academically in his first year in college and failed one course despite his very superior intelligence and scholastic aptitude test scores. In subsequent years, however, he did much better and considered himself an above average student. While in his last year of college, he had a romance with a young woman employee at the university. Although Mr. Fletcher says that he never had intercourse with this girl or any other woman prior to marriage, there was a great deal of heavy petting, which usually culminated in mutual orgasm. About the time he graduated from college this young woman broke off their relationship. Mr. Fletcher was extremely disturbed by this rejection and was depressed for a period of about six months.

Following his graduation from college, Mr. Fletcher entered a prestigious university, studying social work. He stated that he threw himself into his studies as an antidote for his depression and disappointment over the break-up of his romance. Around the end of his third year in the university, Mr. Fletcher began courting his wife, whom he had known from a high school association. After a courtship of approximately one year, they were married before Mr. Fletcher began his final year in the university. Their backgrounds were similar in many respects, having both grown up in the same community, and having been very religious members of the same church. According to Mr. Fletcher, neither of them had had any previous sexual experience prior to marriage.

Paul Fletcher received a doctorate in social work (D.S.W.) from the university with the highest of academic honors, and a few months later enlisted in the Army. He considered accepting a teaching assignment near home but decided that it would be good for him and his wife to be a little more distant and independent from their families. Mr. Fletcher also had some concern about being mature and experienced enough to accept counseling responsibilities. Soon, he was ordered overseas. His wife was pregnant at the time and they did not have the money to pay for her overseas transportation, so she decided to remain with her parents. They were separated for the subsequent thirteen months, which Mr. Fletcher spent in Europe.

When Mr. Fletcher returned to the United States, his wife and infant son joined him while he completed his enlistment. He and his family then returned to their home community.

Since he was undecided as to how he should pursue his counseling career, he decided to accept an assignment which he was offered in Europe. He and his family lived in Europe and Mr. Fletcher worked in various capacities. When they returned to the United States, he enrolled in multiple courses in the extension program of the psychoanalytic institute.

While in the extension program, Mr. Fletcher decided to inquire into the possibility of psychiatric evaluation and possible treatment for personal difficulties which had become apparent during his social work training. Mr. Fletcher at that time felt he had two major problems. First, he had difficulty being on time, was frequently tardy, and prone to procrastinate. Second, he felt he overappraised himself and therefore overextended himself. He felt this was not just teaching zeal to be helpful as a counselor but represented some kind of compulsion or need to do a great deal for other people. He felt that he was much too conscientious, and complained that he could not finish a job and relax. Instead, he would always see something else to do, never feeling that his work was quite caught up.

Mr. Fletcher and his family next took up residence in a small, rural community where he became a counselor in a small church. He continued to feel rather chronically dissatisfied with himself and his performance and still complained of the problems of tardiness and procrastination. He also complained of general feelings of inadequacy and the feeling that he was somehow not living up to his potential.

Approximately a year and a half before the start of the analysis, Mr. Fletcher's father died. He felt that he had never really recovered from his grief over this event. He felt a possible reason he had continued to grieve was that he felt his father never realized any of his dreams and lived a life of quiet desperation.

Six months before Paul Fletcher sought treatment, his mother died. He said that although he mourned his mother, he grieved much more over his father's death. He acknowledged, however, that perhaps it was his mother's death and the finality of having lost both parents that precipitated his decision to seek analysis. His parents' death had increased both his feeling of insecurity and his appreciation of the fact that perhaps he was more dependent on parental support than he had been previously willing to acknowledge.

Much of the above material came from his interviews with a psychiatrist, not the analyst, although much filling in and rewriting of Mr. Fletcher's history occurred, of course, during the analysis, which covered a four-year period at a frequency of five fifty-minute sessions per week. Mr. Fletcher had also received psychological testing, which underscored the obsessive, intellectualizing aspects of his personality structure, his neurotic depression of mild to moderate severity, his masochistic and self-sabotaging character style, and an ego organization sufficiently well integrated to warrant a treatment recommendation for analysis. In addition, parts of the historical material came from his wife's interviews with the social worker, who found her to be a warm, steady, practical woman with considerable awareness of her husband's difficulties and some insight into their psychological origins.

In the beginning of the analysis Mr. Fletcher's associations took the form of verbal essays or discourses on various topics. These were usually rooted in two sources: one was history and theology, the other his knowledge of psychoanalytic theory which he had gained from the seminars he had attended. He quoted at length from the writings of Erikson, Fenichel, Freud, on the one hand, and Tillich, Niebuhr, and Martin Buber, on the other. These "lectures" appeared designed to ward off the intensity of his affect and anxiety, to flood the hours with material which kept him safely in control of the analytic situation, and to impress the analyst with the scope and depth of his knowledge of his field. They did indeed impress the analyst, principally with Mr. Fletcher's anxiety, but also with the poignant, neurotic waste of his talents. The man was an honored graduate of one of this country's leading universities. He had the potential to become a major figure in his field. He spoke seven languages including Hebrew, Greek, and Latin and yet his procrastination and his capacity for self-sabotage were such that he found himself counseling in a remote church where the congregation and his colleagues understood little of what he was trying to teach and disliked the liberality of that portion of it which they did understand.

Because these "lectures" occurred early in the analysis, I elected to restrict my comments to (1) pointing out their themes and relatedness to more central conflicts, and (2) noting their appearance in the material when transference feelings threatened to surface. The initial transference paradigm to emerge was that of the analyst as a stern, severe, swiftly punishing figure who demanded compliance and would brook no deviation from a scrupulous adherence to the "rules" of the analysis—as they applied to the fee, the times, and to a presumed demand for copious and regular outpourings of material. Mr. Fletcher got his first transference understanding of the anal submission and sadism contained in this transference manifestation when his thoughts turned, with a compelling and self-surprising insistence, to Martin Luther, particularly as he was described in the Erik Erikson biography. He became preoccupied with Luther's anal rage, dwelling for hours on his anal fury against the Pope, telling with vehemence of Luther's vow to "drown the Pope in farts and feces." While such material was obviously rich in transference content, it was far from easy to demonstrate the relevance of these thoughts to his emerging feelings about the analyst. Some defense interpretive work had to be undertaken to deal with Mr. Fletcher's rigid intellectualizing, his isolation of affect, and his reaction formations against the conscious experiencing of rage and oral longing. I consistently drew his attention to the difference between his tranquil, unruffled manner and the violence and rage of his thoughts. I also pointed out the sparsity of any mention of direct feelings toward me or our work together. In addition, I tried to help him to see the defensive "safety" of recounting material remote in time and distant in space from the immediacy of our relationship. Weeks of such work on these character traits culminated in the following dream: "I had this movie projector, only it wasn't working right. The motor was broken and the pictures could barely move. And somehow the sound and the picture couldn't work together. When the sound was on, the picture was off, when the picture came on, the sound went off. A man came and said he could help me fix it."

Mr. Fletcher's associations were first to a broken piece of equipment at the church and to his chagrin at not being able to repair it himself, and then to his annoyance at how much the man had charged for his work. I pointed out to him some of the links between the dream, its associated thoughts, and what I believed he might be thinking and feeling about our work and some of his reactions to it. That Paul Fletcher was able to utilize the interpretation of the dream as it related to the analysis, to his need to separate his thoughts and his feelings, and to his procrastination (both in and out of analysis), was attested to by some beginning "stylistic" (defensive) changes in his way of working. He began to speak quite directly of using "all these ideas to avoid the wretchedness of my life."

The term *wretchedness* as used by Mr. Fletcher proved, during the first years of the analysis, to be a poignant reference to the nature of his relationship with his wife, his children, his congregation, and his colleagues. It also referred to his intrapsychic life, which was characterized by a strenuously muted rage, rooted in a sense of oral deprivation as well as the more apparent anal sadism.

His attendance at the analytic hours was regular, but punctuated by occasional tardiness rationalized as attributable to his heavy counseling schedule. The analysis, it turned out, was a self-imposed duty, a penance for having inherited a share of his father's estate. He felt guilty over the inheritance, "unworthy" of having it, yet greedily retentive of the money involved. His "solution" to this conflict was to jeopardize the inheritance, by which he was paying for the analysis, through some patently unwise investments. The analyst, mindful of his own countertransferential irritation at Mr. Fletcher's glaring and uncharacteristic financial irresponsibility, pointed out the resistive, treatment-endangering aspects of his recklessness, which was rooted in the same self-punitive guilt as was his lateness to the analytic sessions. The analyst told Mr. Fletcher that he thought that as the analysis progressed, his feelings of "unworthiness" were becoming increasingly intense and that despite his hard work thus far, another side of him seemed determined to undermine our collaboration and sabotage the analysis.

Toward his family he displayed the same sort of moral masochism, based on reaction formations to his own oral needfulness and anal sadism, that formed so prominent a part of his character structure. He himself was perversely proud of the age and decrepitude of the car he drove; it was "good enough" he insisted, even if it was difficult to steer, hard to start, and, most important, painfully uncomfortable to ride in, and singularly unattractive in appearance. In a similar fashion he insisted upon the most meager of appliances for his house, the most sparse of furnishing, the least appealing and cheapest of clothing for himself and his family. Money, he insisted, should only be "spent on nobler pursuits," although what such permissible outlays might be was never quite clear. Occasionally his wife would protest his self-imposed austerity, but the situation was kept from coming to a critical confrontation by the wife's parents, who frequently supplied them with "extras"—clothing, vacations, and gifts for the house. A strict disciplinarian, he insisted upon unswerving adherence to rigid rules of conduct by his children. Paul Fletcher was a scrupulously honest man and there is no reason to doubt what was something of a surprise throughout the analysis: the adequacy and satisfaction of his sex life with his wife. While the preferred form of sexual intercourse was with his wife sitting atop him while he had fantasies of anally penetrating her, both partners enjoyed their sexual relationship. Intercourse was frequent, adventurous, and mutually pleasurable. Mr. Fletcher, it appeared, had other arenas in which to act out his pregenitally derived frustrations and angers.

It was in his work that the most significant aspects of his pathology manifested themselves, for here his self-sabotage was most rampant and most apparent to everyone but himself. The vital written material about activities and assignments was seldom written, printed, or distributed on time, leaving the parishioners in anger and confusion over what would be offered to and expected of them. His communications were often intellectualized discourses on historical and abstruse theological issues, much to the anger and bafflement of his congregation. His counseling meetings with the clients were usually ill-considered and unhelpful.

The issue of "comforting" was a particularly difficult one for Mr. Fletcher. Given the severity of his own superego, a reactive harshness necessitated by the terrifying strength (and consequent repudiation) of his own forbidden oral, anal, and oedipal impulses, and rage at their deprivation and frustration, he was defensively unable to empathize with the pain or uncertainty of a troubled client. He exhorted his clients when they sought solace; he scorned their "weakness" when they sought understanding. He urged them to follow his own pattern of Spartan renunciation and self-discipline when they sought acceptance of human fraility. The same attitude was reflected in his religious beliefs. The twenty-third psalm, particularly, was anathema to him. He vehemently opposed, in life as well as from the couch, what he termed "a flabby and sentimental Christianity," which sought to ease suffering and assuage pain. Obviously, such a perception of religion was replete with transferentially reawakened developmental issues, but, clear as these were to the analyst, their recognition was tenaciously resisted by Mr. Fletcher, who filled the analytic hours with accounts of his daily activities, reports of his lectures, descriptions of church meetings, and summaries of his readings.

In this early phase of the analysis, as well as in his life, we saw the poignant loneliness and inconsolability of this man, struggling against a closeness and intimacy that would be more likely to revive feelings of outraged deprivation than of satisfied nurturance, and far more likely to be infuriatingly frustrating than warmly gratifying. Mr. Fletcher resisted such transference reenactments strenuously and tenaciously. As we were to learn later in the analysis, he feared the destructive consequences of his oral voracity and his subsequent anal sadism, and also feared that his needfulness might prove debilitating and unbearable for the analyst (as, in his fantasies, it had been for his mother). His "reluctance to become a patient," his defensiveness, his strict adherence to "reason" were, therefore, neither difficult to understand nor to describe. While meticulously complying with the fundamental rule that he tell me whatever came to his mind, Mr. Fletcher could only allow his mind to ponder the sort of reality events that I have described. He spoke in an even tone of voice; he was calm, polite, unruffled. He would habitually remove his jacket, carefully fold it, and place it on a chair near the couch. For the most part he lay motionless, but his was not a calm immobility. Rather he was stiff with the effort of restrained movement. His rigid posture was a bodily manifestation of his inner inhibition of affect and spontaneity. To hear his recounting of the events of the day, one would think that he had no feelings about them and that they were being presented as a matter of duty and propriety, much like an obedient child on the toilet with a mother before whom defiance was unthinkable, rage impermissible, pleasure unattainable.

Meanwhile, with an insistence rooted in his long-standing anal character orientation, his identification with the Martin Luther of Erikson's biography became increasingly and usefully evident in his associations. The transference relevance of his preoccupation with Luther's anality came to him clearly one day when, following an hour of regaling me with Luther's "shitting all over Rome," he dreamed that he had tracked mud all over my office and couch and that I had placatingly put my arm around his shoulder and said, "It's all right, you're a good kid." This was the first hint of a benign transference experience. I was uncertain of what this dream would portend, and elected to await further developments, especially since his associations were minimal.

Mr. Fletcher's proneness to speak in highly abstract, overgeneralized ways (reflecting his reliance on intellectualization and isolation as defensive activities) then gave way to a much more direct, experience-rooted, concrete "style." Similarly, he found himself experiencing, with considerably greater directness, certain affects both during the hour and in his ordinary life situation. These were depression, anger, and anxiety. On several occasions, this man, previously described as rigid and obsessional, broke down into tears—particularly centering around themes which touched on the strength of his wish to be nurtured and cared for. I interpreted his crying as a reflection of long-suppressed wishes for the care and nurturance that he now felt himself to be receiving in the analysis.

We found also coming to the fore in dreams, in associations, and in transference paradigms, a greedy, sweeping, overweaning ambition which found him nurturing many fantasies of power in the church, having the pomp and pageantry of a medieval lord, and hailed as a great leader and savior by a thankful world. His spiritual message to the world at such times was a scathing denunciation of the sins, lusts, and pleasures of an all too materialistic society. It is noteworthy that while he scourged man for such material preoccupations, he himself now emerged as preoccupied with food, material possessions, acquisitions. Indeed, what we saw as characteristic of this man was that his ambition, like so many other aspects of his character formation, drew principally upon both the phallic phase and its earlier oral precursors. Much of the analysis involved a working through of his intense competitiveness with his father and his guilt over the oedipal implications of knowledge, achievement, and power, as well as the more infantile, pregenital aspects of these themes.

The emerging material required carrying out an interesting sort of "split-level" analysis in which the analyst needed to keep a careful eye on material which appeared at first glance to be rooted in phallic–oedipal concerns, but which, upon close scrutiny proved simultaneously laden with more regressive infantile pregenital elements. Mr. Fletcher's guilt over ambition and achievement, for example (an important component of his symptomatic procrastination), was also demonstrably linked to themes of gorging and stuffing himself with the feasts of triumph and victory, only to feel himself vulnerable to talionic mutilation as just punishment for his insatiable greed. He dreamed: "I was at some sort of graduation breakfast at which the guests were fed by 'an enormous cornucopia' filled with food of all kinds." In his haste to get at the cornucopia he "ripped it in two."

With this dream, he associated a recent memory of one of his children at dinner, greedily gulping down food, gorging himself, and breaking a milk pitcher while taking it from an older sibling. He contrasted such unruly behavior with the required table etiquette and restraint that had characterized his own upbringing. He said, "I could never have gotten away with such behavior." He laughed when I said, "even if you had wanted to," and said that in the dream he was indeed acting like his young son, or more probably, as he wished he himself could have acted in his own childhood. A later dream (near the second anniversary of the beginning of the analysis) concerned the "Goodyear blimp" which led to associations of his good (well-fed) analytic year—quickly followed by memories of the dirigible Hindenburg bursting into flames. The symbolism of, as well as the association to the Goodyear blimp, followed by thoughts of the flaming crash of the Hindenburg dirigible, suggested to me that two sets of unconscious early memories might be discoverable in the material. One set of ideas, those associated with the "good year" suggested a good, nurturant well-fed year with mother. The other image, that of the fiery crash of the Hindenburg, which Mr. Fletcher recounted with considerable affect as he repeated the broadcast coverage of the tragedy, seemed to portray a sudden, rage-filled ending to the blissful, floating year. These were, of course, my connections, not the patient's but I believe that they remain safely on the sane side of the border of wild analysis. For one thing, Mr. Fletcher *did* appear to have had a reasonably good start in life (note his earlier description of mother as "doting and solicitous"). Also, the absence of severe disturbance in ego functioning likewise suggests a secure early mothering relationship. That such a period was not without its sudden and dramatic interruptions seemed an idea worth exploring and I raised it with Mr. Fletcher as a possibility worth considering. This led him to check some family history with his mother's sister and we learned that when he was a year-and-a-half or two, his mother had been hospitalized for some months following a depression upon the death of her father.

In the next phase of the work we were led to the anal implications of sexual experience which, for Paul Fletcher, turned out to be linked to some strong passive homoerotic wishes, centering around themes of being pierced, penetrated, and drained of body contents by a phallic (enema-giving) mother. Through a series of very striking dreams he clearly demonstrated his equation of penis and feces, and the threat of castration was viewed not only in phallic terms but had far more primitive, anal, eviscerating, and emptying connotations, connected with a number of particularly violent primal scene fantasies.

The following detailed notes from sessions 205 to 220 are

added here to provide the reader with a better sense of the analytic process.

During this phase of the analysis, Mr. Fletcher reported a dream:

> I am with some people and a dead duck is brought to the table. There is some talk about the duck not being in proper condition to be eaten and a woman says that she knows how to prepare it. She reaches into the mouth of the duck with the scissors, gives a couple of snips, works the legs of the duck up and down a couple of times, and a large sickening, stinking, billowy mass of entrails comes out of the rectum.

In associating to the dream, Mr. Fletcher thought about violent movements of the duck's leg and torso, of the heavy breathing of the woman as she manipulated the duck's legs, and he said that he thinks of the billowing mass coming out of the rectum as suggesting in some strange way, the withdrawal of the penis—a smelly, slimy, large penis.

He thought of having observed carefully a woman who was cleaning out a chicken the day before during a home visit, and how smelly the whole thing was. He wondered why he should think of a penis in connection with the thoughts and fantasies of a large billowing mass coming out of the rectum. I told him that in his early childhood thoughts and understandings of parental sex, it seemed violent and frightening and that it seemed to drain and empty a person—like the dead duck. He told me that my phrase about being drained and empty brought back another memory to him. He could not remember the precise age at which this occurred, but the family doctor recommended from time to time that he be given enemas. Mr. Fletcher said that he would lie on his back and breathe deeply when the tube was inserted. His mother would lift his legs up and back and he would have to hold this position to keep the water more easily inside him. He would have to count and then he would run into the bathroom where, he said: "the whole farting, shitting mess would come out." He went on: "The implication seems pretty clear to me that I think that intercourse is a 'Phraaaa' . . . [this approximates the sound that he made] in which it all comes out and it is all mixed up with sex and farting and shitting and being drained and emptied out."

Then, for the next few hours, Mr. Fletcher seemed to take a "breather" from this rather stressful period for him in the analysis. He talked about the roofing job that was going on in the church and its progress, and some plans that he had for vacation, a little bit about historical and religious matters, but signaled the end of the breather with a dream that he had received a telephone call from a person whose name was "Ralston," and who said that he had been trying to call him for the last couple of days because he had something important to say. Mr. Fletcher was pleased to be getting an important phone call, knew of no one named Ralston, thinks of the similarity between the dream name and that of the analyst, and concludes that maybe there is some important message to be communicated between us. Then Mr. Fletcher brings in the following dream:

> I was a boy about twelve and the two of us went to a clothing store. It was a big store, but it was like one of those department stores in Japan where there is a big open space in the center of all of the floors and the merchandise is arranged on each floor around this open space, so that on any floor you can look down through this center opening and see what is going on on the other floors. We were in this store to buy me a coat and we tried on several of them—on and off, on and off, they just didn't seem to be right. When I looked at the merchandise on all of the other floors, especially those below me, there was a lot of women's clothing in this store and there was a girl model trying on stockings. She had very beautiful legs and everywhere there was very alluring women's clothing . . . on all the floors. There were mannekins and models with negligées, underwear, sunsuits, foundation garments, bathing suits, all kind of women's clothing, and finally it got to be closing time and I picked a coat off the counter—a boy's coat and it seemed right. That's all there seemed to be in the dream.

He said that he could remember, far back, going shopping with his mother and seeing and being interested in various items of feminine apparel. He said that in last night's dream he was more interested in the lovely sights around him than in whether he was going to get a new coat. He was particularly interested in the young, beautiful girl trying on the new stockings.

He said that in the dream he felt some kind of temptation to put on the various items of women's clothes, although he cannot remember any such inclination when growing up.

(Up until and even at this point my interventions consisted of some nonverbal vocalizations of participation with the material—a verbal nod of assent, an upward inflection of the voice to question, or a question or two about what he thought the dream might mean, etc.)

Mr. Fletcher continued, as I rather surmised he would, by saying that at some point in his life he must have thought that, with all of the violence and danger and being drained and scraped out by sex that it is dangerous to be masculine and that maybe it is safer to be feminine—but he was puzzled by why he should think this. He said that he could remember another masturbatory fantasy—some gorgeously dressed creature was tempting him by holding her legs or displaying her breasts or her vagina and the woman displaying her legs by putting on the stocking was like that. He said that last night he and his wife had made love and it occurred to him that sex was now more satisfying to him than ever.

I commented that indeed he had many fears as a child that in sex something very dangerous might happen to him—some loss inside himself or to his penis and that to wear the coat of a boy is very dangerous—dangerous at many levels, and I alluded to the feminine clothing on all floors in the dream. He then told me that in the masturbation fantasies as an adolescent he would "ravage" the woman—that he would pin her down and penetrate her hard and extremely forcefully, violently, and that these thoughts gave him particular excitement and pleasure.

Next day, Mr. Fletcher reported a particularly stormy day in which he had indeed provoked some of the congregation and his colleagues. At a regular meeting, Mr. Fletcher began the discussion by telling them that he wondered if his counseling was bearing fruit. He pointed to the dwindling interest of the clients, lethargic participation in the various projects, and confronted the parishioners somewhat angrily with the facts. He told them that there would indeed be a time when he would be leaving and he wondered whether he should recommend another counselor to replace him. Did they want to have pastoral counseling, and he asked them what they thought the difficulty was between them and himself to account for the problems that he had outlined earlier.

To make a long story short, Mr. Fletcher had provoked the parishioners and elders, and they retaliated. The elders told him that he was disorganized, that he didn't show enough interest in clients, and seemed to get so bogged down in details that he didn't have time to take care of what they called "the human side of counseling."

Mr. Fletcher felt that they were not altogether being fair about this, but conceded that he might be more diligent about some of his duties. Then the wife of an elder told him that his wife was wonderful but that he "doesn't seem to have a timetable for anything." She also told him that the clients stood in awe of him, that he didn't come through as a person to them, and he said that the clients were, to a large degree correct, that he preached cooperation but he hadn't embodied it in his relationships with the congregation. He compared it to a mountain climber who is trying to lead a party up the mountain, who knows the terrain and the trails and the rocks quite well, but is neglectful of his relationship to those climbers he is trying to lead.

Actually, this whole matter need not have come up, and I'm not sure that anything useful for Mr. Fletcher was accomplished from his encounter with the elders. I pointed out to him the avoidant, "acting out" aspects of this provocation of the clients and colleagues (which might indeed have gotten him into some hot water). I interpreted the very painful, difficult material with which he was struggling in the analysis, and his telling the congregation about his "one day leaving," and doing so in a way that might conceivably hasten that day, to the detriment of the analysis.

Next day, Mr. Fletcher told me that he had gone straight from the session to his own office, had tidied up his desk, his schedule, and had gotten a good bit done. In fact, he had much of the next month lined up and scheduled in terms of visits and activities.

Then he visited a larger city church, to meet with the minister there. This minister had recently lost his two counselors and replaced one of them temporarily for a year. Although the more senior counseling position, when permanently decided, would obviously go to someone of greater seniority and experience than Mr. Fletcher, he had the thought that perhaps the second position there might be appropriate for him. He would like a large city church much better than the small rural church that he currently served.

He then had the following dream:

> It was a series of encounters with old classmates. I met a few college classmates and friends from way back in high school. It was a big meeting and none of us had seen each other for years. There were husbands and wives and we wanted to hear what was going on. A woman turned up, a girl whom I was very fond of, named Ellen. She had been a very sharp student. I used to take her out. She went to New York State University in her freshman year and contrary to her parent's wishes secretly married a tall, good looking Roman Catholic. I don't know why she should spring into my dream last night. When I saw her (in the dream) we hugged each other and she said that she was married and was

> serving as the Arts & Crafts Director of a big city recreation program, that advertised itself with big posters, some of which she had made and she showed me one. It had the letters on it: BBNBR . . . and it looked like B'nai Brith but that wasn't it. The only other facet of the dream was that I felt some sense of inferiority about being a counselor in a small rural church.

Mr. Fletcher began by associating to the dream: he thought about the letters BBNBR and recalled that he had been showing the kids in Bible School a Hebrew bible and the first chapter of Genesis, which in Hebrew is Barashith. Barashith is the Hebrew word for the beginning of creation, at the start of things.

Now, for some reason, a joke came to the patient's mind. It seemed that an opthalmologist treated the wife of a pop artist and he got a handsome fee and in addition the pop artist gave the opthalmologist a gift—a picture of an eye with the opthalmologist in the center. The opthalmologist thanked his patient very much and said, "It's a good thing I'm not a gynecologist."

Mr. Fletcher continued with the Hebrew word *Barashith* and said that the root Hebrew word is *Rosh* which means head—the head of things. He thought of Rosh Hashanah which means the head of a year. Then he had some more thoughts about B'nai Brith and he thought it meant sons of the covenant. He thought that the word *Brith* was similar to birth. He saw a head emerging as though from the womb as an image which kept cropping into mind. He continued working on the dream during the next hour thinking some more about B'nai Brith, and Bar Mitzvah, all of these Hebrew words having to do with sons and boys.

Then he recalled something that had happened the previous day when he was visiting a client, and out in the field they heard the danger signal from a tractor. It turned out that tractors are equipped with very powerful horns that can be heard for miles around because if a tractor should turn over and fall on somebody he could summon help by pressing the button and be heard a long distance away. Yesterday they heard a tractor horn and rushed out into the field to see if anything was wrong, but the man just wanted them to come and help him with the cows.

I inquired if anything in the material gave him any sense of danger. Mr. Fletcher responded that he did feel somewhat anxious talking about all this but that he didn't know why. He went back to work on the phrase B'nai Brith, then thought up the word *Brith* and it suddenly popped into his mind that the word *Brith* refers to the Jewish ritual circumcision. Now his mind turns to the loss of an appendage and to castration and circumcision and emasculation. He recalls that this girl in the dream

> was young, spontaneous, quick with a laugh, and then he had the dream with the poster involving something about circumcision. It seems to him that there is something dangerous about a young and attractive woman—something that leads him to thoughts of castration and danger.
>
> I commented that in the dream the woman is a Director of Recreation, and he said yes, and that in the dream he hugged her and that was fun and he guessed that his affection for her was sexual.
>
> I commented that in the dream he tells us that a long time ago, very early in fact, near to the beginning of things he had some sexual thoughts and feelings which he felt would lead to a Brith or circumcision or castration.

A number of interesting earlier masturbatory fantasies then emerged involving a type of revengeful anal intercourse with a very masculine, widowed woman. These were related to a current exclusive preference for intercourse with his wife on top, and the sadomasochistic fantasy that she was "sitting on top of his penis" while he "jammed it up her ass."

Side by side with themes and fantasies of the grandiose leader emerged dreams in which Mr. Fletcher presented himself as a tricky, deceitful thief, who used all sorts of clever deceptions to trick the analyst out of time, money, nurturance, and then who felt enormously guilty at "getting away with it," and who then had to confess his tricks in order to relieve himself of his guilt and fear of violent retribution.

The bringing to light of such material and the process of working it through found him becoming considerably freer to use his talents, and he was elected to a major position in the counseling system in the state. He had eagerly sought this job, was enormously pleased at his success, and yet, when elected, made a number of procrastinating self-defeating moves, again related to his overreaching oral greed (linked to, but far deeper and more powerful than his strong streak of phallic ambitiousness and competitiveness). For example, he spoke of "wanting the job so badly he could taste it." On the day of an important interview in connection with this position, he reported a dream in which his (hoped-for) appointment was celebrated by an enormous "victory banquet." The previous night, he had been invited to give an inspirational talk at the local high school athletic banquet and, although he refrained from saying as much, was internally punning with phrases like "our team ate their opponents alive," or "we had 'em for lunch."

At the beginning of his third year of analysis, his wife became pregnant. While, at first, there was a flush of virile, masculine pride, the next reaction (perceived largely through dreams) had to do with his concern over his wife's enlargement (disfigurement) and his concern that the child would in some way internally damage his wife. This centered around thoughts and fantasies about the child depleting the wife, draining her, sapping her of strength, vitality, and, finally, life itself, through its greedy, sucking demandingness. This, of course, was precisely what he felt he was doing in the analysis to the analyst, and the better he got, the more benefit he derived from psychoanalysis, that is, the guiltier he felt. On the oedipal side of this particular conflict, we found Mr. Fletcher first expressing a kind of swaggering hypermasculinity over the fact that he, too, could produce a child, but later expressing through dreams and fantasies some thoughts that the child also might be damaged, as if this was in retribution for his flaunting his potency before the analyst. There were earlier associations of his fear of being discovered at heavy necking and petting by his father and still earlier thoughts of being caught masturbating by him.

The analysis was then ready to embark upon an exploration and resolution of some of the narcissistic and grandiose aspects of Mr. Fletcher's personality structure, which had been so vigorously defended against by his pattern of undoing, reaction formations, and a depressively toned procrastination, indecisiveness, and mildly depressive mood state. The narcissism was an intriguing blend of both oral and phallic instinctual derivatives. Constantly we found Mr. Fletcher reverting to fantasies of himself being the oppressed burden-bearer of the world—angrily serving his family, his clients, his community, without stint or recompense to himself. There was a kind of saintly narcissism in the nobility and secret pride that he felt in his suffering. (This was a man who was quite proud of his humility.) However, in the transference, it became quite clear that the analyst was seen as, in the last resort, the person who would know that he had suffered, would adjudge the nobility and fineness of his character, and would then, in rather direct oral ways, feed, nurse, or otherwise reward him—as, in fact, we were able to reconstruct mother to have done. The problems with taking and being given to, and their relationship to oral-aggressive greed, were also death wishes in a number of transference manifestations, particularly dreams and fantasies. He developed a fantasy, which, in the working through, uncovered some major roots of his character neurosis. He discovered, via a series of dreams, the fantasy that he was the possessor of a "magic penis," which, upon exploration, turned out to be a combination of penis and breast that could "both screw the world and feed the world into well-being." One such dream saw Mr. Fletcher making a hospital call on a friend who was terminally ill. He had in fact visited this woman on the day prior to the dream. Whereas in reality he had felt sadness and impotence in not being able to restore his friend to health and vitality, in the dream he had intercourse with her, she performed fellatio on him, and made a sudden, miraculous recovery. The transference implications of such a dream clearly established him as a far more potent healer than the analyst. In fact, he revealed more than a little scorn and derision as he spoke of how he had "put life into her," far exceeding the medical help that had been given the woman. As in the dream just described, the underlying feelings of helplessness and impotence that this fantasy had long served as a buffer against, also came into the forefront, and for a time the patient became markedly depressed as he gave up his protective, hypomanic fantasy. However, we saw the man's grandiosity and his compelling sense of omnipotence—which he always had to work to keep within bounds—and the disdain that he harbored for lesser persons (i.e., those without his fantasied strength and powers).

Several of the most difficult but rewarding of all the hours in the analysis came when Mr. Fletcher began to think of himself as the woman in the dream who had sucked the analyst's breast–penis, taken his strength and power, and was recovering; thereby leaving the analyst empty, impotent, and as frustrated as he imagined his father to have been.

Concomitant with the uncovering of this material, and the

resolution of the depression that accompanied it, a number of things began to occur in his life. He began to attract regional and national attention as a "young man to be watched" in counseling circles. He traveled and gave lectures and speeches in various places, doing this very well and bringing to light the real talent for counseling and teaching that he possessed. He became sought after at a number of places across the country.

Locally his clients and colleagues found him to be much more effective and they worked together to solve a number of pressing problems within the church. He was even able to spend part of his inheritance on himself and on his wife—buying himself a brightly colored new car to replace the drab one that he used to drive. He discovered that there was more money for his wife and children to enjoy themselves with, also. As a consequence of all of these things, he began to talk of termination.

After some discussion we set a termination date six months into the future which proved adequate for him to bring into the transference his previously inadequately mourned loss of both parents, the giving up of much of his grandiosity, and further resolution of his fantasies about possessing (and losing) the magical penis–breast. Obviously, disappointment and anger manifested themselves in the terminal phase of the analysis. Mostly such feelings were directed from the couch (instead of directing them against clients). He dealt with the loss of the analyst at first by displacing and reversing the feelings. It was he who was leaving, not he who was being left. He repeated at length that he would be glad to leave those ignorant, backward people who had made life so difficult for him, especially while he had been working so hard to improve himself in analysis. It took only the slightest of attentional nudges to help Mr. Fletcher recognize the transference implications of such feelings, which were kept safely within the confines of the analysis and not acted out, as had been the situation before and during the treatment.

Two months before the analysis was to end he received a very attractive offer from a progressive prestigious church which prides itself rather strenuously on the quality of dedication of its congregation. This church, in a major city, has rigorous standards of commitment for its counselors and staff and heard about Mr. Fletcher and sought him out to join the staff when a vacancy occurred there. This is a church with a definite sense of social commitment and social action—much to Mr. Fletcher's liking. After thinking it over and discussing it in the analysis, we both felt it appropriate for him to consider this offer—which he did. Both parties were mutually pleased with each other and Mr. Fletcher accepted a position there, much to the pleasure of his wife and the sadness of the congregation and the colleagues of the rural church. The feeling on his departure was voiced by an elder at a farewell dinner for Mr. Fletcher, who, he said was leaving, "just when we started to like the guy."

Dr. Rosen acknowledges the wisdom and supervisory consultation of Dr. Ishak Ramzy.

A DISCUSSION OF "THE ANALYSIS OF A RELIGIOUS MAN" BY IRWIN C. ROSEN

Alan J. Eisnitz, M.D.

I have long been impressed that the posttreatment review of psychoanalytic cases is a valuable and underutilized approach. It is easy to understand why this method is not used more often; it is time-consuming to prepare an adequate summary, and it requires more complete records of the treatment than may be available. However, it is the best method for viewing the broad sweep of the analysis. It gives a perspective far different from that employed by the analyst immersed in a day-to-day view which focuses on details, without knowing what is to follow. The process of the analysis, the uncovering, in growing depth, of the important fantasies of the patient, the resistances to that process, the flow of the treatment with now an advancing, now a heightened defensive phase, now a regressive shift, the vicissitudes of the transference, the defenses employed, and the effect upon the process of the interventions by the analyst can all be observed. The patient's diagnosis can be confirmed, or modified, his motivations for treatment evaluated, and, it goes without saying, the capacity of the analysis to promote change can be determined. For all these purposes the method has obvious value as a teaching tool, and while best suited for studying technique from a strategic, that is, a broad point of view, if enough detail is provided it can be an excellent method for consideration of day-to-day technical management as well. It is the equivalent of a medical case review, a form of CPC, with some of the features of beside rounds included.

UNUSUAL FEATURES OF THE CASE

Even a cursory reading of the case report indicates that Mr. Fletcher derived a great deal of benefit from his analysis. However, there were a number of atypical features of the case which could have presented serious problems. Fortunately, in the main, while each was an influence, it did not prevent analytic progress.

The major potential problems, all resulting from preanalytic factors, were the patient's intellectual knowledge about psychoanalysis, his deep involvement with religion, and the abundance of outside information obtained from extra-analytic sources.

INTELLECTUAL KNOWLEDGE ABOUT PSYCHOANALYSIS

Today, almost every patient comes to analysis with a certain familiarity with psychoanalysis and some of its main concepts. Many other patients have awareness of other forms of therapy and even some experience with them; sometimes they have, in spite of the fact that they are consulting a psychoanalyst, a skepticism or bias about the usefulness of psychoanalysis. Mr. Fletcher was different. He had a great deal of knowledge about psychoanalysis which he derived from courses that he took as part of his professional work. His work itself even involved doing a kind of therapy. It is not so unusual that a patient should have considerable information about analysis. After all, every analyst in training undergoes psychoanalysis as a part of that training. However, there is always the potential that the intellectual knowledge will be used in the service of resistance and specifically in the direction of encouraging intellectualization on the part of the patient. Mr. Fletcher did make use of intellectualization as a defense and as a resistance to the treatment. Probably if he had possessed no knowledge of psychoanalysis he would have used similar intellectualizing tendencies simply because this was part of his character makeup. The task of the analysis, in such cases, is to work through the resistance by careful interpretation and then to deal with the underlying affect and conflicts. As we will see in reviewing the analysis of Mr. Fletcher, the development of the transference neurosis provides the key to this progress.

INFORMATION OBTAINED FROM OUTSIDE THE ANALYSIS

Both Mr. Fletcher and his wife had provided considerable information during a consultation workup prior to the analysis. Information obtained like this, outside of the analytic setting, can be quite useful. However, it can also bypass or distort the analytic process. For example, the analyst, and presumably the patient, knew factually that the patient's mother had suffered some kind of nervous breakdown early in the patient's life. There is evidence that this event, and even more importantly, the patient's reaction to it, were to some extent denied by the patient. At a later point in the report, it is stated that the patient and his family lived for the first ten years of his life with his maternal grandfather. It is also indicated that throughout this time, the patient's father was placed in a subordinate position to the grandfather. Later in the analysis it was learned through reconstruction that sometime around the end of the second year (the Goodyear blimp dream), the maternal grandfather's death was the precipitating factor for Mr. Fletcher's mother's depression, a truly traumatic time. Mr. Fletcher's father, therefore, could not have been subordinate to Mr. Fletcher's grandfather, nor could they have lived with the grandfather for the first few years of Mr. Fletcher's life because the grandfather died when Mr. Fletcher was about eighteen months old. The contradiction of the facts must have served a defensive purpose for the patient. Only analytic work allowed the real situation to come through. Apparently Mr. Fletcher allowed two contradictory versions of his past history to coexist. He "knew" that his mother had a nervous breakdown when he was less than two years old, and he probably "knew" that his grandfather died at that time. Yet he also believed that he lived with his maternal grandfather until he was ten and that throughout this time his father was subordinate to his grandfather. Thinking of his father as submitting this way to his grandfather partly denied his grandfather's death and his mother's depression. It also denied some of his own oedipal guilt in the sense that competition was viewed as occurring between grandfather and father rather than between Mr. Fletcher and his father. Furthermore, it was Mr. Fletcher's father who was the submissive victim of paternal authority rather than Mr. Fletcher himself, a defense against Mr. Fletcher's passive wishes. Finally, although we know from later analytic data that Mr. Fletcher had great anxiety about submission to a powerful woman, in this distortion of facts, no powerful woman appears in a major role; mother is merely reported to be depressed, the conflict takes place between two men, grandfather and father. In the analysis, the analyst did not simply accept the original report from the consultation as the "correct" version of the facts. Had this been done, the opportunity for valuable analytic work would have been foreclosed. Instead, the analyst had the information available to use when the time became appropriate. Probably it sensitized him to appreciate the significance of the sequence of associations about the crash of the dirigible Hindenberg as relating to the depressive change in the patient's mother. Factual correctness was made secondary to analytic work and was not simply accepted at face value. The reconstruction of the patient's past was accomplished through the analysis and not by other means or historical research. In this case, I believe that the analyst dealt with the material from outside sources in a most expert fashion. He used it in the sense that it helped his understanding; he did not allow it to set aside the analytic work or process needed to arrive at an understanding of the possible distortions or the incompleteness of the patient's memory.

Some analysts do not like to have any information available from any source except the analytic contact with the patient. In their view, this eliminates the danger of distorting the analytic process. As a matter of fact, most analyses do deal only with the patient's history as it is obtained from the patient and for the most part as it unfolds during the analytic work. This does work out best in most cases. However, I do not feel that one need fear learning something about the patient from another source so long as one does not succumb to the temptation to use the information without going through the necessary difficult analytic work which would otherwise be required. It is not simply a matter of stating that the important reality is the patient's intrapsychic reality. Of most importance, the inevitable distortions or omissions in the patient's recollections and *reactions* to the past serve defensive and other functions for the patient. All of these must be analyzed and worked through; this is valuable analytic work. Analysts are very much interested in factual reality, but they recognize that such accuracy must be earned by hard analytic work.

Sometimes, patients do initiate historical research on their own. They may check aspects of their history with other members of the family or with friends from the past, or from other sources—Mr. Fletcher did this himself. Often this is part of their growing capacity to deal with reality and comes about as a consequence of analytic work. Sometimes however it can represent an effort to bypass the work of the analysis or to attempt to evade or displace transference issues. Like everything else in the analysis, efforts at research by the patient must also be analyzed.

RELIGION

Religious beliefs can represent a tricky area for analysis. It is hardly necessary to emphasize that the personal views of the analyst should not enter the picture and that no a priori judgments should be made. Yet strongly held religious beliefs can present a formidable problem. The religious patient tends to accept his religious beliefs as being beyond question. There is a built-in resistance to allowing the analysis to enter areas involving religion. What the analyst must attempt to evaluate before undertaking the analysis is the extent to which this relatively (or potentially) off-limits area is involved in the patient's defensive processes. Religion often represents a method whereby the patient unconsciously views himself as being united with something far greater than himself. Sometimes this represents a union with an omnipotent object and it may be an essential method for promoting the stability of the patient's self representation and ultimately to maintaining his identity. When religious beliefs absorb much of the patient's activities and where they represent a magical and massive defensive system, analysis may not be possible.

On the other hand, successful analyses have been reported in members of religious orders and other devoutly religious people. I have seen patients give up some religious ties during analysis and have also seen patients become more religious as defenses against identification with parents, for example, are analyzed. To state simply that religion is irrational and therefore neurotic is not a useful stand. The analyst must attempt to assess the relative ego strengths of the patient not dependent upon the religious beliefs and must also attempt to assess the degree of conflict which is not bound by the religious beliefs and therefore not accessible to analysis. Like other attitudes of the patient, the analyst must maintain his neutral stance and be willing to explore analytically. Nothing in the analysis must be off-limits from his point of view.

Religion was of great importance to Mr. Fletcher and played a central role even in his profession. It was, unquestionably, a central structuring force for him; he was not simply a religious believer, he functioned entirely within the religious sphere. However, as it turned out there were many areas of conflict which involved Mr. Fletcher's functioning within his sphere of religious activities and outside the area of religion as well. These did not involve his religious beliefs per se, but his application and understanding of them (his annoyance with "flabby Christianity," for example) and in his professional functioning related to them. In other words, religion was not used as an area which could entirely exclude analytic work. It was most important that the areas of conflict involving religion were decidedly ego dystonic. There was effective analytic work done on Mr. Fletcher's passive feminine wishes and his submissive masochistic fantasies, and on his grandiosity. These conflict areas were not completely bound up in the defensive aspects of religious belief, and effective analytic investigation was possible. As a result, Mr. Fletcher's functioning in the religious area did improve, and he became better able, presumably, also to express his views in a more human way.

At the beginning of the analysis it was not possible to know that effective analytic work could be done even in the area of religion. It is apparent that the analyst concluded that the patient would be analyzable, but this was clearly a case where only a trial of analysis could provide the answer. Probably, this is true with any very devout patient. Only with the trial of analysis can one see whether or not effective access to conflict areas is possible. From the point of view of his unconscious, Mr. Fletcher did want to achieve a relationship to the analyst very similar to one of his religious motivations; that is, he wished to submit to a powerful and punitive authority. However, he also had many realistic reasons, which he accepted, for desiring to change, and it was this motivation for realistic change which made the analysis possible.

CONFIRMATION OF DIAGNOSIS

Sometimes, during the course of the analysis, it becomes apparent that the presenting picture of the patient allowed only a superficial glimpse of his character and pathology. As conflicts deepen new emphases become apparent, and sometimes pathology that was not observable before becomes manifest. Following the analytic work in Mr. Fletcher's analysis allowed a confirmation of his initial diagnosis. Mr. Fletcher suffered from an obsessional neurosis and an obsessional character disorder. He also showed some depressive features as well as important sadomasochistic and narcissistic conflicts. All of these phenomena are well within obsessional limits. The analysis progressed in a way characteristic for obsessional patients.

THE COURSE OF TREATMENT

This treatment began with typical obsessional defenses. The patient viewed the analyst, probably on the basis of externalization of his own superego qualities, as a stern and authoritarian punitive figure. Almost in contradiction, he often gave lectures on analytic themes. He engaged in frequent intellectualizing while he effectively isolated affect. Reaction formation was the prominent defense, particularly against his anger and passive longings.

This kind of pattern can be most troubling, particularly to a beginning analyst. The patient's compliant facade may be deceptive at first, but the analyst soon recognizes that intellectualization is not the same as insight. The absence of affect and the lack of deep involvement in the analytic process become apparent to the analyst, while the patient, on the surface at least, blithely proceeds, apparently satisfied with his analytic performance. Below the surface, the patient is attempting to win the analyst's love by means of his submission to the apparent goals of the analyst. This actually portends the development of the transference neurosis. On a deeper level the patient may be trying to provoke or seduce the analyst to "prod" him into action or to becoming attacking or critical. (This attitude was already expressed in the initial view of the analyst as stern and punitive.) The analyst, must, of course, avoid these invitations from the patient and not respond with actions based upon countertransference. Were the analyst to do this, he would provide gratification (instead of analyzing) for important transference aims.

What then can the analyst do? For one thing, he should take solace in recognizing that this is the inevitable beginning of the patient's transference. Similarities can be noted between this analytic behavior and some aspects of Mr. Fletcher's devotion to religion. There are times when some patients who are not outwardly religious have an attitude toward the analysis which in some ways is like a religious attitude. The analyst is viewed as an idealized priest or God, analytic ideas like religious dogma. (The degree of negative coloring of this can vary. Sometimes the analyst is viewed mainly as a loving authority and sometimes as a threatening authority; sometimes loved, and sometimes hated.) Slowly, with effective analytic work, the transference theme will become more defined.

The analyst need not assume that the "intellectualizing"

done by the patient will go to waste. While it is obviously not enough by itself, it does represent a step in the direction of effective analysis. While cure does not result from intellect alone, neither does it result from affect alone. Both are necessary. The intellectualizations of today may eventually, if the analysis develops well, provide a firm foundation for effective insight. It can also become a basis, after its defensive aspects are analyzed, for the analytic attitude which the patient needs. Because intellectualization is used for defensive purposes, the use of intellect and rational understanding has been excessively devalued.

THE ANALYTIC ASPECT OF THE SELF REPRESENTATION

Mr. Fletcher's analysis offers an example of good technique in dealing with the defenses under discussion. The analyst did not bite at the transference bait. Instead, recognizing what was going on, he patiently demonstrated to Mr. Fletcher the defensive aspects of his analytic behavior. He showed him the isolation of affect, the marked differences between Mr. Fletcher's surface calm and his violent fantasies, his distancing techniques, his repetitive and overdetailed reports. Eventually this work paid off, and Mr. Fletcher, utilizing his observing ego, began to establish an aspect of his self representation that is so necessary for analysis. Utilizing ego capacities which are present before the analysis and to some extent identifying with and learning from the analyst, the patient develops a new aspect within his ego, the analytic aspect of his self representation. This relies upon the observing capacity of the ego, but it also relies on new identifications with the analyst. It is this aspect of the self representation which allows the patient to observe himself and his feelings and fantasies and to observe the analyst and their interactions with each other. It allows for the development of an essential quality for the analysand, to experience and accept the reactions as real, and at the same time to be able to experience them as unreal. This allows the patient to truly hate or love his analyst deeply, and then, at the end of the session to be able to "shift gears" and to see and to react to the analyst as the current reality figure he is in actuality. All of this must be experienced within the framework of an acceptance of the absence of action (save for the action of the analysis) and the absence of gratification of the underlying unconscious aims. Unless this basic step is taken, an analytic process cannot occur.

THE STRUGGLES FOR AND AGAINST PROGRESS

The patient must have the capacity to observe the conflicts within himself as he struggles to develop the analytic process. Mr. Fletcher demonstrates this in his dream about the movie projector. The struggle between his wish to reveal things to his analyst and at the same time to oppose this process is clearly shown. From the report, this probably represented the first significant indication of solid analytic progress, although it came after patient and thorough analytic work. Mr. Fletcher reacted in a way typical of many patients. Because a developing alliance with his analyst was threatening to him for unconscious reasons, and because it involved the "danger" of giving up realistically inhibiting but unconsciously gratifying defenses, he struggled against it. Mr. Fletcher demonstrated this with some masochistic provocative behavior; he began to make very unwise investments, thereby jeopardizing his ability to stay in analysis. While part of this was the result of the patient's guilt at being in analysis, part represented his struggle against progress in the analysis which he greatly feared. In this case, the analyst's timely intervention by interpretation turned the acting out into an opportunity for insight.

This entire episode allowed the analyst to work on important aspects of Mr. Fletcher's motivation for analysis. Part of his unconscious aim was to atone for his guilt in relation to his father by paying penance and using up the inheritance his father left for him. Several other themes suggest themselves as being involved in this acting out. One has been mentioned already, that is, the fear of the developing relationship with the analyst and the passive longings which were mobilized. Additionally, there are many aggressive aspects involved. Running out of money is a way of frustrating the analyst—the projector will not be able to work. The acting out thereby demonstrates that neither the analyst nor Mr. Fletcher's father has any say in controlling the way he uses his money (libido).

TENSIONS IN THE ANALYST

The analyst could not deal with all of these issues at once. This illustrates the likelihood that the analyst will experience some inevitable frustrations and some probable psychic tensions which must be mastered. He must be willing to forgo the need for quick narcissistic gratification which could come from cleaning up or at least addressing *all* of the patient's conflicts which he can understand. There are many things which an analyst can understand for himself, but he must be willing to leave some things undone for a time, even to set aside things which he knows to be important, and wait for the opportunity to present itself later to deal with certain issues. In this connection, the analyst must be willing to tolerate a certain amount of apparent passivity which is imposed upon him by the analytic setting. However, he must have the inner sources to recognize that he does this in the furtherance of an active aim; that is, the aim of conducting the analysis to the best of his ability. Compulsive or narcissistic problems (so often interrelated), needs to control, needs to demonstrate one's capacity to be active, can all interfere.

One general pattern of interpretation during an analysis is that interpretations tend to go from the less exact and less complete eventually in the direction of the more precise and thorough. Such was the case in the analysis of Mr. Fletcher. The analyst dealt with the patient's guilt about his inheritance from his father and his need to destroy the treatment. At this time in the analysis, he left it at that. In so doing he demonstrated his respect for allowing the patient's needs and defenses to indicate the direction that the analysis would take. This was quite different from the unconscious offer which the patient had made. Had not the patient "indicated" his willingness to be the passive projector of the themes which the analyst wished to plug in? However, the analyst did not respond to the unconscious offer, nor did he respond to its other side, the implicit offer that the patient could be forced to deal with issues of the analyst's choice. This apparently made a significant impression upon Mr. Fletcher, who throughout the analysis showed one of the qualities of a patient who can be successfully analyzed; he possessed a genuine interest and ability in enlarging upon areas of insight which he acquired and in carrying forward the themes which interpretation brought to his attention. Undoubtedly this was greatly helped by the careful analysis of Mr. Fletcher's initial transference attitudes. Had his intellectualizations simply been accepted at face value with no attempt to call attention to the emotions which they served to ward off, this would not have happened. Similarly, if Mr. Fletcher's view of the analyst as a stern authority had unconsciously been accepted by the analyst out of some need to be authoritative, analytic progress also would have been blocked. The initial phase of working through early resistances to the establishment of the transference and the related therapeutic alliance is most important.

THE DEVELOPMENT OF THE TRANSFERENCE: THE DEEPENING OF UNCONSCIOUS THEMES

Mr. Fletcher's masochistic qualities were then able to come under increasing focus. His masochistic denial of pleasure illustrated in part by his pride in having an old and apparently decrepit car, his imposing upon his family these same masochistic values, his stinginess with his family, his tendency to sabotage himself at work by procrastination and indecision, all came under scrutiny. At this point in the case report the analyst notes the patient's observation that his sexual life was entirely satisfactory. In my opinion it is significant that this observation is recorded here in the midst of a series of observations about the patient's need to express or to provoke masochistic submission. It is partly for this reason that I am somewhat skeptical about the patient's assessment of his sexual life being so conflict free. I will have more to say about this later. An alternative explanation is that the patient feared that in opening up the area of sexuality, his masochistic wishes to submit to the analyst might become too strong and threatening, and it was therefore necessary for him to avoid these issues. Very shortly thereafter, the case report notes Mr. Fletcher's protests against "flabby Christianity." One had to remain strong and disciplined, to accept hardship, suffering, and privation, rather than to engage in efforts to overcome pain or suffering. I suspect that this may also be a reference to the patient's unconsciously determined choice to retain a certain unanalyzed masochistic (and passive) preserve out of the analysis by accepting the restrictions on his sexual gratification and not bringing them into the analysis.

In spite of this, some very important work was accomplished upon significant restrictions of the patient's capacity for empathy. He could not truly appreciate the pain and distress which his clients endured, for to do so required the tentative identification that makes empathy possible. He could not identify, even fleetingly, with those in distress because such an identification exposed him to his own passive and masochistic wishes. In such situations, he reacted to his clients as he reacted, in compulsive fashion, to himself. Instead of offering them understanding and help, he resorted to exortation, urging them to greater self-discipline and renunciation. In other words, his message to them was to be strong, or more accurately, not to be weak. In my opinion, he was primarily attempting to encourage defenses against his own wish for masochistic and passive submission.

The reader should note the interplay between interpretation of transference wishes and defenses, and the expression of the same conflicts in outside areas of the patient's life. This required a coordinated effort by a good analyst and a good patient; that is, a patient who allows his realistic wish to get better to utilize his curiosity and his self perception under the organization of the analytic aspect of his self representation. It will be recalled that this trend in the analysis followed upon the dream of the movie projector which so clearly marked a significant step in awareness by Mr. Fletcher of his conflict between his wish to communicate with his analyst and his wish not to do so. This led to the first masochistic acting out outside of the treatment and then to his defenses against passivity and masochism. We can assume that far more interpretations of these conflicts were made than are actually reported in the case summary. However, the joint collaboration of patient and analyst gradually enlarged the depth of their perceptions and slowly Mr. Fletcher could come to see how he struggled against a closer relationship with his analyst and his passive wishes to be nurtured.

While the interpretations did not seem to deal apparently with the aggressive side of these conflicts very much, there were related fears of "debilitating" the analyst were Mr. Fletcher to express such oral longings. This would repeat the way he had debilitated his mother as an infant. Note that the theme of damaging his mother and his relationship to mother's illness very early in his life will become more explicit somewhat later in the analysis (i.e., with the dream of the Goodyear Blimp). During this first year of the analysis we also note that the analyst continues to express some concern about the patient's use of intellectualization and isolation. Of course, the analyst did not have the advantage of our perspective; he was immersed in the day-to-day associations of the patient and may not have been able to appreciate the gradually deepening focus that was in fact evolving.

The analyst continued working with what was available to him; he interpreted the patient's defenses against affect, defenses against "needfulness," and his struggles against closeness. He connected these with Mr. Fletcher's fears of passivity. This patient work on the analyst's part was gradually rewarded when Mr. Fletcher's identification with Luther became more prominent and more productive for the analysis.

The dream of tracking mud all over the analyst's office following an actual session in which Mr. Fletcher spoke of Luther's "shitting all over Rome" represents a signal, according to my understanding, that the patient was now not so frightened, especially in alliance with his understanding analyst, of his anal sadistic impulses. The hours of work with his defenses had paid off. Mr. Fletcher was now able to reveal things he had formerly kept secret, particularly that the self-sacrificing demeanor overlaid a tremendous ambition, including the fantasy of being an omnipotent Pope.

This sequence in the analysis followed careful analysis of resistances of emerging transference fantasies. It represents an example of the best kind of confirmation of interpretation; that is, an enlargement of the patient's capacity for self perception and the development of new material in the analysis. Apparently a considerable amount of work was then done upon the patient's competitive feelings with his father and Mr. Fletcher's guilt about knowledge, achievement, and power. The analyst notes that much work with preoedipal, particularly oral wishes to gorge himself, was also accomplished.

It is not uncommon for an analysis to appear in what the analyst refers to as a "split level" form. I take this as an indication that in this case the oedipal conflicts were the organizing feature and that they included the inevitable and predisposing pregenital trends. In other words, the oedipal phase with its rich capacity for structure building was colored and influenced by the pregenital conflicts which distorted the perceptions and fantasies of the oedipal phase. At that time they are then organized by the attempts at resolution of the oedipal conflicts into their final form. Sometimes analysis confined only to the oedipal conflicts can produce significant therapeutic results, but unless the pregenital predisposing factors are also worked through, a shaky foundation of the therapeutic change makes future regression and pathology more likely. It is worth noting here that in this analysis, just as there was very little material about Mr. Fletcher's current adult sexual life, there is practically no report of positive oedipal sexual wishes.

A DRAMATIC SESSION

The Goodyear blimp dream undoubtedly represented a dramatic point in the analysis which made it possible for subsequent deepening of the analytic work. Such dramatic sessions during an analysis have a significance very much like a remembered traumatic event. Analytic exploration almost always indicates that the traumatic event is really a screen memory, frequently with an impact of its own, but with many related events and fantasies connected, like overtones, to the main theme. Just as the traumatic event may not have a significant impact without the earlier conflicts, the dramatic session is not likely to occur unless thorough analytic work with related themes has preceded it. Note the response of Mr. Fletcher's to the analyst's interpretation of his wish to be able to seize food aggressively the way his own child had done. The patient stated: "I could never have gotten away with such behavior." It is very shortly after this that the blimp dream appears. I believe that the patient, in effect, was stating that he had in the past tried to seize food aggressively, but that he did not get away with it. His mother's depression and absence from the home were viewed by him as his punishment for his oral sadistic wishes along with the additional punishment of the partially repressed death of his grandfather. This unconscious fantasy, that his unconscious wishes had the power to destroy, undoubtedly served to augment his passivity. It also helps to understand the confusion about the time of grandfather's death. At one point in the report it stated that the patient lived for ten years in his grandfather's home and that during those years Mr. Fletcher's father was subordinate to the grandfather. Here is an additional reason why Mr. Fletcher externalized his own competitive wishes to dominate his father to his grandfather. By having his grandfather competing with his father, Mr. Fletcher avoided the feared event of having his own aggression result in his losing his father just as he lost his mother. I believe that this would have been an important factor to clarify and to work through with Mr. Fletcher. This may have been done, but it is not reported as such in the case material.

ANAL REGRESSION IN THE TRANSFERENCE

It is rather difficult to have an accurate picture of time relationships from the case report. Apparently, however, shortly after the Goodyear blimp dream there was a very significant and clear shift in the material to anal fantasies and wishes, with a focus in the transference. These were expressed as wishes to be penetrated and pierced by the analyst who seems to have represented both a phallic mother as well as the penetrating father. From our knowledge of what evolved in the analysis subsequent to this point, I think it is possible to reconstruct certain important elements of Mr. Fletcher's life. He undoubtedly experienced the events at the time of his grandfather's death as a double loss. It was not only the loss of a revered (certainly in the eyes of his mother) man but also led to his mother's depression, and, at least temporarily, her unavailability to him. Apparently, many of his passive needs could not now be fulfilled by his mother, and so he transferred them and attempted to live them out in his relationship with his father. The fear that he "debilitated" his mother resulted in further repression of his sadistic wishes and the shift to his father augmented what was already a natural anal phase dominance. Unfortunately, at the same time, probably because of both her own predispositions as well as her defenses against her sadistic death wishes (this was just after the death of her father), his mother herself became much more involved in the anal aspects of her relationship with her son. Enema giving became frequent, as Mr. Fletcher so vividly recalled. Pregenital, mostly anal, coloring was given to his character as well as an impetus to his passive anal homosexual wishes. Anal sadistic wishes were even more carefully defended against. As a result we can speculate that Mr. Fletcher's involvement with religion might very well similarly express an anal submission to a revered grandfather-father-God. Certainly Mr. Fletcher's sadomasochistic acting out in provoking confrontations is consistent with this view. A predisposition to an anal regression was established at the time of grandfather's death, a reconstruction which is supported by the flow of the analytic material. Naturally, the developments in the analysis also point to the anal regression as being of extreme importance in the analysis as well as in the development of Mr. Fletcher's character.

THE DUCK DREAM

The duck dream stands out as one of those segments of an analysis which allows the organization of so many of the intermingling conflicts and fantasies. The analyst's first interpretation to Mr. Fletcher was his understanding of sexual intercourse as a violent, draining, and dangerous, even killing activity. It also allowed the interpretation of the equation of the penis with feces, and then via the recollection of the adminstration of the childhood enemas, it dealt with the reconstruction of an important part of actual life events as well as introducing the tremendous fear of castration which so much influenced Mr. Fletcher. It also helps in understanding how, in his passivity, Mr. Fletcher expresses both sides of his oedipal conflict, albeit in a passive mode. He passively establishes a regressive anal sexual relationship with his enema-giving mother as well as with his penetrating father. Mr. Fletcher followed this piece of analytic work with the dream of shopping for female clothing, and his fears of being masculine could be directly approached in the analysis. It also led to his reporting fantasies which expressed his own sadistic sexual wishes, adolescent fantasies in which he would "ravage" the woman, or fantasies during intercourse of assaulting his wife through the anus.

Quite obviously this sequence dealt with the patient's regression to anal sexuality. His anxiety about the wishes derived from this phase have apparently been important factors contributing to his compulsive and submissive personality organization.

The task of the analysis at such a time is to help the patient integrate the formerly repressed elements into a reorganization of his self representation so that he can function effectively at a new level. In the duck dream we can see some of the important elements of his self representation which were involved in his pathology. Considering the duck as one aspect of his self representation, we can understand how his submissiveness was based upon his passive wishes. We can also see the importance to him of the reaction formations against passivity (i.e., his protests against "flabby Christianity"). Viewing the person cleaning out the duck as another aspect of his self representation, we can understand his need to express his sadistic wishes (and the resultant conflict) as well as his identification with the aggressor. Recall, for example, his lectures to his clients, admonishing them to be strong and disciplined instead of offering them the empathy which they really needed. Here we can see his sadism operative in his profession.

Working through in analysis always involves the reintegration of what was formerly unconscious and the giving up of old patterns of defense and reaction. A problem arises, however, in that even though these patterns are at the foundation of the patient's pathology and therefore cause him pain, they also provide him with a certain amount of comfort. I am speaking not only of the gratification of infantile aims which the old patterns provide, but also the fear of giving them up. The new and the untried, that is new and untried ego patterns, also represent the possibility of narcissistic defeat and therefore they are extremely frightening to every patient. As a result, progress in analysis, as occurred here, is frequently followed, in many analyses, by regressive efforts to undo that progress.

It was precisely in this fashion that Mr. Fletcher responded; he expressed his need to regress by engaging in some provocative masochistic acting out with his Board. The analyst was quite understanding of what was happening and interpreted the patient's struggle with the difficult material in the analysis and his unconscious attempts to have the treatment interrupted. Mr. Fletcher reacted to this interpretation by getting right back on track. He took appropriate action to undo the effects of his acting out, and in the analysis he went back to working progressively. I must confess to a bit of surprise upon reading how readily Mr. Fletcher gave up his resistance at this point. In my experience, this phase of work usually progresses much more deliberately, and takes longer. I will have a bit more to say about this later. Mr. Fletcher then had the dream of his old girl friend and the posters with letters on them which looked like B'nai Brith. In his associations he noted that the girl married out of her religion, suggesting the likelihood that she represented an oedipal object. Of great interest to me, however, was the chain of associations about B'nai Brith, Rosh Hashanah, and circumcision. The analyst notes that the image of a baby's head emerging from a womb kept occurring to the patient. He also commented on the theme of sons and boys. A most interesting association was then reported, of the tractor horn used as a call for help.

Obviously this material emerged over a period of several days, and is full of allusions to many themes. The task of the analyst at such times is to select the theme which is most appropriate to the current struggle of the patient, that is appropriate to the progress of the analytic sessions and their relationship to the patient's external reality. In this instance the analyst, not unreasonably, focused on the castration threat which was connected with some sexual thoughts and feelings which the patient had "very long ago."

One can have little quarrel with the interpretation of castration, but there is an equally important theme which seems not to have been explored. The preoccupation over several sessions with Hebrew words and Jewish concepts coupled with the tractor horn call for help suggests to me that the patient was attempting to move closer to his (apparently) Jewish analyst, looking for an identification as well as a libidinal bond with him. This was just as he once wished to do with his father so that he would not be so frightened of his castrating, enema-giving mother. The report does not make clear how effectively this theme was analyzed either at this time or in other portions of the analysis. The patient did report sadistic fantasies of jamming his penis, in anal intercourse, into a widowed woman. This again sounds like an oedipal object. Whether this fantasy represents simple retaliation against his mother, a regressive sadistic representation of his oedipal wishes, or a magical attempt at denial of his own weakness vis-à-vis the woman (perhaps because the analyst neither gratified his wishes for identification, nor, seemingly, were they interpreted adequately) is not clear. The next fantasy reported, however, is of the grandiose religious leader. This suggests an attempt to deny his weakness in fantasy by means of a magic identification with an omnipotent object. Earlier in the analysis there was a fantasy of being an omnipotent Pope. Here we can see a link between Mr. Fletcher's intense involvement with religion, his anal passivity and sadism, his defenses against the anally castrating woman, and his wish for an omnipotent bond and identification with the analyst. This need for the omnipotent bond probably is lived out in his being part of the religious establishment.

Good things began to happen in Mr. Fletcher's life. There

seems to be little question that this is an instance of good fortune coming to someone who now is ready for it as a result of growing maturity. His analysis enabled him to get a more important job and very shortly thereafter his wife again became pregnant. As he felt stronger, he developed more fears of being punished as well as fears of the child draining and depleting his wife from within. I believe that these represented his own oral sadistic wishes as well as his own fears of castration.

The analyst reports that it was now possible to embark upon an exploration of the narcissistic and grandiose aspects of the patient's personality. However, I believe that this was already happening in the analysis of many of his anal conflicts. What appeared in the analysis now were some of the oral components, or more accurately, phallic oral conflicts. These were expressed in the magic breast–penis fantasy in which he cured a terminally ill woman by means of fellatio. Further realistic advances took place as the patient became known as a "young man to be watched." It was shortly after this that the issue of termination appeared. While the termination phase was only sparsely reported, it appeared to deal with feelings about the loss of the analyst and the loss of some of the grandiose aspects of his self representation as well as some regressive revival of conflicts.

EVALUATION OF THE ANALYTIC RESULT

This appears to be a well-conducted and quite successful psychoanalysis. Mr. Fletcher seems to have achieved a great deal of benefit. He functions more freely, and is more tolerant and aware of his emotions. He seems capable of greater empathy, a lack which caused him great difficulty before the analysis. Recall how he provoked antagonism by giving his clients lectures rather than truly understanding them. He seems more appreciative and accepting of his own and others' feelings. He does not appear to be so constrained by procrastination, nor does he appear to have the same need to provoke disfavor and punishment. He is able to seek out and effectively to relate in situations wherein he can promote advances for himself in his profession. His ability to accept and also to seek pleasure for himself has increased. An important indicator of therapeutic progress and possible structural change, he is capable of greater reflection upon and modification of his behavior in advance of action. His grandiosity seems to have been abated. Apparently, his superego is not so much influenced by sadistic qualities, and his need for self-punishment as well as his tendency toward depression is no longer the major factor it had been.

There are some important areas of his life about which relatively little has been reported. One concerns his functioning as a father, and, in general, his relationships with his family. There are implications that he has become more understanding and giving with his wife and children. It is hard to see how this result would not have been derived from the treatment. However, there are practically no references to these people whom he presumably loves and with whom he lives most closely. This is an analysis which was mainly focused, at least in the report, upon his work functioning and relationships. Undoubtedly, this is a reflection of the emphasis in the report upon those areas where pathology was most manifest and where Mr. Fletcher was most troubled. These were the reasons for which he sought treatment. However, one could gather that intimacy was not highly developed in this patient's life and that it may still be restricted. There are indications that his attitude toward his wife and children did change in that he became more willing to make money (and presumably love) available to them. However, there is no consistent analysis of his relationship with either his wife or children reported. In fact, although some of Mrs. Fletcher's positive qualities do come through in the nature of the information she was able to provide during the preanalytic consultation, there is little in the report of the analysis which conveys any picture of her or of the children as individuals. While it is a very difficult standard to impose upon a case report, one usually expects that in psychoanalysis the analyst derives a fairly good picture of the important objects in the patient's life. Naturally, this includes impressions of their emotional interaction. Of course, this is one of the most difficult qualities to convey in a written case report; part of the paucity of information might be a reflection of the method of reporting.

However, it is an area of the patient's life which could have been expected to come through at least somewhat more clearly.

There is also relatively little reported about the patient's sexual life. There is abundant evidence that sadomasochistic conflicts played a very important role in his sexuality. In spite of this his sexual relationship with his wife was said to be quite satisfactory even before the analysis. While Mr. Fletcher may very well have been free of physical symptoms in sexual performance, I would expect that with all of his emotional isolation and with his violent sexual fantasies that sexual functioning would show some restrictions. This is consistent with the impression that the more intimate areas of Mr. Fletcher's object relationships did not come in for full attention. It is my suspicion that Mr. Fletcher's recollection of the adolescent "assault" wherein his fellow campers held him down and painted his nipples with mercurochrome served as an unconscious organizer of fears which prevented him from more fully approaching sexuality in his analysis, lest, in retaliation, his fears might become fulfilled in the transference as his masochistic and passive feminine wishes were mobilized. The duck dream is strongly suggestive of this theme. Also consistent with it is the relatiive absence of positive oedipal sexual fantasies. Most of the work on the positive side of oedipal conflicts was related to competitive struggles with his father; very little is reported about the sexual side (at least the heterosexual) of this conflict, or of feelings for his mother.

Mr. Fletcher's religious beliefs are another area which did not receive much attention in the case report. Mr. Fletcher was not simply a devoutly religious man, he was, in addition, a member of what could be called the professional religious community. For people whose entire lives are so intimately involved with a structured organizational setting like the Army or Church, the organization can function as part of the psychic structure. In such cases the outside organization can be analogous to a kind of psychological exoskeleton for the individual. This can be most difficult to deal with in an analysis.

There are numerous references to religious connections with unconscious themes. Among these, for example, are the patient's identification with Luther and his magic anality and anal sadism and that patient's fantasy of being an omnipotent Pope or a magical religious leader. These suggest that Mr. Fletcher certainly used aspects of religion as part of his efforts to resolve his infantile conflicts. His religious beliefs were apparently ego syntonic, and may very well have represented a well established, stable and, at least in relation to other areas, relatively conflict-free aspect of the patient's self representation. The conflictual aspects which remained may have been, and probably were, reduced with the analysis of underlying conflicts, especially his sadomasochistic provocation and submission to authorities and his grandiose needs. I do not believe, nor am I suggesting, that a good analytic result would require that the patient abandon or modify, in major ways, his religious beliefs. I think that religious people can be analyzed and can remain religious (or conversely can change their beliefs) during analysis. However, in some respects the analysis of Mr. Fletcher's bonds with religious groups may have been incomplete. There was indeed good analytic work done on the patient's sadism, grandiosity, and masochism as it affected his functioning within the religious and professional spheres, and as a result, without question his functioning in these areas was favorably influenced. However, the close affiliation with religious groups retained by the patient was not explored. Am I saying that the patient should have left the sectarian field in order for the analysis to be considered more successful? Not at all, but I would be more comfortable if Mr. Fletcher's religious involvement had received greater scrutiny in the analysis.

Some patients are so dependent upon the outside affiliation for the maintenance of their psychic structure that exploration of this type is a risky undertaking. However, Mr. Fletcher seems to have had a stable personality organization and would not have been unduly stressed by such a direction in the analysis. There are times, however, in most analyses, where certain incompletenesses are accepted for reasons of economy. Analysis can be interminable and is costly in terms of time and money. There are many good analyses where the practical applications of effective analytic work limits the furtherance of that work. By that I mean that patients improve and new life opportunities arise for them as a result of their improvement. Sometimes this involves new jobs or other changes in their life situation and may even involve moves away from the city where the analysis is taking place. Sometimes there is a loss of motivation as the patient finds himself doing so well that his reasons for treatment are no longer as pressing.

Such situations must be distinguished in the analysis from flights into health or flights from treatment. However, they can be genuine expressions of growth. The analyst must recognize, like a good teacher, when enough is enough and when the patient can be expected to further his growth on his own. As long as the major conflict areas have been worked with effectively and as long as the patient shows indications that he can expand their application during the treatment, his continued growth after analysis can be anticipated. This case may well have been an example of such an outcome.

A DISCUSSION OF "THE ANALYSIS OF A RELIGIOUS MAN" BY IRWIN C. ROSEN

Edward D. Joseph, M.D.

I would like to start my discussion of this clinical case report by referring to the very end of it. A church colleague of the patient's is quoted as saying that the patient was leaving "just when we started to like the guy." That one phrase summed up the change that had occurred in this patient in the four years of analysis. He had started the analysis as a distant, aloof, unenthusiastic, procrastinating, ineffectual, and chronically depressed human being. In some way during the four years of analysis this individual was able to emerge from his cocoon and be transformed from a caterpillar to a butterfly. The makings of the butterfly must have been there, but the question that I wish to discuss is, what allowed for the emergence of this potential that had previously been hidden? What was it the analysis accomplished, and how was it accomplished in such a relatively short time so as to transform this individual?

This analysis, like most analyses, was begun with a therapeutic intent on the part of both analysand and analyst. The goal is to gain benefit and relief of disabling symptoms whether these be direct symptoms, or the characterologic manifestations such as this patient displayed. There is presumedly enough distress and discomfort on the part of the analysand that he is willing to undertake a lengthy, time-consuming, expensive therapeutic procedure that he hopes will give him some surcease from his misery. There is the anticipation on the part of the analyst, based upon his theoretical knowledge and clinical experience, that the psychoanalytic procedure will enable him to understand enough of the unconscious conflicts, however these may be expressed, to gradually bring to the patient's attention something of the nature of these unconscious processes. By these means, the analyst expects to be able to alleviate the misery or discomfort the patient experiences. Thus both analysand and analyst have the same therapeutic goal but the analyst knows in advance that the achievement of this goal will involve not only transference manifestations of varying natures, but also a number of resistances and barriers that will stand in the way of readily achieving the goals of the analysis. The analysand does not understand this and rather anticipates that the analyst will, perhaps magically, provide the missing ingredients that will rapidly enable him to achieve his therapeutic aim. It often takes the analysand quite a while to realize that the goal of understanding his own mental processes involves a laborious process and that while both parties are working in the same direction, the analysand often works at cross-purposes, seemingly, to the goals of the analyst.

The goals of the analyst are to help the patient gain insight into his unconscious conflicts, both current and those derived from the past, which play a part in producing the symptoms and character structure that the patient brings to the analytic situation. The gaining of insight by the analysand is a long process requiring the piecing together of bits of evidence from current life, fantasy life as best revealed, dreams and their associations, the defensive maneuvers manifested during the analytic session and most of all, the transference evidence as these manifest themselves or fail to manifest themselves, as the analysis progresses. Moments of insight that occur may often be lost only to reappear later in the course of the analysis, often with further additions made to them so that they become deepened and more encompassing. Insight requires the conscious awareness of unconscious mental content, some of which may never have been conscious before and much of which may well have been warded off and defended against in a variety of ways (Joseph, 1984a). The establishment of these new connections or the reestablishment of old connections that had been broken off for whatever reason, allows the ego's intergrative function to work more effectively in the restructuring of psychic systems.

The achievement of insight in the course of an analysis is not a one time instance. It is usually not a flash of light which once it occurs illuminates everything that has gone before and follows after. Unlike the dramatic version portrayed in drama, television, or Hollywood films, insight in the analytic situation is usually the product of much working through of defenses, of transference manifestations and interpretations, of various behavioral acts occurring both within and outside the analysis, and the slow piecing together of various bits and fragments of both historical and individual history or reality (see Spence [1982] for a discussion of narrative truth versus historical truth). Most of all, what clearly emerges from almost every ongoing psychoanalysis, and this one describes it so well, is that the achievement of insight is an ongoing, continuous process throughout the analysis, with varying bits of insight being achieved at different moments as part of the ongoing psychoanalytic process itself rather than a sudden revelation to either patient or analyst. The insight gathering and achieving situation, while illuminating, comes at the end of periods of intense analytic work and involves both cognitive and affective components dovetailing together for effective insight to be achieved.

In the protocol of this patient, such insight was shown, for example, when in association to the dream of being at a graduation breakfast his thoughts led to a description of one of his children:

> [G]reedily gulping down food, gorging himself and breaking a milk pitcher. . . . [After further associations] he said, "again I could never have gotten away with such behavior." He laughed when I said, "even if you had wanted to." His insight then followed that in his dream he was indeed acting like his young son or more probably as he wished he himself could have acted in his own childhood [p. 143].

The patient had provided his own insight and his laughter in response to the analyst's interpretation. This seemed to have served as a sign of recognition of the validity of the interpretation and of the emotional connection and identification with the young son, together with the memory of a wish from his own childhood.

The important point of this insight was that it came, not at a given moment out of the blue, but followed at least a year and a half or more of ongoing work requiring much analysis of Mr. Fletcher's rigid defenses of isolation and intellectualization, and the working through of other components of what are described as his "phallic–oedipal concerns." Also, as an indication of the important role of this insight, it opened the way to a widening inclusion of aspects of his greed for gratifications at an oral level in his present-day life as well as the reconstruction of an early period of such a gratification in his own early life—a reconstruction of a probable bit of historical reality. It is of interest that this reconstruction could be confirmed by his appeal to the memory of relatives, thus providing a degree of outside validation of the analytic reconstruction.

Having cited this example, it seems to me that much of the work in the various phases of the analysis as detailed in the protocol was productive of insights similar to the example just described. These insights were not dramatic in and of themselves, but were important for the analysand in bringing together various aspects of his current behavior and concerns with portions of his unconscious life, both in terms of reality and fantasy, in ways which made sense out of them. While this sense may not have been that of pure logic, it was consistent with his experiences and with his fantasies, fears, anxieties, and most particularly, his needs to protect himself from anticipated dangers.

Striking in the section of the protocol given in detail is the analysand himself presenting insights into his own behavior through his associations. These bespeak of his understanding himself and of his making connections between his own thoughts, feelings, and behaviors which he apparently had not made before. While we are not given details of his associations in the early part of the analysis, from the description given, his associations of this later phase of the analysis seem quite different. They seem to be meaningful to the patient and significant to him, being both cognitive and affect-laden. From the description given by the analyst, his associations early in the analysis were distant, intellectual, and isolated from himself. These associations at this point are far different, bespeaking of the successful working through of at least some of his defensive, isolating intellectualizations.

Thus it would appear, from the content of these sessions, in contrast to those much earlier in the analysis, that the psychoanalytic work with Mr. Fletcher's defensive structures had been successful, allowing for him to make connections between previously unconnected portions of unconscious mentation, affect, and other aspects of his mental life. These new connections made at a more conscious level and in a way which was meaningful and affectively experienced by him consciously, allowed for a degree of restructuring and modification of ego structures which previously had been rigidly maintained, particularly in regard to his relationship with objects. It is notable that this particular segment of the analysis ended with a marked modification of his behavior at church, in his relationship to his work and to the congregation, an area of his life that had been previously fraught with many difficulties.

Needless to say, during this period of insight gain, the transference played an important role, and much of Mr. Fletcher's behavior, fantasies, and other activities took place within the framework of transference manifestations. While this is commonplace in the course of an ongoing analysis, it does require explanation. The explanation has many aspects, only one of which, in relation to insight production, will I touch upon in this context. From early on in his writings on neuro sogenesis, Freud had emphasized the importance of early traumata, fixation points, and fantasies serving as the focus of unconscious conflicts which continue to be operative and to have their effect in later life. It was to the undoing and uncovering of defenses against these unconscious conflicts and the making of the conflict conscious that Freud attributed the therapeutic benefit of psychoanalysis and his claim that insight formation was the therapeutic avenue for such improvement. However, the problem is and was that of providing a sense of reality, a sense of conviction, about the nature of such unconscious conflicts so that their restoration or reconstruction would be more than an intellectual exercise for patients, but would rather be a meaningful experience. As knowledge about the nature of transference and transference manifestations became more and more evident, it became clear that what was lived out via the transference was a new and current edition of early relationships with their accompanying feelings, fantasies, disappointments, and potential traumatizations. Thus the early memories would be recovered through the transference and acquire a current reality in relationship to the analyst in a variety of forms of transference phenomena. Within the psychoanalytic situation, the transference in its myriad forms could then be understood and interpreted not only in terms of the present—the here and now—but also in relationship to its genetic origins in ways that would give it life and currency, bringing both affective and cognitive insight and validity to the patient. This certainly seems to have been what happened to this particular patient at this particular point in time in regard to the detailed examples.

It seems to me that there is another aspect of the work with this patient that accounts for the therapeutic gain achieved by him. I am referring to the organization of this individual's fantasy life, and I have in mind the concept delineated by Arlow (1961) in which he spoke of the hierarchy of fantasy life "which reflects the vicissitudes of individual experience as well as the influence of psychic differentiation and ego development" (p. 377). I elaborated on this concept (1984b), to suggest that the same conflicts would produce successive fantasy formations as the ego apparatus matures in its ability to develop functions and be adaptive. I added: "each of these [fantasies] would play its role in later structure formation within the maturing ego apparatus and, through a feedback mechanism, would influence and be influenced by each other" (p. 213). In that same paper it was suggested that it is possible, through the work of a thoroughgoing psychoanalysis, to enter into the various layers of these fantasy formations and gradually uncover the different levels of fantasy formation, proceeding either forward or backward in time, depending upon the point at which the analytic situation entered into the inner life of the analysand.

Looking at it from this point of view, successive levels of fantasy formation dealing with the patient's dependency needs and feelings of abandonment and weakness (impotence) were uncovered in various phases of the analysis. Needless to say it was not only the fantasy per se which had its impact, but also the range of defenses and struggles against the fantasy that were also worked out. Thus, although his active sexual life with his wife was a happy and successful one throughout the analysis, it was accompanied by a conscious fantasy which, while serving many functions, among others, also defended against an unconscious fantasy of being disemboweled and emptied out "like a chicken." The fantasy formation uncovered in the later phases of the analysis of his possessing an all-curing and all-powerful phallus was restorative and restitutive as well as protective against the feelings of abandonment, weakness, and narcissistic insult occasioned by those feelings. Equally, the fantasy of himself as all-engulfing and all-devouring was guarded against by reaction formations which rigidly prohibited any gratification of such desires. Thus, he did not gain the narcissistic gratifications sought nor the replenishment and replacement of the feelings of weakness associated with the deprivations occasioned by his mother's illness or his disappointment in his paternal image.

However, it is not merely the uncovering of such layers of fantasy formation which enabled the therapeutic gain to be achieved. It is rather the psychoanalytic work carried out by the working through of resistances, particularly in regard to transference neurosis and transference manifestations, which allow for the emergence of the fantasy formations into consciousness and for the gradual alteration of ego and superego structures, making for therapeutic gains. The totality of the analytic work, manifested through the gaining of insight, through the uncovering of fantasy, achieves the desired effect. The therapeutic gain comes about not through any one single aspect or one single finding at a given moment. Unlike the early cases that Freud described with Breuer, the removal of symptoms through the "lifting of repression" does not come about dramatically, but rather comes about slowly and gradually through the cumulative effect of the totality of the psychoanalytic process.

There is suggested in the protocol, although not clearly enunciated, that still another factor contributed to the ultimate therapeutic benefit achieved. This individual's early life was not as deprived of good caretaking individuals as his initial presentation suggested. Rather, it seems probable that the mother was a reasonable caretaker until her illness when he was about two-and-a-half and that the father, in spite of Mr. Fletcher's disappointment in him, was equally concerned about the patient and the family. In fact it is in regard to the latter that there are suggested issues, not clearly spelled out in the protocol, although there were indications these played an important role. The father was an admired figure until eventually came a disappointment when the father, according to the patient's account of things, went overboard and made a miscalculation, losing money on a shell game. We do not know from the protocol to what extent this was looked into, but it is not hard to imagine that his disillusionment with the father, who had been previously admired and idealized, is represented in this screen memory as father's losing the gamble with life, changing his goal direction from teaching to a business career.

Yet it is striking that the patient seemed to proceed in the opposite direction to the father by trying various ventures before ending up in a progressive counseling career, as though he were intending to reverse father's footsteps and yet was afraid to be too successful and outstrip the father in "the shell game of life." How much of this aspect of the oedipal relationship was actually worked out in the analysis is not clear from the case report, which after all could not possibly include all the details of a lengthy analysis, yet is suggested by the clinical material.

Therefore it seems that a further therapeutic benefit was achieved by the working through, more successfully at this point, of the patient's oedipal rivalry, no doubt achieved through the transference, and through his pride at sireing another child. This latter, which is described in the protocol along with his pride in the achievement, as well as his fears about it, suggests his ability finally to move beyond the level of his father and a willingness to outstrip him both in terms of procreation as well as educational and vocational achievement. Lacking further details though from the protocol itself, it is not possible to know how much this contributed to the ultimate gains that he made from this psychoanalysis. It would seem, however, that this is another important component.

The patient gained a great deal from a relatively short analysis. It was a difficult analysis for him and for the analyst. The analyst could speak of some of his countertransference difficulties as he saw this patient with obvious abilities doing things that were, at best, self-destructive and seemingly self-defeating, and mocking of the therapeutic efforts of the analysis. One of the difficulties of conducting any analysis is that the insights of the analyst often outstrip those of the patient. The analyst is often aware that premature confrontation with such insights will increase the resistances on the part of the patient or be totally wasted. With a patient such as this where intellectualization was a principal defense, it would have been anticipated that any premature confrontation in a desire to ward off the untoward effects of self-defeating behavior, would have fallen into the trap of his intellectualizing defenses and merely increased his isolating resistance, prolonging the analysis or perhaps precluding a successful analysis. Obviously the analyst did not fall into this trap and a successful conclusion was reached.

REFERENCES

Arlow, J. (1961), Ego psychology and the study of mythology. *J. Amer. Psychoanal. Assn.*, 9:371–393.

Joseph, E. (1984a), Insight—Psychoanalytic perspectives. Brill Lecture. New York Psychoanalytic Society, November.

——— (1984b), Further comments on the therapeutic action of psychoanalysis. In: *Psychoanalysis: The Vital Issues, Vol. 2,* ed. G. Pollock & J. Gedo. New York: International Universities Press, pp. 205–225.

Spence, D. P. (1982), *Narrative Truth and Historical Truth: Meaning and Interpretation in Psychoanalysis.* New York: W. W. Norton.

4. THE ANALYSIS OF A NEUROTIC BOY

Introduction

Psychoanalytic methodology has been successfully and increasingly applied in the treatment of adolescents and children of all ages in the past few decades. The vivid fantasies of child patients readily confirm the validity of the concepts of oedipal and preoedipal development and infantile neurosis. There has been controversy about the intensity of transference phenomena in preadolescent children due to the availability of the parents and the children's dependence on them. The following selected verbatim report of the analysis of a latency age child by Dr. Colarusso provides the reader with a first-hand opportunity to examine many of the above issues.

Dr. Colarusso's patient was a latency age neurotic boy with symptoms of unhappiness, temper tantrums, and difficulty making friends. Following establishment of a working alliance with the parents, the boy was brought into engagement with the analytic process. A wide range of communication and play was used to complement the boy's remarkable verbal expressiveness. Early in analysis, Jim expressed the fear of the analyst getting angry with him for dirtying his walls, which was interpreted. He then became aggressive toward the analyst but defended it by the feeling of boredom and attempted to join the analyst rather than compete with him. The fear of aggression was interpreted. Jim then resorted to compulsive drawing. The interpretation of his anxiety paved the way toward the unfolding of oedipal themes in the transference when Jim attempted to beat the analyst by cheating at games. The interpretation of Jim's wish to be big resulted in fantasy plays with the analyst where he played king and general to the analyst playing slave and private. The analyst verbalized the subject's feeling of helplessness, anger, and fear. The appropriate interpretation resulted in the revelation of Jim's wish to castrate the analyst. The boy's fear of the analyst in the transference was related to the fear of the father. The interpretation of the above feelings resulted in a lessening of the fear of the father. The deepening of the positive relationship between Jim and his father occurred as a parallel to the increased positive transference. This in turn gave rise to the discussion of penises and erection. The possibly premature timing of interpretation of this material resulted in Jim's acting out by stealing a lighter. The discussion of masturbatory fantasies revealed Jim's bodily sensations, anal squeezing, curiosity about the parents' sexual life, and revelations of Jim's habitual huddling with the mother. The expression of sexual aspects of the positive oedipal fantasies continued with the revelation of the fantasy of sexual intimacy with the mother and retaliatory fear of castration. The inquiry by the analyst about Jim's interest in women doing things to him revealed a fantasy of being caught in quicksand and the dangers emanating from women, such as biting off the male's penis.

The fear of rattlesnakes, expressed in the evaluation phase, reentered analysis in the second year and the patient's associations revealed the connection between the phobia and fear of losing his penis in retaliation for his sexual interest in his mother. The discussion of this fantasy allowed the reconstruction of the rattlesnake phobia of the oedipal period. This later resulted in revealing a clear oedipal fantasy of sexual interest in the mother and the wish for the father to leave and be killed.

The termination phase of Jim's analysis is described in detail. The termination issue was initially introduced defensively by Jim and discussed periodically during the second year of analysis. A mutually agreed upon date was established three months before termination. The rationale for termination was the resolution of Jim's symptoms concomitant with the analytic work on his castration anxiety and construction of his oedipal phase. The positive feelings toward the analyst and the father became more readily apparent at the time of termination. A range of feelings and issues was expressed and worked through during this period including the expression of sadness.

Dr. Glenn describes the child's means of communication, including play, role-playing, story-telling, drawing, speech and dreams to complement the relatively limited use of free association. He comments on the seesawlike phenomenon of alternating between interpretation of defense and drive in Jim's analysis. Jim readily transferred to the analyst his feelings about his parents, both those originating in the present time as well as his repressed feelings toward the parents of yesteryear.

Dr. Glenn discusses the reconstruction of the rattlesnake phobia rooted in the original conflict of the oedipal period. He provides a discussion of the impact of the latency age child's limited cognitive ability and interest in the past on reconstruction phenomena. He states that the analytic process of Jim's treatment provides a clear example of interpretation of repression resulting in the surfacing of competitive feelings toward the father and sexual feelings toward the mother. The modification of the superego resulted in lowering of the guilt and the ability to experience a wide range of feelings. The impact on the therapeutic alliance of the gift giving to Jim by the analyst, analysis of negative and positive transference, and insight formation is discussed. A wide range of issues in meeting with the parents, ranging from the establishment of a working alliance and gaining information while avoiding the pitfalls of double transference and advice-giving, is described.

Dr. Glenn provides a clear discussion of the issues involved in termination, including resolution of Jim's symptoms, his sense of maturity, return to the developmental mainstream, and ability to control the upsurge of instinctual drives during preadolescence. Jim was initially in an unstable latency state with breakthrough of his prelatency fantasies, but at the end of analysis had moved to the preadolescent stage of development. Jim's feelings about termination in different phases were tactfully handled, a termination date was mutually agreed upon at the proper time, and a three-month termination phase was established. Jim's feelings of sadness and wishing to hold onto the analyst were interpreted. Dr. Glenn raises a question about handling the feelings of anger and worry in the termination phase and the adequacy of the analysis of Jim's need for narcissistic perfection.

Dr. Bernstein provides a broad discussion of indications and contraindications for child analysis, the child's ability to undertake analysis, and the parental ability to support analytic treatment. He describes the analyst's "benevolent neutrality" and the child's capacity to trust the analyst, primarily based on adequate parenting in early childhood. The analyst offers the child an object-related interest in contrast to the parental object relations which may be narcissistic or anaclitically based. The examination of the analytic process reveals that interpretation was the primary tool used to diminish defensiveness, clarify conflict, and reveal unconscious fantasies.

Dr. Bernstein questions that Jim, like many latency children, felt unhappy when entering analysis. Jim exhibited the latency age interest in the world outside. However, he had not initially achieved a stable latency state due to the breakthrough of oedipal and preoedipal conflicts resulting in primitive discharge mechanisms such as temper tantrums.

Dr. Bernstein feels it was proper for the analyst to refrain from the early interpretation of guilt and anxiety over anger which was rooted in Jim's conflict over anal play and messiness. In analyzing Jim's wish to be big, the analyst facilitated the emergence of the competitive feelings toward the father but may have inadvertently made it difficult for Jim to talk about his feelings of weakness and his passive homosexual wishes; the analyst assisted Jim to defend against such feelings. Jim's castrative wishes and fears toward the father, masturbatory fantasies, and positive oedipal feeling toward the parents were analyzed. Dr. Bernstein wonders if the lack of interpretation and analysis of Jim's passive homosexual wishes, commonly seen in early adolescent patients, may represent one area of incompleteness in Jim's analysis.

Dr. Bernstein questions the advisability of giving gifts to Jim as it may have blocked the expression of negative feelings and emphasized the real aspects of the relationship with the analyst thereby creating a barrier to the unfolding of transference phenomena.

Jim's case exhibits that analysis of masturbatory fantasies can play an important role in the analysis of children similar to its role in the analysis of adults. The transference reaction to the analyst was apparent and analyzed although the main cathexis, as it is commonly seen in latency age children, remained with the father and mother. Bernstein raises a question about the lack of reconstruction of forerunners of oedipal conflicts, particularly during the anal period, in light of the historical information about Jim's negativism and refusal to comply with toilet training in that period.

THE ANALYSIS OF A NEUROTIC BOY

Calvin Colarusso, M.D.

Jim was nine years, nine months old and in fourth grade when he began analysis. Handsome, outgoing, and strongly built, he lived with his parents, both of whom were in their thirties, and his younger brother and sister. Mother brought Jim for evaluation after discussions about him with her therapist. She and her husband were concerned about his general sense of unhappiness, temper tantrums, and difficulty in making friends. The evaluation consisted of: (1) a series of four interviews with both parents during which details of the presenting problems, developmental history, and family background were obtained; (2) two diagnostic interviews with Jim; (3) psychological testing; (4) a summary conference with his parents during which the results of the evaluation and the recommendation for analysis were presented and discussed.

Jim's unhappiness, which began in the first grade and seemed to be self-generated, was expressed in concerns that his parents didn't understand or like him and preferred his brother. "He can't be satisfied or comforted," said his mother. His temper tantrums had been occurring since age two; they usually followed episodes in which Jim felt neglected or abused. For example, while Jim was talking on the phone someone in the family made a noise. He screamed, shouted, banged the table, and threw a book. On another occasion he threw himself on the floor and screamed. The difficulty with friends appeared to result from his attempts to control his relationships with other boys or a need to avoid them entirely.

A phobia was described by Jim but not by his parents. He had nightmares a few times a month and was concerned that rattlesnakes were in his bed. Jim knew they weren't really there, but wondered if the snakes might be invisible. His fears led to mild obsessional preoccupations that sometimes made it difficult for him to get to sleep.

DEVELOPMENTAL HISTORY

Jim was a planned child, the product of an uneventful pregnancy and delivery. During his infancy the mother–child relationship was close and constant. Mother felt that the problems precipitating her own analysis had little to do with Jim and did not interfere with her desire or ability to love and take care of him. "He was a good baby, healthy and calm. I particularly loved to feed him. He was so responsive at those times."

Jim was weaned from the bottle by eighteen months, except for a bedtime bottle until he was two-and-one-half years old. Bowel and bladder control were accomplished by age three. In all likelihood toilet training was accompanied by occasional outbursts of anger and frustration from both parents, generated by Jim's negativism and refusal to comply. Mother would back down and give in; father would become more rigid. In essence, their respective attitudes toward Jim's impulses continued throughout the oedipal phase, latency, and his analysis. There were no prolonged parent–child separations during his first three years of life. Jim became increasingly assertive, insisting on doing things his way. By age three he had developed a strong sense of self.

Historical data from the oedipal phase, ages three to six, were difficult to obtain because of the striking amount of anxiety in both parents. However, they did recall that between four and six Jim feared that rattlesnakes were in the house. He asked many sexual questions which were usually answered in great detail. His parents observed him masturbating frequently. One day at dinner, his father casually told Jim to eat so he would grow big and strong. A few minutes later Jim showed Father his erection, saying it was growing big and strong too; Father responded by telling Jim to go to his room if he wanted to masturbate. During those years Jim clearly preferred his mother and particularly enjoying opportunities to crawl into bed with her or watch her dress. His parents maintained an "open door policy," with free access to the parental bedroom and bathroom.

In school Jim was moderately successful academically but had mild difficulty sitting still and finishing his work. He did not keep friends very long because of his demanding ways and immaturity.

Both parents were bright, successful individuals. Raised in intact families, they remembered their childhoods with mixtures of pleasure and regret. Both demonstrated neurotic symptomatology: considerable anxiety in mother; shyness and inhibition in father.

DIAGNOSTIC INTERVIEWS

Jim's parents were encouraged to tell him why he was being brought to see the analyst and to be prepared to answer any questions he might have about the analyst, the office setting, and the length of the interview. It was suggested that he be told several days in advance of the interview to allow time for him to consider the idea and form his questions and concerns. Father would bring Jim to the interview; he was asked to make the introduction and then to wait for Jim in the waiting room.

After the introduction Jim bounded into the office and sat on the couch. Obviously nervous, he paused a moment to take in the surroundings before beginning. "I wanted to see if you were like the psychiatrists on TV. You're not; you're not bald and fat." The analyst was struck by the anxiety, openness, and desire to relate in this bright, engaging child. Without prompting Jim began to talk of his worries. Father had encouraged him to do that. He had known what psychiatrists do anyway and he agreed with his parents that he was unhappy. When the analyst asked about the reasons for his unhappiness Jim replied that his parents favored his younger brother. He was blamed for things his brother did. The intensity of Jim's feelings and his excellent verbal abilities were increasingly obvious. Later, after complaining that his parents didn't pay enough attention to him, Jim looked straight at the analyst, his eyes almost pleading for understanding and acceptance, and said: "I don't think adults understand how kids think." Here was a child in considerable pain, eager for understanding and help. When asked about other worries, Jim replied that he couldn't get people to do what he wanted them to do. That morning his brother and a friend had messed up his bedroom. He yelled to his mother to come and help. All she did was yell at him for yelling. As Jim talked, his considerable problems in peer relationships became obvious.

"Can you tell me about your dreams?" asked the analyst.

"Well, I don't have many anymore," replied Jim. "But I worry about going to bed. I saw a movie about snakes and now I'm afraid there are rattlesnakes in my bed." He explained how he lifted the covers before getting into bed to be sure that it was safe. "Maybe somebody sneaks in my room and sprays the snakes with invisible spray. I sleep with my legs up just to be sure." The analyst was impressed by Jim's readiness to reveal his thoughts and by the revelation of the phobia, a symptom unrecognized by his parents.

Near the end of the interview the analyst explained the steps in the evaluation and the need for psychological testing. Jim readily agreed to go and eagerly accepted the invitation to return for a second diagnostic interview.

The second interview was much like the first. Jim seemed less anxious. He continued to express resentment at his parents and his brother, at anyone who did not do things his way. Noting the absence of any play, the analyst invited Jim into the playroom which adjoined the office. After surveying the toys, Jim decided to draw. Over the next twenty minutes he obsessively drew a monster. When asked to tell about the monster, he revealed this fantasy: "He lives alone. People don't like him. He goes out and gets food and comes back. Maybe he'll get a friend someday." The lonely monster was understood to represent Jim's feelings about himself—ugly and isolated.

Psychological testing provided the following information:

> In summary, this boy presents the picture of an anxiety neurosis, fueled by oedipal conflicts and a prominent sense of castratedness, but underlaid with conscious pregenital conflicts (oral-dependent and oral-aggressive), such that he typically experiences the call to appropriate competitiveness and sharing as a call to battle, with a resultant regression in adaptive and defensive (obsessional) ego functions and modes of object relatedness (he becomes increasingly infantile) as depressive feelings come to the fore.
>
> On the WISC his Verbal I.Q. was 118–125; Performance I.Q., 100–113; Total I.Q., 110–121. There was "a developing characterological preference for acting reasonably and rationally, and thinking things through before acting on them. . . . His depression seems related to guilt over his competitive–aggressive wishes."

Because his psychopathology was primarily neurotic, Jim was considered an excellent candidate for child analysis. The operating diagnosis was a psychoneurosis, anxiety type, with phobic and obsessional features. Pregenital components were represented by the temper tantrums and self-centeredness. Jim was bright, verbal, eager for help, and clearly aware of his problems and the suffering they caused. Equally important, his parents were stable, psychologically minded, and able to support the treatment.

During the summary conference with his parents the nature of Jim's psychopathology and the recommendation for child analysis were presented and explained. They were encouraged to consider the matter seriously and to feel free to ask any questions. Four days later they called, announcing their decision to begin the analysis.

Jim was seen four times a week. Parental conferences were held weekly during the opening phase and approximately twice a month thereafter. Both parents provided excellent support throughout the analysis, bringing Jim regularly for sessions, observing his behavior, and considering their own interactions with him.

COURSE OF THE ANALYSIS

The remainder of the case presentation consists of descriptions of the unfolding of the analytic material, illustrated by selected clinical vignettes, and the thinking of the analyst as he conceptualized the material, formulated interpretations, interacted with the boy, and considered the effects of his interventions. The intention has been to focus on the neurotic process, as illustrated by the gradual emergence of oedipal themes and oedipal transference. A separate discussion is not included since the case report will be accompanied by two formal discussions.

During the initial sessions Jim acted like a young adult. He sat politely and talked, albeit quite seriously and openly. An exchange in the sixth analytic session illustrates this characteristic.

Session 6

Jim: I was playing baseball with my father yesterday. I almost broke a window and he yelled at me. I asked him why he yelled at me and he told me to be quiet so I quit and went to my room. Then I heard him playing ball with my brother so I went out and got my ball.

A: What did your father do?

Jim: (feeling indignant) Nothing, it was my ball.

A: How did you feel at the time?

Jim: (with animated anger) Like a dog, like a slave. I felt ordered around when he yelled at me so I wanted him to feel the same way. My mother feels that way sometimes, she knows how I felt. . . .

Such animated conversation did not continue very long. The sessions became largely silent when Jim began to spend his time meticulously filling in page after page of an elaborate coloring book that he brought with him. After ten to twelve sessions of such activity, the analyst decided to approach the resistance by encouraging Jim to play. Jim was invited to the playroom and told that it might be helpful and fun as well if he spent some of his time playing. This early technical intervention was based on the assumption that play is a childhood equivalent to free association, a necessary form of expression for a latency age child, even a verbal one like Jim, because language is not yet developed enough to convey the full richness of the intrapsychic world. Although tempered by the rapid expansion of verbal abilities during latency, motoric discharge, particularly through play, remains an important, phase-appropriate mechanism for expressing thoughts and feelings. The intervention was also meant to promote the working alliance, and to educate Jim about his own role in the analysis. It was the analyst's feeling that an interpretation too early in the analysis of Jim's inhibition about playing would be experienced as an attack.

Thus encouraged, Jim began to build lincoln log houses—and to destroy them—with obvious concern about the analyst's reaction. The following material illustrates the unfolding of this theme.

ATTACK ON THE ANALYST–FATHER: THE POSITIVE OEDIPUS

Session 24

Jim decided to build a lincoln log house and then to knock it down.

A: You seem uncertain about whether it's okay to knock the house down.
Jim: Yeah. My parents would get mad if I did it at home because I might mark the walls.
A: I thought so. It's okay to play like that here. I understand that boys play like that, and it may help us understand your worries. I know you think a lot when you play; you can tell me about it.
Jim: Sometimes I put people I hate on the bad side.

He knocked down the house, leaving plenty of time to clean up his "mess" at the end of the session.

Session 25

Jim: I'm building the Empire State Building. I was there last year. Then I'm going to bomb it.
A: (inquiring into the fantasy) Who's inside?
Jim: No one, a siren warns them.

Jim used "superbombs" to destroy the building. In the process a small lincoln log hit the wall. Jim looked at the analyst apprehensively, consciously fearing that the analyst would be angry at him for marking the wall. The analyst understood this play as a vehicle for the expression of the boy's aggression. By verbalizing Jim's fear the analyst hoped to demonstrate his acceptance of Jim's feelings and pave the way for further elaboration of the fantasies involved in his play.

A: You look worried; do you think I'm angry?
Jim: No, I just don't understand why you let me play like this when my parents don't.
A: What do you think?
Jim: Maybe you see children every day and they don't.
A: They see you and your brother.
Jim: (uncertain) Yeah. Maybe you do understand more about children.

The superbombs were thrown with increased abandon after this exchange.

Gradually, stimulated by the acceptance of Jim's aggression by the analyst, the play became more defined, and transference themes began to emerge. Jim began to attack first the "Japs," who were fighting the Americans, and later the analyst as well.

Session 35

Jim: Today it's going to be my soldiers against yours.

As the opposing forts were built Jim mentioned that he had built a fort at home. His mother had not objected. When the forts were built Jim changed his mind and decided that he and the analyst would be brother and sister rather than opponents. He began to bomb the fort which had become their house. For the time being, the analyst did not question the deflection of aggression from himself. As the bombing began, with the mother and father dolls serving as bombs, the brother and sister were suddenly inside the house.

A: Okay, what shall we do brother, I'm scared.
Jim: Just be calm. We'll be all right.

The house was destroyed with enormous power and abandon, but at the end brother and sister were pulled from the rubble, miraculously unharmed.

Session 37

Two sessions later the play became increasingly violent. All of the bombs were dropped at once on the helpless Japanese. Immediately afterward Jim said: "I'm bored, help me draw a car." The analyst decided to begin to approach the patient's conflict over his aggression.

> *A:* Gee Jim, what happened, first you were involved in the war and suddenly you say you're bored. You sure didn't seem bored.
> *Jim:* Well, I was.
> *A:* Maybe, but maybe something else happened. I wonder if you became nervous about how open you were about bombing the houses like that. Like you thought you were too tough. Maybe you were worried about what I would think of you for acting like that.
> *Jim:* No.
> *A:* Didn't the same thing happen last week? First you were going to fight against me and then suddenly we were brother and sister on the same side. I think you must have had similar feelings then and changed the sides because of them.

Jim denied the interpretation but he had obviously heard it. He began to draw and talk about his fear of doing poorly on some upcoming tests in school.

After a return to compulsive coloring and drawing, which was interpreted as a resistance, Jim began to bring a deck of cards to the sessions and invited the analyst to play with him. The analyst agreed. Here was a competitive situation, chosen by the patient, that could lead to a further understanding of Jim's conflicts. As with all play, the analyst made no attempt to determine its form or structure. Jim chose the game, defined the rules, and adhered to them or broke them as he wished.

Like the lincoln log wars, the card games gradually began to allow the emergence of aggression and castration themes through a developing transference. At first Jim scrupulously followed the rules that he himself proposed; then he began to cheat occasionally. His pleasure in beating the analyst and neurotic responses to winning became more apparent and were eventually interpreted. The development of these themes is contained in the following clinical material.

Session 81

Jim: We're going to play cards all day today. I have to leave three minutes early for soccer practice. Is that okay?
A: Sure.

Jim won each game, becoming more excited—and anxious—as his cheating became more blatant. Finally he made up a game called "14-card stud." As the analyst dealt him card after card, on his command, he rejected the low ones, throwing each across the room, insuring that he won with five aces each time. He laughed wildly as he compared the analyst's hand, always a losing one, with his own.

The analyst understood this play as a transferential vehicle for expressing positive oedipal impulses and wishes for power and control, originally directed toward the father. Not surprisingly, a mild anal regression followed this attack. Jim announced that from now on this game would be called "stud-a-roo-poo-poo." Despite his involvement in the session, he did not forget to leave early for soccer practice.

Session 82

Jim repeatedly referred to the analyst as "my friend." He was sincere about the statement, enjoying the relationship and the newfound freedom of expression for his impulses in the play.

During a card game he asked, "Do you know I'm cheating?"

A: Yes (accepting and inquiring). Why do you think you're doing it?
Jim: I don't know why, do you?
A: I thought you wanted to beat me a lot.
Jim: (with a huge smile) You're right!

In the card games that followed Jim continued to cheat and to win. He was still anxious, but less so.

Session 83

Jim seemed depressed and listless. He again played cards, cheated, and won, inquiring if the analyst knew what he was doing.

The depression and listlessness were considered to be the result of a punitive superego response to the acknowledgment by both patient and analyst of his cheating. The analyst decided to interpret this aspect of the transference because by now Jim's wish to dominate and control the analyst–father had been demonstrated in many sessions and he was likely to be receptive to the interpretation because he was in pain and had asked the analyst for help in understanding his feelings.

Session 85

Jim began the session by playing cards.

A: I notice you're not making up rules as you go along today.
Jim: Yeah, I decided not to.
A: Oh, how come?
Jim: I don't know.
A: I think I understand why. Remember how sad you seemed after I told you that I knew you were cheating? (Jim nods his head in agreement.) My knowing seemed to ruin what you were trying to tell me through the card games. (He nods again.) Let's see if we can figure it out. Maybe you were telling me by beating me how much you enjoy feeling big and strong like your father and me.
Jim: (emphatically) I was.
A: I also thought that you felt that big people, particularly your parents, didn't want you to be big and strong.
Jim: (with certainty) They don't want me to be big and strong because they don't want me to order them around.
A: Why would they think that?
Jim: I don't know, why?
A: I guess you feel that's what you would like to do.

After this interpretation of his wishes to dominate and control, Jim withdrew from the discussion briefly. Then he seemed attentive again. The analyst decided to continue.

A: There was another idea I wanted to tell you. When I went along with your cheating I was trying to understand how you felt, and I did, but I guess you feel that I was playing a trick on you (he nodded) and since I figured out what you were doing that I was smarter than you. You felt little and dumb. (He nodded again in firm agreement.) Do you remember what you did next?

Jim: (curious) No.

A: You played solitaire, as if you were saying to yourself and to me, I can't win no matter what I do, I might as well go off by myself.

Jim then became more animated and played a game of cards, honestly, which he tried very hard to win. He did and was very happy. The analyst felt that Jim's response was evidence that the interpretation had been understood and accepted. Then Jim played blackjack, acting as the dealer. After losing a few times he became very dejected, slapped the floor and began to play solitaire.

A: I think the same thing just happened again. You tried so hard to win. When you lost a few times you felt weak and withdrew.

Jim nodded and decided we should play a game with both of us on the same side. As we began to do well Jim said, "You don't have to be very smart to win at solitaire."

Session 86

Jim won a number of poker games honestly.

A: You're winning without cheating. It seems to make you feel good.

Jim: (pleased that the analyst noticed) Yeah.

A: In some ways, like playing cards, you can be as good as adults.

Jim: Do I seem sad today?

A: No.

Jim: Our talk yesterday made me feel better.

A: Good, but I still don't understand one point, your idea that your parents wouldn't want you to get big and strong.

Jim: Well they don't. Why should they? They don't want me to boss them around.

A: I see, they wouldn't because you would like to boss them around.

The first time that interpretation was made in session 85 it had met with resistance, but Jim readily acknowledged his wish this time.

Jim: It's true, I would.

He then proceeded to another game of cards in which he obviously cheated. He feigned horror and laughed, in essence saying that what he was doing was obvious.

> *A:* Now we *both* know what's going on and we can laugh about it.
> *Jim:* Yeah.

He decided to have us play solitaire together.

> *A:* We're going to combine our power.

The patient–analyst team lost the first two games. Jim was disappointed. Then they won. With a rush of pride and shared masculine power, basking in the warmth of identification with the analyst–father Jim proclaimed, "That's the first time I ever won at solitaire."

Six months into the analysis the therapeutic alliance was developing nicely. Jim was overheard by mother extolling the virtues of analysis to his best friend, saying "Analysis is good for you, it's fun, and it helps with your problems." He had become less demanding with his friends and had fewer temper tantrums. The material thus far had confirmed the initial diagnosis of a psychoneurosis as evidenced in the transference by the pervasive and growing presence of positive oedipal impulses (wishes to control and dominate the analyst–father) and by the ever-present defenses against them. With the expectation of continued parental support, the analyst was optimistic that he and the patient would be able to explore other facets of the neurosis.

THE EMERGENCE OF CASTRATION WISHES AND FEARS

About 100 hours into the analysis, Jim introduced new play situations in which he was the master or general and the analyst was a slave or a private. If the slave or private manifested the slightest deviation from the impossible standards set by the master or general, "punishment" was forthcoming, and it eventually included beheading and cutting off all appendages.

In dynamic terms the analysis of Jim's competitive, controlling wishes (and the expectation of retaliation) during the first six months of treatment allowed wishes to castrate the analyst–father (and again the expectation of similar retaliation) to be expressed. This phase of the analysis is illustrated by the following clinical material.

Session 102

> *Jim:* I'm the king and you're my subject.
> *A:* What is your decree, oh king?
> *Jim:* First, no more double solitaire. Clap, you should be glad. (Analyst claps.) Second, all psychiatrists will be killed.
> *A:* Oh, oh. What for, oh king?
> *Jim:* For making the people bankrupt. We'll set a trap and get all the psychiatrists in one place, then we'll cut off their heads.

Session 107

In this session, within the framework of the play, the analyst tried to verbalize another aspect of the boy's neurosis, his feelings of passivity and weakness. By assuming the role of the subject and expressing the subject's feelings of helplessness, fear, and rage, the analyst hoped to draw attention to Jim's similar, strongly defended feelings. This conclusion grew out of the observation that Jim always assumed the dominant role in his play (identification with the aggressor) and studiously avoided any role that caused him to feel weak and passive.

Jim, as the king, scattered cards about the room and ordered the analyst, as a subject, to pick them up quickly. He set a time limit and counted faster and faster. The subject could not succeed within the time limit.

> *A:* Oh king, I feel so weak, I can't seem to succeed, but I'll try harder.

Later, as the game continued,

> *A:* I wish I could tell you how angry I am, oh King, at what you

do to me but I am afraid. You are so big and powerful. What will you do to me if I speak my mind?

Jim: Nothing, speak.

A: I don't like. . . .

Jim: (interrupting) You're fired!

But the subject did express his feelings of anger and helplessness and the king listened, seriously considering what the subject said.

Jim: Do you mind playing the subject?

Jim's question conveyed his willingness to address these feelings.

A: No, I think it helps me understand you. But I don't like to feel what the subject feels. I think everyone does at one time or another. Didn't you feel like that when your parents wouldn't let you buy the tape recorder right away?

Jim: Yeah, I did.

A: Sure, nobody likes to feel like that. Those feelings hurt.

Session 114

The theme of Jim's aggression toward the analyst and expected retaliation from the analyst was played out with a new variation when he brought a Polish/Italian joke book to the session. After reading to himself, while closely watching the analyst's face for a reaction, Jim began to read the Polish jokes. Since Jim knew that the analyst was of Italian ancestry the analyst assumed that he chose to read the Polish jokes first to test for a negative response. After reading a few jokes he asked if the analyst were Polish.

A: You seem very worried that I might be.

Jim: Yes, if you are you won't like the jokes and will get angry at me.

A: What do you think I would do?

Jim: (anxious) I don't know. What are you anyway? I want you to tell me now.

A: I think you knew that my ancestors were from Italy. Do you remember when you mentioned it early in the analysis?

Jim: (straining to remember) No. Here, you read the Italian jokes. (As the analyst read Jim commented that the analyst wasn't smiling.)

A: What do you make of it? (A look of exquisite fear crossed Jim's face.)
Jim: You don't like them.
A: Now we can see how afraid you get of me when you feel you've attacked me. I hope we can understand more about that fear so you can be more comfortable with your feelings and with me.

Session 116

Working through continued when Jim returned to playing general to the analyst's private. The general ordered the private about. Later the private became a Japanese soldier attacked by the general. For the first time, in the play, the analyst was killed. Jim provided the scenario wherein the analyst was shot, hung, drowned, and eventually buried in a small grave. Jim enjoyed his play and was not anxious during it.

A: What do you make of this general–private play?
Jim: I knew all along. The general is my father and the private is me. The general orders the private around.
A: But the private doesn't like it, he says so and he stands up for his rights.
Jim: Yeah, but he has to obey or be killed.
A: Yeah, but he wasn't afraid like before and he understood how both the general and the private felt.
Jim: Yeah. I sure feel better, too. I understand more.

Session 124

After sentencing the private (analyst) to the guillotine for disobedience, the general (Jim) systematically "cut off everything"—arms, legs, fingers, toes, chin, nose, head, mouth, and ears. He gently used a book as his weapon and never actually touched the analyst's body. He was only mildly anxious and he obviously relaxed when the analyst went along with the play.

Later in the session Jim related the transferential play directly to his father and himself.

Jim: (on the phone to the commander of the police) I have a *son* killer here.

After discussing the play in relation to Jim's father and himself the analyst again interpreted his fear of his father, the expectation that his father would hurt him for his assertive thoughts and behavior.

Jim interrupted to say he *used* to be afraid of that, but not anymore.

Session 125

Jim repeated the guillotine play, symbolically cutting off everything on the analyst's body except his penis. The exception was so obvious that the analyst chose to speak directly about the genital. This was the first time in the analysis that the word had been used.

> *A:* I think I understand something about this play. You and I are both males so we know about the male body. Right?
> *Jim:* Yeah.
> *A:* Well, did you notice that you cut off every part of my body but one, which you seemed to be thinking about but avoiding. (Jim broke into an embarrassed smile which indicated to the analyst that his assumption that Jim was thinking about the analyst's penis was correct.) Did you notice that?
> *Jim:* Yeah.
> *A:* What part was it?
> *Jim:* Your penis.
> *A:* Right.

Jim began to make paper airplanes, obviously interrupting the conversation. After several minutes the analyst continued.

> *A:* You've become good at analysis, what do you think is happening?
> *Jim:* (continuing to fly his paper airplanes) I guess I'm avoiding my feelings.
> *A:* Seems that way.
> *Jim:* I was surprised when you mentioned it. It was like you knew more about my thoughts than I realized.
> *A:* That sounds like you had realized and were thinking at the time that you had cut off everything but my penis.
> *Jim:* I was but I didn't know how you would act.
> *A:* It sounds like you're still learning that in analysis we really can talk about any thought, including the private ones that you have about penises. You know all men and boys have special feelings about their penises, you're not any different; but usually those thoughts don't get talked about.

THE PENIS—PLEASURABLE, POWERFUL, AND DANGEROUS

Through a series of derivative productions centering around the movie *The Towering Inferno,* and comic book figures called the Fantastic Four (Plastic Man, The Flame, The Thing, and Spider Man), Jim's feelings about the penis as a hot, expandable, powerful, but dangerous part of the body were brought into the analysis and eventually interpreted. The analyst hypothesized that this material became part of the analysis at this time because of the analysis of Jim's castration wishes and fears. Talking about the penis became relatively safe.

But possibly not as "safe" as the analyst thought because during the course of these discussions Jim sheepishly confessed that he had stolen a cigarette lighter from a store. He had never stolen anything before, what should he do? The analyst understood this isolated episode of stealing as a reaction to the discussion of erections and sexual excitement which preceded it, probably precipitated by premature interpretation of this emerging masturbatory material. The analyst did not give Jim the advice he asked for but discussed his options instead—keep the lighter or return it—and explored the meaning of the episode. Some of the interchange is illustrated in Session 133.

Session 133

Jim: I decided to give the lighter to my mother.

A: I've been thinking more about the lighter. I'm sure you have too.

Jim: Yeah.

A: Do you remember what you asked me to read about yesterday?

Jim: The Towering Inferno movie. (Then it dawns on him.) About fire!

A: Yes, but even more than fire, a towering inferno.

Jim: Are you thinking that I'm saying something like the other day when I was talking about playing with matches and I thought you thought I wanted to light my penis on fire?

A: Not for real, but the idea does seem to be there of a boner (Jim introduced this expression for erection) being hot or on fire like a building or a match.

Jim: But it's not hot.

A: Isn't it hotter when its erect than when it isn't?

Jim turned away at this point and began to play. After a few minutes he reestablished eye contact.

> *A:* What else did you ask me to read about?
> *Jim:* The Fantastic Four (the comic book characters).
> *A:* Do you remember their names?
> *Jim:* Spider Man, The Thing, The Invisible Lady, and Plastic Man.
> *A:* Right, except for one.
> *Jim:* (surprised) Which one?
> *A:* You think about it.
> *Jim:* (struck by the connection) The Flame.
> *A:* Yes, a boy whose body becomes a ball of fire. Like a hot boner. And the others probably represent thoughts about the penis too. It has different shapes like Plastic Man, it stretches like Spider Man, and with a boner its hard and big like The Thing. Now maybe it's clearer what I meant the other day. Taking the lighter seemed to be your mind's way of trying to handle your sexual feelings about your penis, particularly when you have a boner. Bringing in the comic book and talking about *The Towering Inferno* were more of the same, ways of beginning to tell about these private thoughts.

Jim was quiet for the few minutes left in the session. He seemed to be processing and digesting what had been said.

In subsequent sessions Jim began to talk about boys stimulating their penises to make them erect. He knew his brother and his friends did this, but not Jim himself. "Boners are torture," he said, why would he want to produce one? Further, the penis could be injured. This was initially expressed when he came to a session with a fake nail through one of his fingers.

The acceptance of Jim's sexual feelings by the analyst led to further involvement with both the transference and Jim's real father. Jim was still fearful of his father and avoided him much of the time. However, he wanted a new skateboard badly enough to consider asking his father. The analyst helped the patient understand his fear of approaching his father. With help from the analyst, father began to understand the significance of his son's reaching out to him in a less frightened way. During the regularly scheduled parent conferences Jim's father frequently described the interactions between Jim and himself and often asked for assistance in understanding his feelings about Jim. Instead of advice, the analyst usually provided a developmental context within which to place Jim's behavior or requests. Such was the case in regard to Jim's request for a skateboard. Father eventually decided to help Jim build one rather than buy one.

In the transference the analyst was able to interpret to Jim that he had felt unable to approach his father or his analyst because he thought they would not accept him because of his wish to attack them. As they had learned from the play, his fear was connected with his sexual curiosity and his thoughts about his penis. Through reconstruction, these current fears and curiosities were related to similar ones when Jim was a little boy.

With the interpretation of these basic oedipal themes Jim's sexual curiosity flowered. Many hours were spent discussing the sexual relationship between men and women, conception, and birth. Infantile distortions were revealed, some related to the patient's castration anxiety; for example, "If a lady cuts her arm, will the baby be born without a penis?"

Eventually Jim returned to the subject of masturbation when he again described observing his brother's sexual play with friends. As before, Jim steadfastly denied that *he* had ever played with his penis. A two-week patient vacation followed. The first hour back, home less than three hours, Jim revealed that he had decided on the airplane to tell the analyst that he did touch his penis.

In a sense Jim's reaction to this vacation characterized his attitude toward separations throughout the analysis. There were no lengthy interruptions since Jim attended a year-round school and the analyst was not away for any extended periods. Jim had four three-week vacations spread throughout the year. The analysis continued through most of these since his parents were working during these intervals.

Jim never expressed any feelings of missing the analyst during separations. Consciously, he either seemed to forget about the analysis and enjoy the break (confirmed by his parents) or to continue the analytic work in a most concentrated way, as exemplified by the revelation of his masturbation following this vacation. He always seemed pleased to see the analyst upon his return but frequently complained about the intrusion into his free time.

Attempts to interpret the defensive aspects of such behavior were largely unsuccessful. The analyst understood this as partly defensive against preoedipal feelings of dependency and aggression but also the result of a deep sense of security in relationship to primary objects and continued gratifying interaction with them. Development during the preoedipal years was essentially smooth and positive, particularly in regard to the separation–individuation process. Clearly Jim had the ability to maintain mental representations of the analyst in his absence and a rather remarkable capacity to continue the analytic work on his own—when he chose to do so.

In following sessions Jim, now ten years, nine months of age, discussed his conflicted feelings about masturbation and without conscious awareness began to connect his masturbation to thoughts about his parents. The analyst understood this connection as a step toward the still unconscious masturbatory fantasies about the parents, particularly the sexual wishes for the mother. To this point in the analysis Jim had dealt with his oedipal competitiveness with his father but not his oedipal love for his mother.

Session 177

Jim: How long will I have to come here? I was thinking about that on the airplane. This keeps me away from play. I want to work faster to get finished. It's been slow in here lately.

A: We have been stuck a bit lately.

Jim: We've been talking about penises a long time. That's slow. Where did we get stuck?

A: Where do you think?

Jim: I don't know.

A: I think we got stuck when we talked about your brother and his friends touching their penises (material from the weeks preceding his vacation). Your brother seemed to enjoy his feelings and when your parents saw him touching his penis they didn't punish him.

Jim: That's true.

A: You seem to be troubled by those same feelings. One of our current problems is understanding why you struggle over these feelings. (Jim accepted this comment and began to work with it.)

Jim: I sorta get a boner sometimes from squeezing my rear end together after having a B.M. I guess it feels okay. It also happened when I had pinworms.

A: Do you ever get a boner at other times?

Jim: No.

A: I think that's part of the problem. Your mind hides from the feelings by blaming your erections on pinworms or B.M.s. What's missing is the idea that you might cause the erection yourself. (Jim is listening seriously.)

Jim: You think my mind forces me to think that way?

A: Yes, it's a way of denying that you can make erections just for pleasure.

Jim: I think I did know that. I just didn't want to tell you. I decided on the airplane to talk about it. Sometimes I get a boner when I'm in bed. If I squeeze it, it gets real hard.

Jim seemed visibly relieved. He went on to report that sometimes while watching TV he put his hands in his pajamas and "played" with his penis.

A: You really seem relieved at being able to tell me.

Jim: Yeah.

A: Well, you're saying that you're like other boys, not different.

Jim: I also do it sometimes when I'm in the bath tub. I flick my penis on top of the water. (Seriously but proudly) I really overcame my mind to tell you. I thought a lot on vacation about whether to tell you or not. (Pause) My dad is away. I asked my mother to have a party for him when he comes back. I want the cake to say "we're all together again."

Session 178

Jim invited the analyst to play gin rummy. He did not cheat. The card game was distinctly different, no longer the main vehicle of communication.

As the game progressed Jim talked about his thoughts on the plane ride home.

Jim: . . . if I tell him we'll get done faster but if I do he'll think I'm abnormal.

A: Why abnormal?

Jim: Because you would think I was the *only* boy who played with his penis.

A: I think you know that I don't think that. I know that boys do play with their penises. So the thought that it's abnormal to play with your penis must have come from inside your mind. Also, you knew all along that you weren't the only one. Rob (his friend) had told you about his erections and you saw your brother and his friend playing with their penises.

Jim: (letting these ideas sink in) I think we found another piece of the puzzle today.

Session 179

Jim's father had returned from a trip. Jim was very glad to see him. A new sense of warmth was evident, which the analyst related to the better real relationship that Jim and his father were developing and to the deepening positive transference.

In the session Jim described further the way in which he played with his penis by vigorously rubbing his head. "It tickles a whole lot." For the first time, pleasure was evident as he talked. Jim's associations turned to his father again. "I never saw my father with an erection but I guess he must have them like I do. You know, you never think of your parents like that." Toward the end of the session Jim revealed a new fantasy, laughing nervously as he did. "Maybe a ropelike thing goes up in the penis into the balls and pulls the sperm out."

HUDDLING WITH THE OEDIPAL MOTHER

These themes were coupled with feelings about "ladies," particularly Jim's mother. The woman was seen as powerful and castrating. Maybe there were wires or teeth in her "uterus" (meaning vagina) which would burn or cut off the man's penis. Through dreams and fantasies he began to approach the theme of his parents' sexual life as well as his own sexual interaction with mother. Jim later described this phase of the analysis as the most painful part for him.

According to Jim, when father went away on trips the two boys took turns sleeping with mother, at her invitation. "Come on, Jim, let's huddle," mother would say. This meant lying in bed together with arms around each other. This material was revealed with only the slightest embarrassment, indicating to the analyst that Jim did not recognize his own wishes to huddle, he was merely going along with mother's invitation. Through a series of dreams and free associations Jim began to approach the still unconscious and forbidden wish that his mother would touch his penis. It became clear why he had been so resistant to any idea that he masturbated like other boys.

Session 196

In previous sessions Jim had discussed a weekend vacation his parents took recently. Continuing a discussion of whether his parent's "mated" or not at the hotel, Jim first said they probably did, then denied it.

Jim: But they went with another couple, they probably slept in the same room.
A: (skeptically) You think so?
Jim: Yeah, I guess you're right. My mind is trying to avoid the idea of my mother and father mating.
A: When you do think of it what comes to your mind?
Jim: They probably hug and kiss when they mate. They love each other.
The analyst nodded in agreement.

Later in the session, in an attempt to reconstruct Jim's infantile wishes for sexual involvement with his mother, the analyst commented that it was difficult to think of his parents mating because he had been curious about it for a very long time, likely since as a little boy he first wondered about the sleeping arrangements.

Jim: I think that's a good idea.
A: What do you think you wanted the sleeping arrangements to be when you were a little boy?
Jim: For my parents to sleep together.
A: (accepting and questioning) I'm sure you had that thought. Any others?
Jim: For them to sleep in separate rooms?
A: Yeah, any other thoughts?
Jim: (with a smile, acknowledging that he had been witholding the obvious) I guess I wanted to sleep with my mother.
A: Yes. Boys first learn about hugging and kissing and loving from being taken care of as babies by their mothers.
Jim: Yeah, that's true but they don't know about mating.

The analyst sensed new ground was about to be broken, and indeed, the interchange allowed Jim to reveal the following sexual material about his relationship with his mother.

Jim: Sometimes my brother and I take turns huddling with my mom when my father goes away. We sleep with her and be close for warmth.

> *A:* I think you're a better analyst than that. Can you think of other possible reasons?
> *Jim:* No, it's for warmth, my body gets hot all over. (Jim smiled knowingly after using the word *hot*) I know what you mean, getting an erection. Well I don't. Anyway my father doesn't mind.
> *A:* Why should he?
> *Jim:* Well, if I was old enough to mate he might, but I'm not and he doesn't.

The session ended at that point, but the work continued in the next session.

Session 197

> *Jim:* My mother will say (imitating a sexy voice) "Come on Jim, keep me warm." (suddenly anxious) Would my mother be mad if she knew what I was telling you?
> *A:* Why do you think she would?
> *Jim:* Because I'm telling you about her private life. She wouldn't want anybody outside her family to know and I don't either. My friends would tease me. It's her sexual life, not mine.

The analyst decided to ignore for the moment Jim's denial of his own sexual involvement and interpret his projection.

> *A:* I think your worry about what your mother and your friends would think is really your mind's way of expressing your own concern.
> *Jim:* I guess you're right.

Session 198

Jim's birthday was approaching. He comfortably discussed his hope that the analyst would buy him some skateboard wheels, and the analyst agreed. This was not the first time that a special occasion had arisen in the analysis. The analyst chose to give the patient a gift on each of his birthdays and at Christmas time. On the first such occasion Jim asked if he would be receiving a gift and was told that he would. On subsequent occasions his wish for a certain gift was analyzed as was his response to receiving the gift. For instance, the wish for skateboard wheels was eventually related to Jim's fear of, identification with, and aggression toward his father. The rationale for giving gifts is based on the assumption that children (in most instances, through latency) expect those adults who are especially close to them to acknowledge important occasions in their lives. Not to do so is experienced as a rebuff that cannot be fully comprehended. Within the conceptual framework of the young child a gift is a sign of caring, an indication of a special relationship. By giving a gift the analyst furthers the therapeutic alliance. However, like all other aspects of that relationship, gift giving may be analyzed.

The discussion of huddling continued, leading to an elaboration of Jim's thoughts about his parents' sex life and intercourse in general, a subject first discussed twenty to thirty sessions before. Was the lady hurt when the man puts his penis in? Could the man be hurt, his penis "chewed up" or burned by wires in the vagina?

> *A:* That sounds like what we talked about a couple of months ago, your thought that the lady might be dangerous to the man, that she might hurt and control him.
>
> *Jim:* You have a good memory. Maybe these ideas are my mind's way of covering other ideas but I don't know what.

The analyst had been waiting for the time when Jim might be receptive to further interpretation of his own wishes for sexual involvement with his mother. Because Jim raised the question of "other ideas" and seemed to be asking for help, the analyst decided to make the following interpretation.

> *A:* I have a thought. Maybe they cover what you would like ladies to do to you.
>
> *Jim:* I have a picture flashing in and out of my mind of my mother. Now hands and feet are grabbing my penis and stomping on it. It's not in the lady. Now a naked lady is dancing around me. I'm in quicksand up to my waist.

This remarkable free association, which led directly to Jim's infantile sexual wishes toward his mother, indicated that the interpretation preceding it was correctly timed.

> *A:* The quicksand is covering your penis. The naked lady can't put her hands and feet on it.
>
> *Jim:* Isn't quicksand dangerous?
>
> *A:* Yes. I agree, that's probably what the quicksand means.

Not surprisingly, this thinly disguised material containing wishes that mother would stimulate him and touch his penis was followed by strong resistance during the next few sessions. Jim returned to playing cards. He smilingly said he forgot what had been talked about and openly stated that he didn't want to talk about the quicksand anymore. The analyst did not interpret the resistance because Jim was aware of it. Instead he waited for the boy to take the next step after integrating the breakthrough to consciousness of the sexual wishes contained in the quicksand associations. That occurred five sessions later.

Session 203

Jim talked about a fantasy of a man and woman sleeping together.

> *Jim:* The lady pretends to be asleep and when the man is asleep she bites off his penis and spits it out. In the morning when he goes to the bathroom and reaches down to hold his penis to pee, it's gone. He says, "Marjorie, where is my penis?" She says she doesn't know, but he sees it on the floor. It had her teeth marks in it. So he has her arrested and as punishment her nipples are cut off by the guillotine.
>
> *A:* Who is Marjorie?
>
> *Jim:* I don't know, I just made it up.

He then reveals with mild embarrassment that he first thought of his mother's name but he didn't say it because the analyst would think he was talking about his parents.

The analyst understood this material to be a reaction to the breakthrough of the wish to have mother fondle his penis. Both the wish and the fear of castration were expressed in the fantasy.

THE RATTLESNAKE PHOBIA

By this point in the analysis, approximately 200 hours into treatment, the patient's symptoms had largely disappeared. He had more friends and was doing well in school and regressing less at home. His father was making a major attempt to spend more time with Jim in a supportive way.

In a dream about rattlesnakes in his bed, Jim continued to elaborate his many infantile sexual fantasies about intercourse and expected castration as retaliation. The meaning of the rattlesnake phobia, presented in the evaluation by the patient but absent from the analysis until now, became clear.

Session 211

Jim began the session by relating a dream. "I got out of bed one morning. When I put my feet down I heard two rattlesnakes. I was in shock and I sat very still. One snake was on my leg and it bit me. I jumped over the snakes and ran out of the room. A lady with glasses and frizzy hair, not my mother, rushed me to the hospital."

Jim presented dreams occasionally and had learned how to work with them analytically. He began to associate.

> *Jim:* Maybe the rattlesnakes were there because my mind was punishing me for thinking about ladies in my other dreams. Do you remember a long time ago when I was afraid that there were rattlesnakes in my bed. Maybe it came back.
>
> *A:* Yes I remember, you told me that at the very beginning of the analysis.
>
> *Jim:* When I moved it crawled up my leg and bit me. Maybe it was reaching up my leg to get to my penis and bite it. (Jim said this almost triumphantly, enjoying his ability to associate and interpret.) I would think my mother would be there. I don't even know this lady. My mom sure doesn't have glasses and frizzy hair.
>
> *A:* Do you think that could be the purpose, to be sure that it wasn't your mother?
>
> *Jim:* Why would my mind want to do that?
>
> *A:* You said the rattlesnakes were there to punish you for your interest in ladies. Maybe for your interest in a particular lady, and maybe for a particular kind of interest that you don't feel is okay.
>
> *Jim:* (smiles) You mean for wanting to huddle with my mother, don't you?
>
> *A:* Yes.
>
> *Jim:* That was in bed too, wasn't it?

As a result of this analytic work Jim was now fully conscious of the fact that we were talking about his mother and him, not his father and mother, not some vague man or lady. This insight now became an integral part of the continuing analysis of his relationship with his mother.

In a skateboard dream in which he "showed off" for a group of admirers, the exhibitionistic aspects of both his current and infantile wish to display himself to his mother were obvious. In the course of these sessions through reconstruction, the analyst was able to connect Jim's wish to exhibit his penis and his rattlesnake phobia during the oedipal phase with their current day equivalents. A skiing dream followed, stimulated by a ski trip Jim took with his father. In it the wish to have mother for himself was presented in the form of a reversal.

Another period of very strong resistance followed this work, but the material eventually continued with a song that contained his mother's first name in the title. This was a popular song about a stepmother and early adolescent boy who became sexually involved while the father was away. Mother was a seducer and Jim's wish to respond became the central focus of the analysis, as painful aspects of the infantile oedipal situation were analyzed.

Session 229

Jim insisted that he was ready to stop. He wasn't having problems anymore and he wanted more free time. His mother said it was up to him and the analyst. Jim asked the analyst for his opinion.

> *A:* I think the decision should be made by you and me, and I do know that your problems are a lot better. But I think we have one important question to ask and answer and that is, have we understood enough about what caused your problems so that they won't come back again?
> *Jim:* I think I understand enough, and anyway I could come back if I needed to. But I don't care about that. How do we stop?
> *A:* Well, you and I decide when it's time to stop and how much longer we'll meet.
> *Jim:* (surprised) You mean we don't stop right then?
> *A:* It's better if we take time to talk about how it feels to stop.

Jim was satisfied. The analyst could almost feel him gearing up to work again, overcoming his wish to run. Jim began to talk about his mother, cutting through to the heart of the matter.

Jim: I used to think that my mother was very powerful but I don't anymore, and I don't sleep with her anymore either.
A: I know that, but I'm not sure we understand all about your feelings when you did sleep with her.

Jim reluctantly agreed and said he would try hard because he wanted to stop. He went back to the quicksand, to the idea of the quicksand keeping the lady away from the man's penis, to the dream being about his mother and himself.

Jim: This is hard to think about. I see my mom and me in bed. The covers are up to my stomach. I have my arms around my mom (embarrassed but determined) and she has her hands under the covers on me. She's squeezing me.

Session 230

In the midst of the continuing discussion the analyst, in an attempt to clarify the issue of motivation, asked Jim why he thought his mother invited him into bed.

Jim: She was probably lonely with my father away.
A: So she turned to you.
Jim: Yeah. It reminds me of a song. (The song title was a woman's name, the first name being the same as his mother's. Jim went on to explain the song.) The father marries a stepmother. There is a boy who is thirteen. The father goes away on business and the mother gets it on with the boy. They hear a noise and the boy says, "What's that?" like it's someone. The mother says "it's only the wind." Later the sheriff comes and says the father died in a car accident but he wasn't the kind to have accidents. The song ends when the mother wonders if it really was the wind.

As the analyst listened he recognized the introduction of the last remaining unanalyzed component of the positive oedipal conflict. Jim had acknowledged his sexual wishes for his mother; here he introduced the wish to take the father's place as mother's lover, to kill him. His superego, represented by the sheriff, reacts immediately to the unacceptable wish.

Jim fell silent, pondering his own detailed description of the song.

A: What does the song mean?
Jim: That the father committed suicide because it was him and he

saw them having intercourse and stuff. (Another pause) Do you remember a long time ago when I said that my mother wanted sex and my father just went along with her. He didn't really want to, he wasn't interested?

A: Yes, I remember.

Jim: Well, the boy was the same way.

A: I'm not sure about that. It seems like the boy wanted to have sex with the lady but he didn't feel that he should.

Jim: Yeah, I guess you're right. The first name (in the song title) is my mother's name.

A: Yeah. The song does seem to be another way of talking about you and your mother and father, particularly your father because of what happens to the father in the song. What do you think would happen if your father knew that you wanted to do sexual things with your mother.

Jim: Well, he could hurt me, (pause) or commit suicide, or run away with another woman or maybe see a psychiatrist.

Near the end of the session Jim reiterated that he wasn't going to sleep with his mother anymore. Now he understood, even if she didn't.

Session 231

Jim again insisted that he was ready to stop. The analyst interpreted his wish to avoid the current material. Jim acknowledged the interpretation and later in the session returned to the boy's feelings in the popular song, announcing at first that the boy did it to please the stepmother. Then thinking out loud he began to consider the analyst's idea that the boy was a willing participant. His willingness would be "announced" by his erection. That was "proof." Near the end of the session the analyst drew together Jim's previous difficulty in acknowledging his interest in his penis, his masturbation, and now his interest in sleeping with his mother; in a broader sense his masturbatory fantasies. Although he acknowledged and agreed with the analyst, he also reported that his mind was wandering.

Session 232

The interpretation in session 231 seemed to have been accepted because Jim talked about his masturbation and masturbatory fantasies with greater openness than ever before. He played with himself in bed, in front of the TV, and in the bathtub. "I like the bathtub because my penis is slippery and it feels real good. I rub harder and harder and my mind says more, more!"

When asked what he thought about while rubbing his penis Jim responded with the following fantasy: "I think about lying on my parents' bed with a girl friend. She's my age and we are in love. There are hearts all around my head and my penis is in her." This wonderfully naive, age-appropriate fantasy, although partly defensive, was taken as an indication that the patient was moving toward a resolution of his infantile neurosis. For the first time, the analyst began to think about the prospect of termination.

In subsequent sessions Jim's feeling that his father was opposed to his sexuality was thoroughly explored; both his castration fears and his failure to see that his father wanted him to enjoy his sexuality and grow up to be a sexual man.

A change of developmental phase became apparent to patient and analyst at this time. Jim noted that he was growing rapidly and pointed out the dark hair on his arms and legs. These prepubertal changes seemed to increase his resistance to the oedipal material being analyzed.

In session 235 Jim stated categorically his wish to stop. His problems were gone and he was fine. He felt the analyst was trying to keep him in the analysis to control and manipulate him. "You'll never let me go, you want to make money." His anger and fear were discussed, and transference interpretations dealt with the themes of seeing the analyst as (1) the hostile oedipal father who wished to control him, castrate him, and make him passive, and (2) as the seductive mother who tried to get him to talk of sexual themes which were anxiety producing. "You mean talking in here is like huddling with my mother?"

In the continual unfolding of the sexual interaction between mother and child, Jim told of seeing his mother use a tampon, then quickly denied that he had said it. From mother in the next parent conference it was learned that she had shown him one as she gave a detailed explanation of menstruation. A series of similar seductive activities on the part of the parents became more apparent. The boys used the parents' bathroom to bathe and brush their teeth, frequently seeing the parents nude in the process. Mother kept Jim's unfolded clothes in her bedroom. A second TV was there. All of this meant frequent trips by the boys into the parents' bedroom.

The analysis of this material covered many sessions and was difficult because it represented the incestual tie to the mother and the actions themselves produced considerable sexual gratification. Gradually Jim began to use his own bathroom, stay out of the parents' bedroom, and set limits on the seductive interaction between himself and his mother.

Resistance during this difficult phase of the analysis took the form of silence (one entire hour of silence, which was accepted and then interpreted in terms of the patient's anxiety and anger); regression to previous forms of behavior (playing cards, throwing cards, etc.); and continued wishes to stop. Eventually it was interpreted that Jim was seeking independence by trying to rush away from the feelings about his parents, but that no real independence was possible without understanding the feelings. When mother finished her analysis around this time it allowed for further discussion of Jim's wish to stop. Jim questioned the nature of mother's relationship with her analyst, seeing it in sexual terms ("maybe they had an affair"). As his fantasies about that relationship were elaborated, connections were made with his own sexual wishes for his mother.

LOVE FOR THE ANALYST–FATHER—THE NEGATIVE OEDIPAL CONFLICT

Aggression toward the analyst–father became more pronounced. If the analyst did not let him stop he would curse him, he would not come, he would complain to his parents that the analyst was mean to him, he would not analyze. When retaliation was not forthcoming the fear of hurting the also loved analyst–father emerged. "Am I mean to you?" At one point when the analyst blew his nose Jim thought he was crying and asked if he had made him cry.

Session 272

Jim demanded to play cards. Looking directly at the analyst he announced his intention to play forever. He began to sing and throw the cards about the room.

> *A:* I think you're angry at me.
> *Jim:* (singing) I agree.

Session 273

Jim began the sessions by demanding again to play cards all day.

> *A:* You really want to control things don't you?
> *Jim:* Yeah.
> *A:* As I mentioned last time I think you're angry at me and want to be the boss in here but you say it in actions, like the cards, not in words.

At first Jim said no. Then he described a series of ways in which he "teased" the analyst—turning the radio on and off, changing the time on the clock, and pushing chairs around. Jim regressed and became silly.

> *A:* Have you noticed, almost every time you're teasing me in some way you act silly?
> *Jim:* (seriously) I'm mad at you and I want to tease you, but I don't want to hurt you.

Session 278

In this session the analyst brought together a "developmental line" of Jim's aggressive feelings as they had been expressed in the transference, tracing the initial reluctance to play; playing cards, first carefully, then cheating; followed by the master–slave play in which Jim avoided cutting off the analyst's penis, leading to open discussions of sexuality. Then in a sense Jim reacted by being a good boy, a good patient, working hard with the analyst to understand his masturbation and his sexual feelings about his parents. When the analyst pointed out to Jim that it was no more natural for a boy to work all the time in analysis than it was not to play (at the beginning of the analysis), he relaxed some. Now he seemed to be angry at the analyst, yet unable to express his feelings directly in words. His anger showed itself in teasing and silliness.

Jim listened intently to the long clarification, becoming sadder as the analyst continued. When the analyst finished Jim said that he was picturing the analyst crying, "I want you to know that I don't hate you."

> *A:* I guess your problem is to figure out a way to be comfortable liking me and being angry at me.

Session 282

Jim openly and knowingly teased the analyst in a card game, closely watching for a response. As he won and rubbed it in his concern burst through. "Am I mean to you?" he asked.

The interpretation of Jim's conflicting wishes to hurt and love the analyst and his father were connected with his sexual wishes for his mother and desires to displace his father. Gradually, all aspects of the positive and negative Oedipus were brought together. This series of interpretations was followed by an increased drive for age-appropriate prepuberal autonomy. Now eleven years, six months old, Jim began insisting that his parents, particularly his father, give him permission to go to the movies with friends, stay up one-half hour later, go to the park after supper. His parents were at first threatened by his new assertiveness but eventually agreed to allow greater autonomy. In a dynamic sense this change marked the beginning of the termination phase of the analysis.

Jim's activities and most of the analytic material began to revolve around age-appropriate themes. He announced to his parents and the analyst that he liked a girl (from a distance). Discussions of kissing, holding hands, and petting followed. His preadolescent naiveté was not interfered with or interpreted since it was considered developmentally appropriate. Jim relied less on his parents, stopped using their bathroom, and spent less time with his mother. His behavior with peers also changed, as he made close friends and volunteered his home for a farewell party for his soccer team. His growth could be summed up by the decal on a shirt he bought for himself. It read "Captain."

As Jim grew closer to his father, negative oedipal issues continued to be analyzed. In the transference he expressed wishes to leave, but said that he would miss the analyst since he liked him very much. "How do guys be nice to each other?" he asked. The analyst verbalized Jim's concern about his loving feelings toward his father and the analyst. "Yeah," he said, "our whole school is messed up about that. One guy put his arm around another guy and he was called a queer. I'm confused."

Spurred on by the hormonal upsurge of preadolescence —evidenced by a broadening torso, increased muscle mass, and the appearance of darker hair on his arms and his legs—and by the removal of blocks to development by the analysis, Jim became adolescent in appearance and action. He began bringing his radio to sessions, always tuned to a rock-and-roll station. While lying quietly on the floor listening, he tapped his feet to the music. Jim talked of music, girls, passing notes, his friends. He became very invested in his body, showing his biceps and asking if they were big. The analyst was allowed, indeed privileged, to observe this developmental process at close range. Jim's demands to stop the analysis ceased, but his interest in termination did not.

TERMINATION

Session 314

Jim related with enthusiasm his success in Little League. He drove in four runs in the last game and was one of the stars. He felt good playing ball, quite a change from the beginning of the analysis when he stalked off the soccer field because he didn't like his teammates.

The analyst sensed that Jim was manifesting a readiness to terminate.

Further, he added, his father said he was not watching TV as much and he didn't have to be told what to do so often. His mother was glad because he was playing with friends more and not bugging her.

> *Jim:* I know I'll have problems in the future but I know that I can handle them. That's what stopping means, doesn't it?
> *A:* Yes, in part. What kinds of problems do you think will be coming up in the future?
> *Jim:* Drugs. My friend and I decided not to take them because they screw up your brain. And I know I'm going to have to get better study habits. The work will be harder in junior high but I'm not perfect. You don't expect me to be perfect, do you?
> *A:* No, I'd like you to be able to enjoy doing the things people your age do and to be able to handle being a teenager.
> *Jim:* I think I can do that now.

In essence Jim began to show considerable evidence of (1) a sense of stability and maturity; (2) a return to the developmental mainstream, the prime goal of child analysis; and (3) a controlled response to the instinctual upsurge of preadolescence. For these reasosns the analyst felt that the termination phase of the analysis had been reached.

In session 318 the analyst agreed to discuss termination seriously. Within that hour Jim showed a variety of responses: (1) reasonable anticipation—"I'll be free to play with my friends. At the beginning of the analysis I didn't mind coming because I didn't have any." (2) Regression—he grabbed a large stuffed lion from the playroom and lay on it. His wish to remain safe and secure was interpreted, as was his fear of being on his own. (3) Sadness—he immediately began to mourn the loss of the relationship with the analyst.

Session 318

> *Jim:* I still want to stop. Everything is great in my life.
> *A:* Let's talk about it seriously. I think I see some signs that you're ready to stop.
> *Jim:* (big smile) No kidding? That's the first time you've said that.

Jim reviewed the areas of improvement—at home, in school, with friends. He continued:

> *Jim:* "*I've* decided not to go to the rock concert."
> *A:* Oh, how come?

Jim: Well, my friend can't go and my parents don't want me to. I'm not disappointed. I'll have plenty of time to go when I drive.
A: That's a few years off. Knowing what you can handle and what you're not ready for is one sign of being ready to stop.
Jim: What problems do I have left?
A: What do you see?
Jim: None really. I know I'm not perfect but I don't think I'm going to be.
A: Analysis isn't intended to make people perfect. That's impossible. I think you used to think you had to be perfect.
Jim: Like at the beginning when I was afraid to play. I can come back if I want to, can't I?

A sense of sadness began to be evident in Jim at this point.

A: Sure, any time.
Jim: I don't think I'll need to. I'll be free of the chains. I'll use the time to play with my friends. I liked the first part of the analysis best.
A: Why?
Jim: Because I didn't have anything to do then.
A: No friends then.

Jim went into the playroom and picked up a large stuffed lion (which he hadn't touched in months). He threw it on the floor and plopped on it. A shy, almost embarrassed smile followed.

A: (taking the smile as a nonverbal communication of feelings about getting the lion) What do you make of it?
Jim: I guess it's being like a little kid. Maybe it has to do with the end of the analysis.

A detailed discussion followed on how Jim would feel on his own.

Although termination had been in the air for several months, it was not agreed upon by analyst and patient until this time. Jim wanted to stop immediately but listened to the analyst's suggestion that he needed a period of time to deal with his feelings about leaving. Although he was amazed by the analyst's suggestion that sessions continue for three or four more months—"*That* long!" he exclaimed—he reluctantly agreed when the analyst explained that he might have many thoughts and feelings about leaving the analysis. These should be explored just as we had analyzed all his other thoughts. Jim's parents were not directly involved in this decision, although the analyst knew they were very satisfied with the results of the analytic work. When Jim informed them that a termination date had been set they congratulated him warmly, in the process supporting the analyst's suggestion of an extended termination phase.

In subsequent hours the theme of separation was expressed in many ways. One day Jim put on the analyst's jacket. His wishes to hold on to the analyst and become a man like him were interpreted. Jim attempted to initiate physical contact through playful touching, tickling, or arm and leg wrestling. This allowed a reworking of the seductive physical contact with mother and the expression of warm feelings toward men as well as a more specific interpretation of the desire for physical contact stimulated by termination.

With a few weeks to go in the analysis Jim asked if the analyst would see him for nothing if his parents wouldn't pay anymore. "You're wondering how much I really care for you as a person, huh?" was the interpretation.

Angry feelings related to leaving the analyst played little part in the termination phase. Jim was consciously pleased to leave. He readily acknowledged his loving feelings for the analyst but clearly preferred his peers. The analyst chose not to force the issue since it would have seemed dissonant to Jim and in a sense out of harmony with the strong developmental surge of early adolescence.

Jim started junior high school three weeks before termination. Anxious at first, he handled the transition from grade school without incident. Jim offered to make the analyst a ring in leather shop but said nothing more until the last day when he proudly brought in the leather ring with "Dr. C." on it. He had made it himself and paid the quarter for the leather from his allowance.

Five days before his twelfth birthday Jim left for the last time with a smile, a firm handshake, and "Goodbye, Dr. Colarusso." Despite having left 355 times before, he reached for the door knob on the wrong side of the door. A knowing smile followed. As Jim left the analyst was keenly aware of how tall he had become.

A DISCUSSION OF "THE ANALYSIS OF A NEUROTIC BOY" BY CALVIN COLARUSSO

Jules Glenn, M.D.

Dr. Colarusso's description of his analysis of Jim, a ten- to twelve-year-old boy, illustrates the psychoanalytic process beautifully. Jim was eager to be cured of his symptoms and quickly got the idea of how analysis could help him. He started by talking and then retreated to coloring a book. As Dr. Colarusso encouraged him to play, he engaged a full range of communication with his analyst, interrupted at times by anxiety.

Early on, Dr. Colarusso was able to interpret the patient's fear that the analyst would become angry if Jim dirtied his wall, a fear the patient recognized as originating in his fear that his parents would have similar objections. With that interpretation, Jim's play became more aggressive and he even attacked the analyst. Defenses against aggression manifested themselves anew as the patient became bored and joined the analyst as an ally in play. Interpretation of these defenses led to a brief engagement in compulsive drawing and then a new means of communication—Jim brought cards into the sessions, a phenomenon the analyst did not interpret as a defense but rather as a means by which Jim could express conflicts over competition and aggression. Jim cheated in order to beat Dr. Colarusso, but became anxious and briefly employed regression to anality.

Thus far, as will continue to be the case, we see the seesaw shifting from interpretation of defenses to interpretation of drive derivatives as each facet becomes more prominent.

Things became a bit more complicated when Dr. Colarusso, in response to Jim's questions, acknowledged that he knew the patient was cheating and added that Jim did this to feel big and strong. Jim became sad, and before long Dr. Colarusso realized he felt tricked, defeated by the analyst, an outcome that he interpreted, releasing the patient from his distress. A minor complication occurred when the analyst went further than the patient could go as he showed him that he would like to order his parents around and control them, not simply because he felt they did it to him and wanted to keep him weak, but because of his own aggression. Possibly this early drive interpretation was premature, but after the analyst repeated it a second time, Jim agreed.

Jim was now caught up in the treatment, making his own observations, even when he cheated. He introduced a new game which Dr. Colarusso could interpret. He played king to the analyst's slave or general to the analyst's private soldier. Dr. Colarusso felt that he, the analyst, represented the patient and made interpretations about the patient's bad feelings about feeling weak, bad feelings which included anger and led to fear. This allowed Jim to attack Dr. Colarusso through getting him to read anti-Italian jokes, but the attack led to fear of retaliation which the analyst then interpreted. The analyst explicitly stated that Jim feels afraid when he attacks him, and this enables Jim to go further—*kill* Dr. Colarusso in a game and then cut off all appendages except his penis.

When the analyst observed that one part was not extirpated, Jim agreed that he had spared the penis. The displacement had defended against his expressing his aggression fully.

Now Jim could talk of penises with relative safety, but a degree of displacement was necessary. He talked of the movie, *The Towering Inferno,* and stole a lighter. Soon he came to realize, through Dr. Colarusso's explanations and his own astute observations, that he was talking about his hot erect penis. His preoccupation with certain superheroes—Spider Man, The Thing, The Flame, and Plastic Man—was based on his fascination with his penis. Defenses having been interpreted, once more drive derivatives appeared more clearly. Jim recognized his sexual feelings.

Jim's diminished fear of his own sexual feelings and father's changing attitude to his son enabled Jim to become less fearful of his father and talk to him more, to ask him for a skateboard. Dr. Colarusso was able to reconstruct and to relate present fears of father to similar earlier fears of his father and sexuality—fears that occurred during the oedipal period.

Now Jim could deal with his oedipal competition with his father, but not as yet with his sexual feelings toward mother.

Again displacement became an important defense as Jim talked of other boys touching their penises. When Dr. Colarusso pointed out this defense, Jim talked more about his bodily sensations. Again defenses were interpreted—this time his attributing his erections to pinworms and anal squeezing rather than to the *idea* that actually caused the erections.

Jim kept away from the *idea* for a while and concentrated on the act and related sensations. But soon he was telling his sexual fantasies—a ropelike thing goes up in the penis into the balls and pulls the sperm out—and discussing his parents' mating. Dr. Colarusso dealt with his denial that they slept alone in a room of their own on vacation with skepticism and soon Jim was talking about his mother's wanting to take him into her bed and "huddle" with him when his father was away. The interpretation of the projection involved didn't lead to further clarification immediately, but in a few weeks Jim came back to the "huddling."

When he talked of the possibility that men hurt women, Dr. Colarusso suggested that Jim was talking of "other ideas" to "cover up what you would like ladies to do to you." The interpretation had an astonishing effect. Jim told of a sexual fantasy of being immersed in quicksand, a fantasy associated with mother and danger. The analyst didn't interpret the resistances that followed because Jim knew of his fears. He waited patiently for five sessions until Jim told another version of the fantasy—a woman (associated with mother) bites off a man's penis and is punished for it. This in turn was connected through a dream with Jim's fear of rattlesnakes. Dr. Colarusso interpreted his fear of being bitten by them as a punishment for thinking of ladies (mother). The rattlesnake phobia of the oedipal state could now be reconstructed.

Not surprisingly, Jim wanted to stop the treatment at this point. Things seemed to be getting too hot to handle. But he persisted and soon more fantasies about mother and patient being in bed together appeared; mother squeezed the patient.

The oedipal configuration became even clearer as Jim talked of a song in which the father leaves and kills himself because mother had an affair with her stepson. Jim recognized his own wish to get rid of father and have mother for himself. After this Jim avoided giving in to his mother's actual advances.

As Jim entered prepuberty, masturbatory fantasies and acts were discussed more than ever and Jim again wished to leave treatment, be independent, avoid sexual feelings toward mother and father. Interpretation led to Jim's remaining in treatment and discussing the negative oedipal aspects of his feelings as well as his interest in girls. He teased the analyst more and more, expressing both antagonism and attraction, which he could discuss with Dr. Colarusso.

Soon he was ready to enter the terminal stage of treatment, but I will defer discussion of this phase of the analysis.

I have underlined the swings from defense analysis to analysis of drive derivatives. Other aspects of the analytic process are clear as well. Often a particular unconscious conflict first manifested itself in reference to feelings toward the analyst, and then appeared as derived from feelings toward Jim's actual parents; eventually transference from the parents of yesteryear, the oedipal period, becomes clear. The feelings that appear need not be toward the parents as they actually were or are, but rather involve the *representations* of the parents. At first Jim hesitated to mess in the playroom, a displacement to the analyst of inhibition because his parents, especially father, objected to it. Later his fear of his father, and hence the analyst, could be seen as a result of anger toward his father, an anger traced to sexual wishes toward mother.

The analyst was able to do a reasonable amount of reconstruction, but not as much as one usually sees in adult analysis. He reconstructed Jim's conflicts during his oedipal period, in particular his fear of rattlesnakes, because he feared punishment for his wishes to possess his mother and get rid of his father. He felt he should be bitten for these desires, including his wishes to be huddled, hugged, and squeezed by mother. The limited reconstruction in child analysis has been understood in terms of the child's limited cognitive ability and his relative lack of interest in the past, his concentration on the here and now. Jim, of course, had a remarkable capacity for insight. He could see connections between defense and drives warded off when Dr. Colarusso pointed these out. Later he made his own connections, a reflection of his recognizing cause and effect. That he was a bright boy is not sufficient explanation for his capacity for insight. Tactful interpretation enabled him to use his limited logical capacity, and as Jim entered prepuberty, with its beginning formal logic (Flavel, 1963) he acquired greater maturational capacities on which interest in the past and present could be built. It was in prepuberty that the reconstruction mentioned above became effective. It was then that he could talk of termination with an eye to the future.

Conflicts were not resolved all at once. They appeared repeatedly in different forms. Hence defenses and drives were recognized and interpreted again and again. This repetitive working through is not described in full in the case summary because of needs to condense, but sufficient evidence of the process does occur.

Not that everything went smoothly all the time. In analysis the unconscious forces that resist insight and recovery can be potent indeed, and the analyst's own unconscious needs will, at one point or another, almost always facilitate the patient's resistance. Sometimes, conventional analytic technique will serve to slow things.

As a result of the interpretive work, a change in the balance of defenses occurred. Repression diminished remarkably. Jim soon became more aware of this antagonism to his father and later recognized his sexual feelings toward his mother. He stopped attributing his huddling solely to his mother's desire for this activity (i.e., projecting his wishes for his mother to his mother). He no longer attributed sexual feelings to other boys, but owned up to his own wishes. Displacement of fears from parents to the rattler who would bite him and thus punish him for his illicit sexual desires ceased, but displacement came to be used adaptively in his new object seeking; his feelings toward his mother transferred to girls his age.

As these defenses altered, Jim became more able to tolerate hostility, affection, narcissistic hurt, and anxiety (which diminished). The greater tolerance also reflected a superego change; Jim did not experience the severe guilt he had early transformed into symptom formation.

Not only did Jim's symptoms disappear, but he also made developmental advances. At the start of the analysis this ten-year-old's temper tantrums, difficulty maintaining friendships, trouble sitting still in school and completing his work signified that he was not firmly established in latency. Latency children are able to maintain a proper balance between sublimated activity and the use of isolation and reaction formation on the one hand, and less controlled outbursts of drive dominated behavior on the other; Jim leaned too much toward the latter.

As the treatment proceeded, Jim became a latency child. By the 200th session his "symptoms had largely disappeared. He had more friends and was doing well in school and regressing less at home" (p. 223). Sexual interests and activity were present but did not dominate the picture. By the 235th session, bodily changes revealed that Jim was entering prepuberty. He started the growth spurt and grew dark hair on his arms and legs. Jim's psychological reaction to prepuberty was to seek more independence and to avoid consciousness of incestuous involvement. Regression was minimal.

To Dr. Colarusso's credit he analyzed the boy's reluctance to continue the treatment tactfully and without disrupting his developmental advance. Eventually the analysis ended with Jim's preadolescent status firmly established. As Dr. Colarusso notes, achieving appropriate developmental level is a prime criterion for termination.

Dr. Colarusso raises the question of the justification of his giving Jim birthday and holiday gifts. He appears to offer gifts to latency children as a matter of course in order to fortify the therapeutic alliance and to keep the patient from developing an unanalyzable antagonism toward the analyst. As he points out, children expect gifts from their friends.

Many analysts advocate a more flexible approach to gifts. Analysis works best when there is an optimal balance of frustration and gratification. If an analysand is too frustrated, and especially if he cannot understand the reason for the frustration, he will become angry at the analyst, be convinced the anger is justified, and will not engage in its analysis. This may well be the case when the analyst does not offer a gift to his child patient.

For adults we assume the frustration will lie within tolerable limits and the patient will understand our not giving the gift. In fact most adults would consider gift giving peculiar and seductive in the context of the physician–patient relationship.

Similarly, many children are capable of understanding the analyst's reluctance to give gifts, and are able to tolerate the frustration. These children recognize that the chief method of the analysis is understanding and that receiving presents might interfere with that goal. Under such circumstances, the patient will be able to understand his reactions to his strong desire for a gift and his not receiving one.

The problem, then, is to decide which children require presents to keep the treatment going and when gifts would interfere with the analysis. Although Dr. Colarusso does not address this issue in his discussion, his judgment in this case appears to be proper. The gift seemed necessary to maintain the therapeutic alliance. It did not interfere with the analysis of the positive transference as far as I can see; the patient's affection for Dr. Colarusso was subject of scrutiny later in the treatment (of course one cannot be certain that without the gift, the analysis would have progressed smoothly as well).

In child analysis, a working alliance must be established with both the patient and his parents. The parent–analyst cooperation starts with the consultation and continues throughout the analysis. Dr. Colarusso obtained the history of the child's present and past life from the parents, a necessary step in evaluating and diagnosing Jim's condition, and in ascertaining the optimal treatment. Because children often do not have the capacity or interest in describing their symptoms and surroundings, information the consultant needs, this data must be obtained from the parents. Only then can the assessor gauge the patient's developmental progressions, arrests, and retreats, as well as their causes—environmental pressure, organic disorders, or psychophysiological disturbances.

Dr. Colarusso was evaluating the parents as well as the child, trying to understand their role in Jim's illness and their reliability as supporters of therapy. They were eager to get help for Jim and Dr. Colarusso's tact and understanding enhanced their avidity. They were willing to see Dr. Colarusso regularly and reveal to him their family intimacies. They imparted their pleasure and confidence in having Dr. Colarusso as his doctor and were able to tell Jim, with the analyst's help, enough about how the doctor and patient would proceed.

Dr. Colarusso saw the parents for a number of reasons. Their continued contact fortified the parents' support of the treatment. Father and mother provided information that would help the analyst understand his patient, make appropriate interpretations, integrate reality into his comments, and thus avoid excessive symbolic interpretations and the isolation of reality and analytic work. The analyst did not engage the parents in treatment, did not offer interpretations of their behavior. He maintained his patient's confidentiality, never revealed what Jim had told him. He did not advise the parents, but did explain certain things about child development which helped the parents reach conclusions that altered their behavior. In particular, father became able to deal with his son with greater warmth and to help him build a skateboard. So far as I can tell, the analyst never urged the mother to stop huddling with her son; through the analysis, Jim resisted mother's "advances."

The principles behind Dr. Colarusso's cautious behavior were varied. One should try to maintain an analytic stance, restrict oneself to a great extent to interpreting the patient's conflicts to him. Giving advice to parents can lead to the child's looking to the analyst as a manipulator of his environment rather than someone who helps through insight. (Of course, if the parents' pathological activity is so fixed as to produce a stalemate in the analysis, the therapist may have to give advice, but this did not occur in Jim's treatment.) Another finding is that treating parents along with the child can create unanalyzable competitive transference reactions which will hinder the treatment. Antagonism to the analyst can appear from other sources as well when the analyst attempts to interpret the parents' behavior. Dr. Colarusso avoided these pitfalls and retained his alliance with the parents. Jim's improvement was more stable because it grew primarily out of changes within him rather than alterations in his environment.

Dr. Colarusso helped establish the therapeutic alliance with Jim with tact and care and without trickery. He explained something of how they would understand Jim's problems, but mainly through correct, empathic, and timely interpretations, the analyst provided Jim with a model of treatment that worked—that relieved Jim of his distress while providing the pleasures of insight. Jim identified with Dr. Colarusso as an interpreter, as a seeker for inner truth, got the hang of the method, and loved the work. At the same time that he was the observer and understander, Jim remained the player, the communicator, the experiencer who provided the data to be understood.

Dr. Colarusso had to help Jim through encouragement and through providing him with age-appropriate means of communication. First, let us discuss the encouragement. In the 114th session, after Jim became fearful that Dr. Colarusso would object to the anti-Italian jokes, the analyst supplemented his interpretation by reassuring him. He did not do so through telling Jim he wasn't angry, but through emphasizing that they were trying to understand his feelings. I assume Jim's reality testing was sufficient so that he could perceive the analyst's benign attitude.

> A look of exquisite fear crossed Jim's face.
> *Jim:* You don't like them (the jokes).
> *A:* Now we can see how afraid you get of me when you feel you've attacked me. I hope we can understand more about the fear so you can be more comfortable with your feelings and with me [p. 211].

For the most part in adult analysis the interpretation would suffice, but in child analysis the child often needs a modicum of reassurance to support his reality testing and sustain his narcissism.

Children normally retain the cloak of narcissism and feel naked without its protection. Hence, without narcissistic gratification most children have difficulty engaging in the treatment. Dr. Colarusso recognizes this when he tells Jim, "You've become good at analysis, what do you think is happening?" Jim, encouraged, acknowledges a defense: "I guess I'm avoiding my feelings" (p. 213). The analyst, through his tact, succeeded in eliciting understanding without Jim feeling criticized by him.

At times, however, Dr. Colarusso seems to employ encouragement more than I would do. Along with interpretation, he seems to push the patient to become more overt in his expressions. At one point, Jim played general and private with the analyst. Jim took the role of the general who treated the private, enacted by Dr. Colarusso, poorly, but identified with the mistreated private. The following interchange took place:

> *Jim:* The general is my father and the private is me. The general orders the private around.
> *A:* But the private doesn't like it, he says so and stands up for his rights.
> *Jim:* Yeah, but he has to obey or be killed.
> *A:* Yeah, but he wasn't afraid like before and he understood how both the general and the private felt.
> *Jim:* Yeah, I sure feel better, too. I understand more [pp. 212].

The dangers of too great encouragement include interfering with the patient's autonomy on the one hand, and acting in a way that the patient will find seductive, arousing sexual feelings and gratification which, when based on reality, may be difficult to analyze. We should note that the analyst eventually did analyze the patient's positive transference. The therapeutic alliance remained intact as the patient revealed and understood.

Jim had difficulty finding satisfactory age-appropriate means of communicating with Dr. Colarusso and the analyst skillfully helped him along those lines.

Children's means of communication differ from those of adults. Children are incapable of free association except for brief periods. They fear the ego and drive regression necessary for free association. The latency ideal of being sensible and logical, not disorganized and dominated by primary process thinking, runs counter to the requirements for free association. Their superego opposes it and they are apt to employ vigorous defenses—denial, reaction formation, and isolation—when primitive feelings surge forth.

However, the child has means of expression, even of the primitive. He uses play, story-telling, and drawing to give vent to feelings. Jim used these means of communication along with speech, dreams, and a bit of free association.

At the start of the analysis, Jim talked like a grown-up for a while and then retreated to filling in a coloring book he brought with him. Rather than interpret the inhibition which prevented age-appropriate communication through play, Dr. Colarusso elected to encourage Jim to play. "Jim was invited into the playroom and told that it might be helpful and fun as well if he spent some of his time playing" (p. 202). Having toys, paper, and pencil and crayons available is, of course, standard operating procedure in child analysis because these provide opportunities to the child for his own means of "talk." It is not clear to me why the analyst did not introduce Jim to the play material immediately. I can understand his delaying interpretation of the child's inhibition over play early in the analysis. I note, with admiration, how the causes of Jim's reluctance to mess started to emerge in the transference. The fear of the analyst as a prohibiter could soon be interpreted as a result of displacement from Jim's father.

Jim brought his own play materials, the deck of cards, into the office, and used these to express his conflicts over aggression. I presume that Dr. Colarusso, like most child analysts, did not have structured games, like playing cards, in his office, lest the structure interfere with the communicative potential. Once Jim brought the cards, Jim and Dr. Colarusso used his playing to understand the boy's feelings. During the play, of course, Jim talked, further clarifying his difficulties. The play expanded to include enactments of stories. The analyst played the roles Jim assigned him, but at times Jim failed to recognize that they were using the dramatic play for communication. He thought the analyst was actually enjoying his masochistic activity—a phenomenon akin to but different from an adult patient's loss of perspective when he thinks his analyst is engaging in countertransference interplay even when he is not. A child is more likely to incorrectly interpret his analyst's behavior because the doctor *does* engage in play. Dr. Colarusso of course used Jim's misperception to help him gain insight.

As the child communicates in his own way, the analyst must communicate in a way the child will understand. Dr. Colarusso uses plain, down-to-earth speech, nothing "high falutin'," to interpret to Jim.

> "You look worried. Do you think I'm angry?" [p. 204].
>
> "Gee, Jim, what happened. First you were involved in the war and suddenly you say you're bored. You sure didn't seem bored" [p. 205].
>
> "My knowing [that you were cheating] seemed to ruin what you were trying to tell me through the card games. . . . Let's see if we can figure it out. Maybe you were telling me by beating me how much you enjoy feeling big and strong like your father and me" [p. 207].

Sometimes, Dr. Colarusso made an interpretation through talking of other boys, a way of reassuring Jim so he could tolerate the anxiety the analyst's comment evoked. Dr. Colarusso does this rarely, an indication of Jim's ability to tolerate anxiety and accept his frightening wishes. The instance I found occurred after Jim recognized his wish to sleep with his mother.

> *A:* Yes. Boys first learn about hugging and kissing and loving from being taken care of as babies by their mothers [p. 220].

At other times Dr. Colarusso made the interpretation through altering his role in the play. During the king/slave game, the analyst wanted to tell Jim how angry and afraid Jim felt when a huge and potent person pushed him around. As the game proceeded, Jim, as the slave, introduced his own thoughts. He said, "Oh, king, I feel so weak, I can't seem to succeed, but I'll try harder. . . . I wish I could tell you how angry I am, oh king, at what you do to me but I am afraid. You are so big and powerful . . ." [p. 210].

Let us return to and conclude our discussion with the terminal phase of Jim's analysis. The analyst discussed succinctly the reasons for planning the ending of treatment. The symptoms for which Jim had entered analysis had disappeared and Jim felt confident in himself. In addition, "Jim began to show considerable evidence of (1) a sense of stability and maturity; (2) a return to the developmental mainstream, a prime goal of child analysis; and (3) a controlled response to the instinctual upsurge of preadolescence" (pp. 232–233).

Jim had progressed from being an immature child not firmly into latency to becoming a latency child and then a preadolescent. He was now more interested in being with his friends than spending time with his analyst.

One of the indications for an optimal ending of adult analysis, the ability to mourn, to decathect the analyst, is usually absent in children. Children may feel sad and angry about ending, but, as Wolfenstein (1966) has noted, the capacity to mourn fully does not occur until adolescence has been well established. The child cannot tolerate the sustained pain of losing the object and uses denial and displacement to avoid the painful affects. Some analysts (Furman, 1964) believe that children can mourn when reality is pressed upon them and the therapist interprets denial vigorously, but Dr. Colarusso wisely deals gingerly with his patient's disavowal of the impact of the loss of him.

In child analysis, the terminal phase is an important part of the treatment, but it is usually not as crucial or emotion-laden as in adult analysis. Whereas the adult generally develops a profound and highly organized transference neurosis, the resolution of which depends on extensive analysis during the termination phase and before, the child's attachment to his doctor is usually less intense. The child lives with his parents who provide much direct satisfaction of libidinal and aggressive urges. As a result, although displacements to the analyst occur and require analysis, they are generally less potent than in the adult.

Jim introduced the possibility of stopping by, seeking reassurance that he could handle future problems and that the analyst didn't want him to be perfect. On the one hand Dr. Colarusso used this to further the analysis; he asked Jim what problems he thought could come up. On the other hand, he did not go into Jim's worries about being perfect. Instead he agreed that the patient did not have to become an ideal person, possibly reassuring him too much. At any rate this approach led to the mutual decision to terminate because Jim was doing quite well.

Jim and Dr. Colarusso made the arrangements for termination together. His parents, who had known that the conclusion of treatment was in the air, supported their plans. This approach precluded any realistic basis for the patient's feeling, as some do, that he was being maneuvered out of the analysis. Doctor and patient discussed the basis for the decision to stop and decided that three months would suffice to deal with feelings about ending. Jim had not anticipated such a long terminal period, but agreed with his analyst's suggestion that it was wise.

Concerns about bringing the analysis to an end soon became more prominent. Jim became sad and tried to eliminate this feeling by grabbing a stuffed animal from the playroom and lying on it. Dr. Colarusso interpreted this as a result of his worries about being on his own. When Jim put on the analyst's jacket, Dr. Colarusso interpreted his wish to hold on to the analyst and become a man like him. The defensive function of holding the stuffed animal and wearing the coat was not fully dealt with. I believe Jim wanted to keep the analyst or a substitute with him to identify with Dr. Colarusso, in order to avoid irritation, disappointment, and sadness. Jim rather poignantly wanted to make sure he could return to the analyst and do so even if his parents could not pay. Dr. Colarusso chose to reassure him directly that he could return and attempted analysis of his worry that the analyst would treat him for free if need be. These concerns and the anger were not sufficiently dealt with, so that Jim's uncertain feelings and sadness about ending manifested themselves right up to the last moments of the analysis as he gave the analyst a gift and had difficulty opening the door through which he left.

Many patients are upset because they feel the analyst is leaving them, often as parents had left them earlier, and because they feel the analyst does not care for them (a thought that Dr. Colarusso and Jim had discussed a bit), and because they regret not becoming perfect, fully grown-up, and without conflicts.

They may be upset by not achieving a narcissistic ideal of perfection and full phallic competence. I would have analyzed Jim's defenses against anger more thoroughly with the expectation that it would appear and be understood, thus stabilizing the therapeutic result. However, I recognize that the intensity of irritation and disappointment may have been damped by the reassuring and supporting presence of Jim's parents.

Dr. Colarusso intentionally chose "not to initiate further analysis of negative feelings since it would have seemed dissonant to Jim and in a sense out of harmony with the strong developmental surge" of preadolescence.

Dr. Colarusso, of course, was there in the playroom with the live patient and we must recognize his feel for what was appropriate. Throughout the analysis he interpreted with the empathy a skilled analyst lives with, and I would assume that empathy remained intact to the end. Jim's was a successful analysis of his major oedipal conflicts and regressive defenses as they appeared. Nevertheless, the reader will appreciate that in many successful child analyses, hostility and defenses against it, appear more prominently, especially during the terminal phase.

REFERENCES

Flavel, J. H. (1963), *The Developmental Psychology of Jean Piaget.* Princeton, NJ: D. Van & Nostrand.

Furman, R. (1964), Death and the young child. *The Psychoanalytic Study of the Child,* 19:321–329. New York: International Universities Press.

Wolfenstein, M. (1966), How is mourning possible? *The Psychoanalytic Study of the Child,* 21:93–126. New York: International Universities Press.

A DISCUSSION OF "THE ANALYSIS OF A NEUROTIC BOY" BY CALVIN COLARUSSO

Isidor Bernstein, M.D.

The report by Dr. Colarusso strikes me as a frank, unvarnished account and conveys a feeling of participating in a dynamic ongoing process. It provides an opportunity to discuss a number of clinical, theoretical, and technical issues regarding child and adolescent analysis. These include: indications and contraindications for analysis; the role of the parents in child and adolescent analysis; interpretations and reconstructions in the course of analytic work with children.

We can begin with a consideration of the suitability of the patient for analysis. The decision will be based on three major determinants: (1) the need for analysis; (2) the capacity of the child to participate in the analytic process; and (3) the ability and willingness of the parents to sustain the analysis.

The need for analysis for a child is rarely determined by the degree of subjective suffering experienced by the child. Most children are brought for analysis by the parents because of parental concerns or because of difficulties in school or poor relationships within the family or with peers. This was the case with Jim. It was Jim's parents' concern about his unhappiness that made them decide to bring Jim for evaluation after the mother had discussed her concerns with her therapist. It is clear that a major problem had to do with Jim's efforts to tyrannize and control his family and friends. Typically, he attributed his unhappiness to his parents' favoring his younger brother. Jim's parents were able to see that Jim was causing his own problems. This was helpful since other parents unconsciously reinforce the defenses of the child when they join in blaming other children.

However, I find it difficult to agree with Dr. Colarusso's statement that "here was a child in considerable pain, eager for understanding and help," although it certainly was helpful for the analyst to have such a positive reaction. My impression was that the boy expected a magical cure of his fears. It was after Dr. Colarusso had explained how they would work together that a therapeutic alliance began to be formed. The particular threat that Jim was responding to was his inability to control his fears and feelings of loneliness. Although the diagnosis was "psychoneurosis, anxiety type with phobic and obsessional features," the main indications would seem to have been (1) the failure to achieve latency as revealed by Jim's involvement in oedipal and preoedipal conflicts, and (2) the increasing failure of his obsessional defenses so that he would resort to primitive discharge mechanisms such as temper tantrums. The likelihood of spontaneous resolution was remote. The boy's conflicts had become internalized to the extent that more superficial forms of therapy such as guidance would not be effective. Finally, the threat to progressive development was sufficiently grave to warrant analytic treatment.

We next turn to the child's capacity to participate in the analytic process. Jim's I.Q. as reflected in both testing and schoolwork indicated a sufficiently high level of intellectual functioning for the needs of analysis. Children do not use the couch for the purpose of free association and they rarely free associate verbally. They do communicate through verbal productions, play, drawings, action, and, at times, dreams. Dr. Colarusso's statement that "play is a childhood equivalent to free association" is a misleading oversimplification. I do not believe that Dr. Colarusso means for us to take his statement literally, as evidenced by the care with which he makes his interpretations. The analyst shows due regard for the need to interpret defense as well as drive. At any rate, the fact that Jim was able to talk, draw, and play (in the sense of dramatizing through play) demonstrated his ability to participate in the analytic process. As we can see from the analyst's report, although Jim was superficially compliant in coming to his sessions in the beginning, he exhibited an intense resistance for the first ten or twelve sessions. This was manifested by his compulsive filling in of the pages of a coloring book that he brought with him. The analyst intervened by encouraging Jim to play. It is of interest that the analyst did not interpret the defensive character of Jim's behavior, a point to which we shall return in a discussion of technique.

The third element to be evaluated in deciding on analysis for a child is the ability and willingness of the parents to cooperate. Some degree of psychological mindedness is helpful here and it existed in Jim's parents. This was demonstrated by the mother's response to the discussion of Jim with her therapist and by the father's cooperative participation. Jim's father "often asked for assistance in understanding his feelings about Jim" to which the analyst responded by providing a "developmental context within which to place Jim's behavior or requests." Apparently this was sufficient to maintain a positive relationship between the parents and analyst. The parents were also able to accept the privacy of their son's personal analysis and to endure their exclusion from Jim's relationship with the analyst. The parents' loving feelings for their son outweighed any feelings of disappointment, shame, or guilt in reaction to his difficulties. This augured well for their ability to sustain a long-term commitment to therapy. Dr. Colarusso undoubtedly made such a favorable evaluation before he agreed to undertake the analysis, and the course of the treatment confirmed his judgment.

We do not want to overlook the analyst's own reactions to the child and his parents. Just as it is important for the parents and the child to have a sufficiently positive transference to the analyst, it is necessary for the analyst to have a *degree* of positive feelings for the child and his parents. This does not mean that he has to identify strongly with either child or parents. Dr. Colarusso reacted with interest and a desire to help so treatment was arranged.

Let us now look at the analytic process. The analysis of Jim can be considered to have begun with the first appointment with the parents. At that time, the analyst started to become informed about Jim, his parents, and their reasons for bringing him to the analyst. At Jim's own first appointment, he revealed his fantasy that the analyst would be bald and fat like the psychiatrists on TV. This stereotyping of the analyst would be part of an effort to deal with the threat of meeting an unknown or unfamiliar person. Jim could also have been trying to deal with his anxiety by making the encounter unreal—just another TV program.

Although Jim reported his fear of snakes and feelings about his parents in the early sessions, he quickly became silent. The analyst's response to the prolonged silences was a suggestion that he enter the playroom; that it might be helpful and fun as well if he spent some of his time playing. This was an effort to circumvent the resistance through action rather than interpretation. One wonders whether pointing out to Jim that his silence occurred after expressing anger and referring back to his statement that "adults don't know how children think" would have opened the way to discussing his guilt and anxiety about angry thoughts. Having been instructed to play, Jim chose to dramatize his angry fantasies of destroying his home and family. In session 25, in response to the analyst asking whether Jim thinks the analyst is angry, Jim responds by saying that he doesn't understand why the analyst lets him play like that when his parents don't. The boy says this even though the analyst had explained to Jim that his "playing" was a form of communication which would help the analyst understand the reason for the boy's worries.

Here we may stop to examine how the analyst functions in his work with children. By his analytic stance, the analyst attempts to convey a benevolent neutrality and wish to be of help. His gain goal is to diminish resistance or defensiveness against the production of verbal and nonverbal communication of material from the unconscious. The lack of criticism and the permissive atmosphere, which nevertheless has some clearly defined limits, are intended to promote the development of trust. Such trust rests on a matrix of basic trust related genetically to the degree of adequate mothering or parenting that has been experienced by the child. Thus basic trust originates in early infancy but develops further as the child gets older, depending on the nurturing and growth promoting attitudes and behavior of the parents. Trust of the analyst depends on the child's perception of the object-related interest of the analyst, sometimes in contrast with the narcissistic or symbiotic needs of the parents. The trust is affected by the child's confidence in his ability to control his urges and to depend on the analyst to help him do this without fear of either seduction or rejection. Furthermore, the child's estimate of his ability to tolerate the regression invited by the analytic situation will influence the degree of trust he can achieve.

Jim's analysis covered a period of two years and three months, beginning when he was nine years, nine months old, and ending just before his twelfth birthday. Although, at the start of his treatment, he was chronologically at the age when he should have been in latency, he was, as was noted before, mired in preoedipal and oedipal conflicts. He did show some of the characteristics of early latency, such as his interests in the world outside of his immediate family, expanding ego interests with greater sublimatory activity, and a striving for autonomy. Typically, the latency child has established an equilibrium between his drives and defenses, controls and gratifications; he has made a more or less adequate adaptation to both inner and outer worlds, and will resist attempts to disturb his precariously balanced situation. Therefore, it is important to proceed cautiously with the interpretation of defenses so that the child will not be overwhelmed by premature confrontation with unconscious material. This careful approach is apparent in the report by Dr. Colarusso. The analyst allowed Jim to express his angry feelings and his fear of snakes without comment. Subsequently, Jim fell silent and devoted his sessions to obsessively coloring a book he had brought. After ten or twelve sessions, the analyst decided to deal with the resistance by encouraging Jim to play. Dr. Colarusso shares his reasoning with us and one must accept his feeling that an interpretation of Jim's inhibition about playing too early in the analysis would have been experienced by Jim as an attack. However, this does not jibe completely with

Jim's ready acceptance of the analyst's direct suggestion that Jim could play; the inhibition could not have been very great. Jim himself explained why the analyst let him play in a way that his parents didn't; namely, that the analyst was different from his parents in that he understood more about children. Unconsciously, the kind of play the boy was making a veiled reference to was "dirty," an allusion to his anal masturbation. This would validate Dr. Colarusso's feeling that interpretation at that point in the analysis would have been experienced as criticism or an attack.

The theme of aggression and the wish to beat the analyst–father so as to reverse the weak situation Jim felt he was in vis-à-vis his parents, more especially the father, then emerged. Jim's perception of the analyst as less restrictive than his parents and the analyst's interpretation and acceptance of Jim's wish to defeat him helped to promote the therapeutic alliance. Thus emboldened, Jim's fantasies of being great and powerful, a king or general with the analyst as subject or private, came out in clear fashion. The analyst points out that, in addition to the positive oedipal aspects in the material, he wished to bring out the boy's feelings of passivity and weakness. What happened, though, was that the boy felt that the analyst was confirming the undesirability of such feelings. I agree that it was too early to deal with passive homosexual wishes; they would be better tolerated after the boy had a firmer sense of his masculinity. However, the impression one gets is that the analyst here conveyed his own attitude toward any passive feminine wishes. This would have the effect of reinforcing the boy's defenses and make the task of subsequently confronting him with those wishes and fantasies much more difficult. As a matter of fact, they are never dealt with, although the opportunity was there later in the treatment as in session 235. This analysis would therefore be considered incomplete, a not infrequent occurrence in the treatment of pre- and early adolescents. When a more stable sexual identity has been established in mid- or late adolescence resumption of analysis would be helpful in resolving homosexual conflicts, and there are instances where this does take place.

The boy's castrative wishes toward his father and his fear

of retaliatory castration were brought out very well and are nicely linked to the masturbatory conflicts. The acting out episode in which the boy stole a cigarette lighter from a store was, according to the analyst, "probably precipitated by premature interpretation of the emerging masturbatory material." Rather than attributing the acting out to premature interpretation, could we consider that it was a result of emerging envy of the father–analyst? It is possible that some of this was brought out in some of the sessions not included in this report. Such analysis of conflicts regarding masturbation and masturbation fantasies is an essential feature of any well-conducted analysis of children as well as adults.

Any effort to critically evaluate this report of the analysis of a latency age boy must take into account that even verbatim reports are incomplete and much goes on between analysand and analyst that is not covered in such a report. I felt that there was an ongoing analytic process with active participation by the analysand. It is accepted that the adequacy of an analysis is not to be judged solely by symptomatic improvement, welcome as that might be. Certain criteria should be met. First, major conflicts should have been brought into the analysis and been examined as to origin, development, and structure. This was done in regard to positive oedipal conflicts, masturbation, and castration wishes and fears. It was not done as fully for passive wishes; for example, when they were alluded to in session 177 where Jim reported "getting a boner from squeezing my rear end together after having a B.M." He further indicated the origin of such anal sensitization. This was from an infestation with pinworms. The analyst by-passed this important material by asking whether Jim got a boner at other times. The passive wishes toward his mother, however, were brought out quite clearly and discussed.

Second, whatever transference reactions develop should be analyzed. This includes the affective, cognitive, and behavior manifestations directed toward the analyst which express repressed infantile relationships. Jim did show some transference reactions to the analyst. For example, he expressed competitive wishes in the games he played with the analyst and in the fantasies of being king or general. The main cathexis, however, remained directed to the father, a not uncommon occurrence in the treatment of latency and preadolescent boys. The same could be said about Jim's sexual wishes. They were expressed toward his mother. This differs from a fuller transference situation where such fantasies would emerge in relation to the analyst's wife. That is what ideally occurs in the analysis of an adult.

Very little in the way of reconstruction is contained in Dr. Colarusso's report. Perhaps not enough was brought into the analysis to enable the analyst to reconstruct preoedipal forerunners of the oedipal conflict. I am struck by the absence of productions relating to the anal period since the history from the parents included data concerning Jim's negativism and refusal to comply with toilet training. Equally noteworthy is the lack of any material related to the birth of the younger brother and sister. Generally, it would be expected that the analyst would at least call the analysand's attention to such gross omissions.

How well did the analyst maintain his analytic stance? Reasonably well, I believe. He did rely mainly on interpretations to clarify conflicts, diminish defensiveness, and enable the boy to reveal unconscious fantasies. There was more reassurance and direction than is optimally desirable. The rule of abstinence was not adhered to so far as giving the boy a gift. Although Dr. Colarusso justifies this on the grounds of promoting a therapeutic alliance, not everyone would agree that giving gifts furthers the analysis. For one thing, it makes it more difficult for the analysand to express negative feelings. For another, it emphasizes a real aspect of the analyst, possibly at the expense of obscuring potential transference reactions.

It can be seen from my discussion that such a report of a lively analytic process provides a base for examining and discussing many important clinical, theoretical, and technical issues. The efficacy of the analysis is convincingly demonstrated. Resolution of conflicts and abandonment of archaic defenses enabled the boy to resume appropriate developmental progress.

BIBLIOGRAPHY

Abate, D. (Panel reporter) (1964), Child analysis at different developmental stages. *J. Amer. Psychoanal. Assn.*, 12:135–150.

Bernstein, I. (1979), On the technique of child and adolescent analysis. *J. Amer. Psychoanal. Assn.*, 23:190–232.
——— Glenn, J. (1978), The child analyst's emotional reaction to his patients. In: *Child Analysis and Therapy,* ed. J. Glenn. New York: Jason Aronson.
——— Sax, A. (1978), Indications and contraindications for child analysis. In: *Child Analysis and Therapy,* ed. J. Glenn. New York: Jason Aronson.
Blum, H. P. (1971), On the conception and development of the transference neurosis. *J. Amer. Psychoanal. Assn.*, 19:41–53.
Blos, P. (1962), *On Adolescence.* New York: The Free Press.
Bornstein, B. (1945), Clinical notes on child analysis. *The Psychoanalytic Study of the Child,* 1:151–166. New York: International Universities Press.
Freud, A. (1965), Normality and Pathology in Childhood. *Writings of Anna Freud,* Vol. 6. New York: International Universities Press.
Glenn, J., Sabot, L., & Bernstein, I. (1978), The role of the parents in child analysis. In: *Child Analysis and Therapy,* ed. J. Glenn. New York: Jason Aronson.
Harley, M. (1971), Transference neurosis in children. *J. Amer. Psychoanal. Assn.*, 19:26–40.
Kay, P. (1978), Gifts, gratification and frustration in child analysis. In: *Child Analysis and Therapy,* ed. J. Glenn. New York: Jason Aronson.
Laufer, M. (1968), The body image, the function of masturbation, and adolescence. *The Psychoanalytic Study of the Child,* 23:114–137. New York: International Universities Press.
Mahler, M. (1968), *On Human Symbiosis and the Vicissitudes of Individuation,* Vol. 1. New York: International Universities Press.
Sandler, J., Kennedy, H., & Tyson, R. L. (1980), *The Technique of Child Psychoanalysis: Discussions with Anna Freud.* Cambridge, MA: Harvard University Press.
Scharfman, M. (1978), Transference and the transference neurosis in child analysis. In: *Child Analysis and Therapy,* ed. J. Glenn. New York: Jason Aronson.
Weil, A. (1973), Ego strengthening prior to analysis. *The Psychoanalytic Study of the Child,* 28:287–301. New Haven, CT: Yale University Press.

CONCLUSION

We hope that the present volume has successfully illustrated the psychoanalytic process and principles. The case material clearly indicates that the treating analysts have based their formulations on the clinical data culled from the patients' associations. The patients' productions have been reported with sufficient objectivity, which has allowed the discussants to construct their own corresponding or alternative hypotheses to those of the treating analysts. For example, Dr. Spruiell uses the same clinical data provided by Dr. Rangell to organize the patient's conflicts according to a perversion model of psychopathology rather than a phobic one. We hope that the readers will be able to use the detailed observations of the treating analysts and the discussants to form their own conclusions, which may vary somewhat from those of the treating and discussing analysts. For example, different analysts have commented on the narcissistic aspects of the pathology of the patient with doll phobia and the religious man, which have been analyzed according to traditional psychoanalytic theory with its emphasis on libidinal and aggressive drives. Other psychoanalysts may use the self psychological model to understand the dynamics of these patients and construct a different course of intervention. Such objective reporting of the clinical data can testify to the scientific validity of psychoanalytic observations.

The comparison of four analytic cases in a time span of fifty years (1930–1980) also allows the evaluation of the shifting emphasis in psychoanalytic theory and technique. As proposed by Weinshel in his contribution, the basic conceptual underpinnings of psychoanalysis have not changed since Freud's original constructions, although there have been gradual shifts in emphasis and refinement in many areas. In the area of diagnosis there is less emphasis on the symptoms and more on the patient's character structure, ego strength, and the developmental level of the conflicts. There is more emphasis on the relationship between the oedipal and preoedipal pathology, as described in all four cases. There is clear recognition of the role of aggression in the patient's neurosis and the patient's intra- and extra-analytic life. Helping the patient gain insight into resistances has become more significant than merely uncovering the content of repressed conflicts. The recognition of the hierarchy of patients' defenses is necessary to achieve this goal. The analytic goal also includes the discovery and reconstruction of the patient's character development and its role in the overall psychic structure by connecting the patient's external and internal worlds and its place in the tripartite psychic apparatus. In regards to therapeutic issues, there is more focus on the countertransference phenomenon (this volume, pp. 72–73).

The insights gained from reading these cases will not surprise a seasoned psychoanalyst, but the verification of principles will be gratifying. It is clear from the case material that psychoanalysis focuses on the patient's inner conflicts, that psychic agencies opposed to drives cause anxiety, and feelings of depression and guilt which the patient must guard against by complicated defenses. The compromise formations that emerge may take the shape of symptoms which the patient suffers from. For the most part, the concentration in analysis is on character which requires extensive scrutiny as illustrated in all cases, especially the case of the religious man. Character consists of the individual's relatively fixed traits which produce stereotyped reactions, frequently maladaptive but not always so, to individuals and circumstances. Careful analysis of defenses results in a change in the hierarchy of defenses with consequent alterations of drive organization and superego configuration. New and more adaptive compromise formations develop. Defenses often become adaptive mechanisms.

The mobilization of the patient's character in the analytic

situation allows a regressive change back into components of the original childhood fantasies, and object relationships from which they were derived. Features of the revived past are channeled in the transference. The reenactment and recalling of childhood, inside and outside of the treatment situation, reveals the pathogenic influences of those forces (Abrams, 1988).

Early in analysis the transferences are usually hidden in the patient's repeated and automatic characteristic reactions to all people, including the analyst, but eventually the individual's reaction to the analyst as a displacement from parental images emerges and can be analyzed.

The psychoanalytic process is the vehicle for therapeutic action. The impetus for such action arises from the ego's integrative capacities in adults and children and is further fueled in children by the pull forward of developmental organizations. The patient introduces the potential for the process by acting upon the ambiguity of the treatment situation in a distinctively individual way. This is the seed of resistance. The analyst searches for the adaptive strategy embedded within the patient's distinctive reactions. This is the seed of interpretation. Resistance and interpretation, the operational dialectic in psychoanalysis, activates the analytic process and sustains it through the anticipated sequence. The patient has the task of reviving and consolidating the infantile neurotic constellation within the transference, while effectively recalling or reenacting the pathogenic past. The analyst functions as the guardian of the psychoanalytic process by concentrating on approaches that permit the transference to consolidate as the embodiment of the decisive, pathogenic past (Abrams, 1988).

The importance of development appears in the cases described. In all of the cases, past, internal, and external events of overriding importance are reconstructed. We see how they reappear in disguised form in current conflicts. In adults, as well as children, maladaptive regressions are halted or restricted so the progressive movement resumes or stabilizes. In child analysis, development manifests itself in still another way as well. The child patient's partially arrested development can be set right through analysis of the inhibiting battles within the child.

The child patient has the specific therapeutic task of searching for ingredients within the analytic situation that will promote whatever developmental phase is being clocked in by maturation. Therefore, in analysis of children the analyst should also be mindful of the requirements of development to attend to the concomitant task of facilitating phase progression. The child analyst's task can be somewhat complex since the evolving developmental process pulls the patient forward, while the analytic process tends to pull him backward (Abrams, 1988).

Finally, the case reports demonstrate the exquisite sensitivity of the analyst to his patient. Empathy enables the analyst to understand his patient's struggles through mobilizing memories of his own experiences. Empathy also helps the analyst to be tactful as he speaks to his patients and to achieve the proper timing of interpretations so that they will be helpful rather than devastating in their effects. The line between useful empathy and interfering countertransference can be blurred. In the cases described, the authors have not dwelt on the analyst's responding to his patient's transferences with transferences of his own, thus repeating his own conflictual relationship with his parents or other significant persons from his childhood. However, these manifestations are hinted at in the material and the reader can sometimes discover them.

Analysis is a cooperative venture, patient and doctor working together in a therapeutic alliance. Despite irrational love and senseless hatreds derived from the patient's past, the patient retains perspective as he recognizes these transferences provide a key to understanding his neurosis. So too does the writing and reading of a book such as this involve an alliance between author and audience. We trust that, as in the ideal analysis, the work continues after the treatment has been ended. The reader will then continue to ponder over the data provided in this volume and the significance of the multitude of insights.

To paraphrase Dr. Leo Rangell in his introductory overview of this book: we cannot but hope that the journey the readers and writers have enjoyed together will continue happily, even after the volume is put down.

G. Pirooz Sholevar, M.D.
Jules Glenn, M.D.

REFERENCES

Abrams, S. (1988), The psychoanalytic process in adults and children. *The Psychoanalytic Study of the Child,* 43:245–261. New Haven, CT: Yale University Press.

NAME INDEX

SUBJECT INDEX